Comedia
Series editor: David Morley

THE KNOWN WORLD
OF BROADCAST NEWS

Roger Wallis is BBC correspondent in Sweden, a journalist for Swedish radio, and a frequent contributor to National Public Radio in the US. He has covered news-making events all over the world. He is also currently completing a PhD in Mass Communications at Gothenberg University, Sweden.

Stanley Baran is Head of the Theatre Arts Department, at San Jose State University, in the US. He has published numerous books and articles on the effects of the media.

THE KNOWN WORLD OF BROADCAST NEWS

International News and the Electronic Media

Roger Wallis
and
Stanley J. Baran

A COMEDIA book
published by ROUTLEDGE
London and New York

A Comedia book
First published in 1990
by Routledge
11 New Fetter Lane, London EC4P 4EE

Simultaneously published in the USA and Canada
by Routledge
a division of Routledge, Chapman and Hall, Inc.
29 West 35th Street, New York, NY 10001

Data converted by
Columns Design and Production Services Ltd, Reading

Printed in Great Britain by Richard Clay Ltd, Bungay, Suffolk

British Library Cataloguing in Publication Data
Wallis, Roger
The known world of broadcast news:
international news and electronic media.
1. Television programmes. News programme
I. Title II. Baran, Stanley
791.45′5
ISBN 0–415–03603–8 (hbk)
0–415–03604–6 (pbk)

Contents

Illustrations

Figures and tables

Tables

Preface

What lies behind the truth?

As we enter the 1990s, the spate of political and generally peaceful upheavals around our globe has provided many examples of both the *power* and the *limitations* of the electronic media. Through the international flow of news via electronic technology, the apparent disintegration of the Soviet Union's traditional sphere of geographical and political influence has been brought speedily, though not always correctly, to the eyes and ears of broadcast news consumers in the West. Domestically, in virtually every nation striving for change, the electronic media have played much more than a catalytic role in deciding the direction of movement, sometimes providing opportunities and sometimes enforcing restrictions.

The pro-democracy movement in China and the violent events of June 1989 in Tiananmen Square, for example, did not lead to radical political reforms in that gigantic country. A major reason for this was the Chinese government's tight control over television. Not only could the authorities literally "pull the plug" on foreign newsteams wishing to transmit material via satellite links, but they were able to impose strict control on domestic news as well. Such was the Chinese government's control of the electronic media that it was difficult for the rest of the world to get more than a sketchy picture of events in the largest country in the world at the time of the Chinese army's move against dissident students. Some of the most comprehensive reporting came from the BBC which reputedly spent £750,000 (more than one million dollars) on the China exercise in May/June 1989, an amount that is more than a year's budget for foreign news for many other national broadcasters.

In Romania, the story was very different. Those who engineered the fall of Nicolaus Ceausescu in December 1989, headed straight for the television centre in Bucharest, using their limited resources to ward off attacks from the Securitate police while the Revolution was transmitted live, not only to the nation, but also via established international video links, to the rest of the world. The capture of Ceausescu and his wife, their trial and subsequent execution were separate parts of this drama. Each was run on television in an order guaranteed to provide maximum psychological effect both domestically and internationally (not least in the Soviet Union). Almost anywhere around the world, people could witness parts of this drama as it unfolded or, at the latest, shortly thereafter.

Technology does indeed provide opportunities and limitations. But does it guarantee that we hear and see the truth, or do the electronic media merely allow more of us to partake more efficiently of current gossip?

Consider again the National Front take-over in Romania. Securitate operations, particularly in the town of Timisoara, we were told, were responsible for no less than 60,000 deaths. The same figure was quoted by an anonymous prosecutor at the trial of Ceausescu. Taken as fact, this information triggered a gigantic operation by international agencies such as the Red Cross to bring emergency medical supplies to Romania. Shortly after the first truckloads crossed the border, a Red Cross official noted that the immediate need was not supplies of medicine, but resources to monitor human rights abuses in the chaos which ensued. After a few weeks, the 60,000 figure had been revised to between two and ten thousand. Three months later, when twenty-one Ceausescu Securitate agents were put on trial before a military tribunal, the indictment referred to forty murders. Still horrific figures, but not the order of magnitude which had shocked the world in December 1989. It also transpired that the much-publicized photographs of maimed bodies in a mass grave, claimed to be the work of the hated Securitate police, later turned out to be arranged pictures involving bodies taken from a local morgue and exhumed from paupers' graves.

A less violent and tragic case where the media got it all wrong is provided by the so-called "English football riots" in Stockholm, Sweden, in September 1989. A small number of visiting English football fans were drinking beer and behaving somewhat rudely, but they caused virtually no damage to property and were involved in virtually no brawls. A few hundred people were temporarily apprehended by the police; most of these detainees were Swedish youths, and all were released after a few hours. The media told a different tale; one of a devastated Stockholm, awash with blood and violence. Six months later, in February 1990, the Swedish Ombudsman presented findings which questioned the legality of certain aspects of the police action during those September football "riots" in Stockholm. This report did not make the international news headlines.

A related story is told from the US side of the Atlantic. It concerns international reporting on the October 1989 San Francisco earthquake. Once again, the quantitative data was all wrong – hundreds did not die in that natural disaster as the first few days' authoritative reporting told the world. Reporters motivating the exaggerations explained that these were the figures given to them by local officials. The BBC's veteran "Letter from America" writer, Alistair Cooke, pointed to a far more disturbing aspect of the international reporting from the earthquake. In one of his epistles from the USA to the rest of the world, he told of reading headlines in the international press such as: "Sick looters try to steal car radios as drivers lie crushed," or statements such as "Families watched horrified as street gangs went from wrecked house to shattered shop stripping them bare." Cooke observed that "there was no looting. Crime on that black night [no power, no lighting] was amongst the lowest of the year. No roaming street gangs, no mobs." As regards the TV News pictures we all saw of sagging buildings on fire down by Fisherman's Wharf, Cooke pointed out that "You would have to roam the city for a week to discover half of the four hundred buildings that were damaged, or even those looking damaged which were later to be condemned: which left only 134,600 buildings untouched."

Much of the improvized truth that the electronic news media feed us has its origin, when it's wrong, in media's preoccupation with *quantitative* (even if correct figures are not available) rather than *qualitative* data. Inaccuracies get magnified even further when we are given the "television's-eye view", focusing on some particularly dramatic visual aspect of an event. This is hardly surprising; after all, who predicted the dismantling of the Berlin Wall or even Ceausescu's rapid fall? When sudden events of this nature occur, the news media tend to "stick to the facts" rather than delve into qualitative analyses of confusing situations.

Pressure from deadlines and hungry competitors all trying to be first also enhance the risk to truth. Especially where on-going developments in Eastern Europe are concerned, the uncertainty and risk of inaccuracy are likely to remain for some time, regardless of whether conservative forces take over again in the Soviet Union or the various nationalist movements are successful in their demands for autonomy (with its attendant confusion regarding national boundaries and conflicts).

It is important not to blame the *technology* for errors in the news. Yes, the technology has increased the chances of stories being broadcast without proper or sufficient checking, but it is those same technological advances that have allowed us to speed and broaden news reporting. Technology provides opportunity, sometimes even for thwarting the activities of those who would use that same technology to restrict the flow of news. The important concern is how the opportunities are met. Many examples, both good and bad, will be highlighted on the pages that follow; one illustrative case, however, should be mentioned at this stage. It concerns the US invasion of Panama in December 1989, where an operation designed to take two days to hunt down that country's military dictator, General Noriega, took weeks to complete.

On the first day of the invasion, several hours after the paratroopers had been dropped, while foreign news media representatives were being hurriedly taken to safety at a US military base in the Canal Zone, Swedish Radio News simply lifted a phone in Stockholm, made a call, and had a stroke of luck. Though only some phone calls to Panama were able to get through as Panama City was being strafed by aircraft and foot battalions, the Swedes were able to reach Noriega's Minister of Trade, Elmo Martinez Blanco, whose Swedish wife has taught him Scandinavian tongue. Blanco was carried live on Swedish national news, with the sound of shooting in the background. Sitting in his office at the Ministry of Trade, he predicted that it would take the US military several weeks to catch Mr Noriega. "He knows this city better than they do," the Minister noted. Elmo Blanco's predictions proved to be correct. This story illustrates well the opportunities provided by unconventional, ambitious use of technology, even one as "old" as the telephone. Many more examples will follow.

This book is about three things, the people and organizations that produce the news we see and hear in television and radio, the differences in coverage between different news suppliers in different countries, and the factors that influence news selection and presentation. It represents a combination of the lessons of years of practical journalism and academic research experience.

In 1986, Roger Wallis, BBC correspondent in Sweden, journalist for Swedish radio, and author of a book on the international music industry, was invited to San Jose State University in California to occupy the Allan T. Gilliland Chair of Telecommunications. One of his colleagues there was Professor Stanley Baran who chaired the Theatre Arts Department.

One of the first things a European notices about American broadcast news is its apparent lack of interest in international news, at least compared to that evidenced by the traditional European news organizations. Not surprisingly, discussions regarding this phenomenon developed between the two authors, leading to the obvious questions of whether there was in fact a difference and, if so, why. Other questions inevitably flowed: if there was a difference between US and European coverage of foreign news, was it inter-nation, inter-media, or both? Would trends evident on one side of the Atlantic eventually make their way across the sea? Rather than speculating (and talking one another's ears off), we undertook a large scale comparative study of nine different news organizations in the US, Great Britain, and Sweden.

Our different orientations, one practical, one academic, produced our choice of format. It includes the literature reviews and descriptions of methodology that typify scientific writing, but it is also full of words from the horses' mouths. As such, the quantitative study has become not the central focus of the book, but a sort of real-life test for the assumptions we developed in our review of the relevant research and our discussions with countless practitioners, both management and line people.

This non-traditional format requires that we offer the reader a few warnings. One of us (Wallis) conducted almost all of the practitioner interviews and was personally involved in some of the actual anecdotes we report. But rather than bore you with "One of us was in. . . " or "As she told one of us. . . " we decided to speak as a team. Thus, occasional references to "we" or "us."

The interviews, too, created a small literary problem. As you read on you will find recurring characters from broadcast news from all around the world. Again, rather than repeat over and over again, "As she said in an interview. . . " or "He recounted for us in a steamy cafe on the banks of the Nile in May of 1988. . . " we simply, in most instances, let the people speak for themselves, identifying them by name and title. You will notice that in a very small number of cases the sources are not identified. This is out of respect for the few requests of anonymity we received.

Three last warnings are in order. Some of our quotes from printed material and personal interviews had to be translated from Swedish to English. We may have sacrificed the literal translation for the sake of readability. We give relatively passing attention to the major international wire services (Reuters, Associated Press, etc.). Here we decided that in as much as our focus was on the news gatherers/presenters in the broadcast media and how they come to make judgements of news selection, the wire services were more providers than players. We also chose not to dwell on detailed discussions of communication theory. We wanted to talk to you about international news in the electronic age. You are free to apply your particular theoretical orientations as you wish. You'll notice, too, that we refrained from presenting a lot of facts and figures that usually appear in a book about news. As we discovered in the relatively brief time it took to prepare this manuscript, these quantitative data change daily – especially in the tumultuous world of electronic media. No doubt they, the ones we excluded and the ones we've included as well, will have changed even more by the time you read this.

The book is divided into eight chapters, with an epilogue designed to move us in a future direction. An introduction offers a pan-Atlantic view of broadcast news based on a telling case study. Chapters 2 to 4 comprise a lengthy segment where we present the important news gathering and disseminating organizations, both the traditional Big Boys as well as newer players. Chapter 7 presents our quantitative study, and chapter 8 brings you our analysis of the factors that govern the decisions of those who select and present the news.

We are not merely content, however, with asking who knows what about the world. A short "where are we heading now?" epilogue demonstrates that developments in broadcast news are not so very different from those in some other media – we use the music industry as an example. With this in mind, we pose a number of questions raised by our study, questions that we believe all of us should address.

There are several people and organizations that made this

Preface

work possible. Channel 2, KTVU in Oakland, California, the
BBC, Swedish radio and television, CBS and ABC in Washington,
NBC in London, the Voice of Kenya, Trinidad and Tobago
Television, and SCANSAT showed us their kindness. Also Allan
T. Gilliland, who established the endowed professorship in his
father's name that Roger Wallis occupied in California during
the academic year 1986/70. Thanks also to the students in
Professor (when he was one) Wallis' classes at San Jose State
University who helped with data collection and coding. They
were crucial to our success. Further expressions of gratitude go
to Hilarie Cutler-Hansson who produced some extraordinary
maps for the cover. Bob Scott of Bosco, Inc. of San Francisco, who
gave graphic representation to our diagrams and tables, was
indispensable. So too were Miral Morris-Jackson and Nina Nolan
from Stanley Baran's staff for their word-processing and manuscript formatting skills. Finally, a number of patient and wise
men gave us the benefit of their counsel and criticism at various
stages of the manuscript's life. Among them are David Morley,
Lennart Weibull, Jeremy Tunstall, George Wood, Kim Massey,
and Daniel Riffe. Above all we must thank our dearest ones,
family members, and close friends who are always subjected to
considerable inconvenience when a book is in the pipeline. In
particular, Goerel, Daniel, and Jonathan who have had to put up
with Roger disappearing regularly into apparent oblivion whilst
thought processes were slowly grinding.

What all this effort has produced is a book that we hope will be
meaningful to different groups of readers. Obviously, we would
expect electronic news practitioners to benefit from our work
because they so infrequently have time to reflect on trends and
developments in their industry. Deadlines are like tides and
taxes. Researchers and their students should find our labours a
reasonable starting point for their own further inquiry and
understanding. And finally, we would be honoured if readers
from the general public, people with a curiosity about the media
and a concern for the world, discover our writing. After all, it is
the audience who ultimately shapes the media that paint its
pictures of the world.

R. W.
S. J. B.
Stockholm/San Jose, March, 1990

1

A day in the life of the world

In the not too distant past many people turned to broadcast news to make sense of a confusing world. Now, though, it seems that it is the world of broadcast news that is topsy-turvy. In the United States, the CBS "Nightly News" programme is a mere darkened screen in homes all across the country as the anchorperson, paid four million dollars a year, fumes in his dressing room. He refuses to go on the air because a late-running tennis match has delayed the start of the broadcast. Hundreds of television journalists are released from their jobs because of budget cuts at all three national commercial television networks. Network newswriters walk out in a labour dispute; 2,000 full-time radio news positions disappear in the US in 1986 alone. Local broadcast stations, using satellite news gathering equipment (SNG), send their own reporters to cover national and international events, reducing their dependence on and the influence of the national networks. Many stations bypass the national networks altogether. The sophistication of news gathering technology grows exponentially, newsreaders' haircuts become more stylized, and the Congress of the United States holds formal hearings on the crisis in broadcast news.

In Europe, a British government report in the mid-1970s contemplated selling two of the BBC's most popular radio networks to the highest bidder or possibly allowing them to become commercially sponsored in order to offset the rising annual licence fee. Now, ten years later, the traditional notion of public service broadcasting is being questioned by that same government – the BBC's licence fee may no longer be sacrosanct;

sponsorship and subscription are to replace it.

The call for "free" radio and television (meaning generally deregulation of the structures governing commercial broadcasting) has become a political campaign issue in Sweden, as of now the last remaining nation in Western Europe that does not have national commercial radio or television channels. Even Sweden, however, is likely to go commercial in the near future. The competitive pressures in European broadcasting are so powerful that even the most ardent supporters of a non-commercial, public-service ideology may not be able to defend their position much longer.

In Germany, where people with cable television can watch satellite-delivered Australian drama, American football, and non-stop news, the national public radio networks and stations convene their journalists in meetings like the 1988 Radio-Borse-Regional in Stuttgart. Their task is to plan strategies to best meet the challenge of the slicker, lighter news offered by the newly created commercial outlets.

The philosopher Plato knew nothing of these events when he wrote his *Dialogues* 400 years before the birth of Christ. One chapter from that work, the Allegory of the Caves, however, suggests a question that we may well ask today: what do we really know about the world around us? Plato's characters are human beings who have been chained in a cave since childhood and are chained to its walls so they cannot turn their heads and, therefore, can look only straight ahead. Behind and above them sits a blazing fire that casts the prisoners' shadows and those of the people that pass between the flame and them upon a far wall. "Like ourselves," Plato says, "they see only their own shadows, or the shadows of one another. . . . To them the Truth would be literally nothing but the shadows of the images."

Like the prisoners in the cave, we too come to know the world beyond the boundaries of our actual experience through the shadows of light and dark electronically beamed into our homes. And if it is true that we know the world (even if only in part) through the pictures of it brought to us by broadcast news, then we need to understand those forces that shape the shadows that shape the perceptions that very often shape our interactions and behaviours in that world.

Plato is not the only ancient author who raised thoughtful questions about how we come to order our experiences of an increasingly complex world. The Udana, a Canonical Hindu

Scripture, offers the fable of the blind men and the elephant. In it, six blind men approach an elephant, each from a different direction. All "experience" a different pachyderm. The first blind man touches the beast's side: the elephant is like a wall. The second fondles the tusk: the elephant is like a spear. The third, the trunk, *ergo* a snake. The fourth reaches for the knee and of course, the elephant is like a tree. The fifth, meeting the elephant at his ear, is certain that this is a fan-like animal and, finally, the sixth, at the tail, gropes and comes away knowing for sure that an elephant is very like a rope. But what does each know of the total beast? John Stevens and William Porter wrote a book in 1973 called *The Rest of the Elephant* (Stevens and Porter 1973), but they meant the broadcast industry itself. We mean the world. If viewers in America meet the world from only one "end" and European viewers meet it from a different angle, what does each really know about the world? And what of those in Trinidad, Mainland China, or Kenya? What is our understanding and awareness of them and theirs of us?

Postdating our two fables by a few centuries is Paul Lazarsfeld. Like Plato and the Hindus, this social scientist, who emigrated to the United States from Vienna, knew a world where television, satellite, fibre optics, computers, cable, video disk, videocassette, and other electronic marvels did not exist. Unlike them, though, he did know a world that harboured mass media and mass audiences. Nonetheless, his view of where our world view is heading echoes accurately those of our two ancient but lasting stories. Writing in 1941 in *Studies in Philosophy and Social Science* (Lazarsfeld 1941:12), he asked,

> Today we live in an environment where ... news comes like shock every few hours; where continually new news programs keep us from ever finding out the details of previous news; and where nature is something we drive past in our cars, perceiving a few quickly changing flashes which turn the majesty of a mountain range into the impression of a motion picture. Might it not be that we do not build up experiences the way it was possible to do decades ago, and if so wouldn't that have bearing upon all our educational efforts?

Let's return to our hypothetical broadcast news listeners and viewers. What experiences of the world do they build from the quickly changing flashes? What truth is contained in the shadows? How would they each describe the world they met on 18 November 1986?

Let's say that the American encountered the beast at 10:00 p.m. PST on "60 Minute News," KTVU-TV's nightly news programme. This offering from an independent TV station in Oakland, California – the top rated news programme in the San Francisco Bay area and, according to the station itself, the "Number One Primetime Newscast in America" – presented the following picture:

Position	Story	Time (min/sec)
1.	Man shoots former District Attorney, police give chase	3' 30"
2.	Bombing suspect arrested in Clear Lake, CA	2' 20"
3.	Cold weather hits America	45"
4.	Man suspected of murdering his wife is arrested	45"
5.	Eighth anniversary of the mass suicide in Jonestown	1' 40"
6.	Larry Lawton (ex-Jonestown leader) on murder trial	1' 25"
7.	NASA simulates launch countdown	30"
8.	Girl kidnapped, molested, and killed in Napa, CA	2' 05"
9.	Sheriff career day in Oakland	30"
10.	Former Presidents Jimmy Carter and Gerald Ford criticize Ronald Reagan and Iran arms deal	1' 00"
11.	Preview of next day's Reagan news conference	2' 00"
12.	French group claims it murdered head of Renault	30"
13.	Wall Street reaction to Ivan Boesky scandal	55"
14.	A New York model returns to work after being disfigured by assailants	50"
15.	Special AIDS report: patient stories	6' 30"
16.	Business news	40"
17.	Vitamin A warning; it is bad for pregnant women	30"
18.	North Korea's President is alive despite rumours that he has been killed in a coup	35"
19.	Toys recalled by Consumer Product Safety Office	45"
20.	Seattle man arrested in East Berlin after falling off the Berlin Wall during a protest	40"
21.	Sports news	4' 30"

A day in the life of the world

At 4:00 a.m. GMT on 19 November 1986 (the 18th in America), the BBC World Service news programme "Newsdesk" paraded this view of the world for a global listening public:

Position	Story	Time (min/sec)
1.	France and Germany adopt new measures in search of terrorist groups	1' 00"
2.	Mrs Thatcher says nuclear deterrence remains the cornerstone of NATO strategy	30"
3.	UN debate on Central America adopts resolution calling on states to respect International Law. Speaking for the US, Senator Trible calls Nicaraguan leadership a "tyranny unimagined in even the worst days of the old (Somosa) regime"	1' 40"
4.	Amnesty International releases report on alleged torture centres in Afghanistan	1' 30"
5.	Another US company signs a deal with China to orbit a satellite in 1988	30"
6.	In South Africa, a government official working with the shanty towns resigns and speaks out on apartheid	55"
7.	Clashes continue in Haiti between anti-government demonstrators and military personnel	30"
8.	Representatives of 300 churches meet in Cyprus to discuss problems of refugees and inter-church aid	55"
9.	Malaysia/Singapore tensions rise in face of visit by Israeli President Hertzog to Singapore	1' 18"
10.	Britain has yet to receive word on fate of an Israeli nuclear scientist believed to have been abducted from Britain after releasing details of Israeli weapons to the *Observer*	25"
11.	British government tries in an Australian court to stop publication of a spy book in that country written by a former agent	1' 21"

Two different elephants? Two different galaxies? It is important to note, too, that half of the BBC stories clearly have more than minor relevance for the US: the UN debate on Central America and Nicaragua, goings on in Haiti after the US assisted removal of dictator Baby Doc, Afghanistani torture chambers, British interpretations of President Reagan's proposal to eliminate nuclear weapons, joint Chinese/American business and scientific ventures. If you had followed any of the five American newscasts we were monitoring on that day, you would have seen nothing of these significant events. Yet the man from Seattle who fell from the Berlin Wall received multiple American coverage (KTVU-TV, CNN and CBS). The ABC Network News had virtually no international news at all that evening. NBC devoted one minute and forty seconds – a very long report in American television news – to the Royal Golf Club of Thailand and its fairways near an airplane runway. CBS, to its credit, ran twenty-second reports on the reactivation of the Chernobyl reactor in Russia and the supply of Soviet weapons to Nicaragua. The arrival of a black US Ambassador to South Africa and a story about drug trafficking in Central America also appeared on CBS.

CNN's "Headline News," described by that cable network as "Around the World in Thirty Minutes," had only two foreign stories on its evening broadcast on 18 November – the murder of the Renault executive and the gravity-plagued man from Seattle.

On the other side of the Atlantic, BBC Television did cover Mrs Thatcher's thoughts on Reagan's disarmament plans. Swedish Television devoted a section of its newscast to the Amnesty International report on Afghanistani torture centres. Both covered the continued fighting in Beirut and an appeal, originally broadcast on Lebanese television, for the release of hostages held in that country. An Eastern European story made Swedish television – a major oil spill into a Czeckoslovakian river had spread into Poland. BBC Network Radio also had an East European item, one dealing with relations between Britain and East Germany.

Both Swedish Radio and Swedish Television gave prominence to a new list of possible World War II war criminals from the Baltic States said to be living in Sweden that was published in, of all places, Washington. Finally, BBC domestic national radio offered two reports from Africa that were only indirectly related to the politics of South Africa. One examined unrest in Zimbabwe and the other dealt with Uganda, a country relegated to news oblivion after Idi Amin was ousted from power by Tanzanian troops.

Why do certain types of international events have low priority on American national newscasts? How can local newscasts, offering a smattering of international news, enjoy apparent rising success (ratings) with their menu of accidents, disasters,

6

violent crimes, and other exceptional (or if they occur with such
frequency and regularity, unexceptional) incidents? Is the
situation so very different in the US compared to other developed
nations?

The answer to this last query is "yes" (at least for now).
Nationwide radio and television newscasts in our two-nation
European sample, Britain and Sweden, cover a much wider
range of activities and geographical areas than do their
American counterparts. But given the tremendous speed of
technological and economic change in Europe, that "yes" might
soon have to be amended.

The ignoring of certain stories and locales is most certainly not
an American-only phenomenon, especially as advances in the
magic of television technology have enchanted news producers
wherever they may live, but it seems to be most acute in the
ratings-driven US system. The desire to produce a fast-paced,
entertaining, slick news "show" is a difficult temptation to resist
in the States. For a time in the early 1980s, for example,
"snappy" was the key word at CBS Network News headquarters
in New York. The New York *Times* special report on the travails
of that news operation quoted one disenchanted producer (28
December 1986), "It was unbelievable stuff, it trivialized
everything. And the correspondents learned that the way you got
on the air was to write a snappy script and be entertaining."
Under conditions such as this, it is not surprising when non-
visual stories like UN debates are ignored. In fact, during CBS's
snappy period, "oddball animal stories" were highly valued. On
one programme two separate stories about eccentric sheep were
included in that network's evening news, a thirty-minute
programme allowing only seventeen minutes for reports, five
minutes for the anchorman, logo, and flashes of things to come,
and eight minutes for advertising. Much of this "dummying
down" of the CBS news product was in response to competition
from the other networks who were gaining ratings points with
new, up-tempo formats.

Such manœuvring led Neil Postman (Postman 1985: 113) to
state in his book, *Amusing Ourselves to Death*,

And so, we move rapidly into an information environment
which might rightly be called trivial pursuit. As the game of
that name uses facts as a source of amusement, so do our
sources of news. It has been demonstrated many times that a

culture can survive misinformation and false opinion. It has not yet been demonstrated whether a culture can survive if it takes the measure of the world in twenty-two minutes. Or if the value of its news is determined by the number of laughs it provides.

More recently, the CBS Network News, according to its own people, has been "hardened." No more sheep. But still not much time for foreign news or goings on at the non-visual UN. Sadly, though, CBS, considered the "class act" of American television news, has been overtaken by other corporate troubles. With eyes firmly directed toward Wall Street, the need to make even more money from an already profitable company has led to labour disputes and significant cuts in the resources allocated to news gathering.

One very logical outgrowth of this financial/technological environment at the national news gathering and reporting level is the explosion of local broadcast news programmes offering a format of local reports with an occasional foreign story being added as filler.

In view of the troubles plaguing the network news organizations, this development is regarded as highly disturbing to many observers of the journalistic scene. Even in the European context of highly regulated broadcast media, many local lobbying groups are agitating for extended regional and local broadcast media. With the growth of satellite news feeds offering national and some foreign news footage for sale to anyone, local stations can claim to be covering the world on a very small budget. All that's needed is a local parabolic dish and a local one- or two-person video team keeping tabs on the police and emergency services (to pick up all the fires, car crashes and bodies of murder victims as they're wheeled off on stretchers). In the totally commercial, virtually deregulated American broadcasting arena, even local affiliates of the major networks are tempted to shun national and international news material, since local news produces local revenue which goes straight into the local stations' coffers.

As might be assumed, the economics of local news become the important driving force behind what and how things are covered. Yet, if asked, most citizens would admit that there are more important issues at stake in news coverage than short-term profits for those fortunate enough to hold a broadcast licence (despite former US Congressman Torbett McDonald's assertion that a broadcast licence is nothing more than a permit to legally print money). One, for example, might be whether or not the general public has a right to be informed by those who operate stations as their fiduciaries (according to the terms of the broadcasters' licence). As one of us wrote elsewhere,

Local television news is good television – fast-paced, exciting, entertaining. The performers are friendly and attractive. It is such good television, in fact, that 40 to 60 per cent of most television stations' profits come from their nightly local news shows. Local news shows have become so lucrative, that most stations hire "news doctors," specialists in improving the ratings of news shows, to help spice up those broadcasts in order to draw more viewers which means higher ratings which results in even more profits. (Baran 1980: 85)

Radio, television, or print as sources of news

The Television Information Office tells us that over 60 per cent of all Americans get "most of their news about what's going on in the world" from television. In addition, over half of the people in the US say that television is their "most believable" source of news. Adnan Almaney (Almaney 1970: 499), who conducted a classic study of foreign news on the US networks, states boldly and simply, "Television is the primary source of news for most Americans."

In fact, newspaper reading in the USA is waning, evidencing a 16 per cent drop in the number of adults who read a paper every day in the period from the end of the 1960s to the end of the 1970s alone. The youth of that country read papers less than their parents did at the same age (McManus 1986).

What is obviously filling the growing newspaper reading void is television news. And in spite the growth of audiences for local newscasts, despite the problems that beset these traditional purveyors of broadcast truth, audience figures for the big three American evening network newscasts are still impressive. Although the proportion of the television viewing audience that tunes in one of the network news programmes each evening has dropped from 72 per cent in 1981 to 63 per cent in 1987 (NBC's "Nightly News With Tom Brokaw" dropped 13 ratings points in that same year), the number of sets tuned in is still impressive. 1989 audience counts show 10.3 million viewers a night for NBC,

10.1 million for CBS, and 9.2 million sets for the ABC Evening News. These figures amount to a sizeable total of the 172 million "TV Households" in America.

Similar sizeable news viewing figures are returned in other countries as well. The main BBC1 evening news at 9:00 p.m. attracts about 9 million viewers on average (20 per cent of the British population). Its prime national competitor, ITN News, does not schedule its main evening news programme at the same time. At certain times of the evening in the USA, on the other hand, a viewer can switch between a variety of different stations and see the same news stories being covered. Many times even the visuals are identical, as the tendency for everyone to sell to everyone becomes more prevalent. Finally, our third sample country, little Sweden with its eight million inhabitants in Northern Europe, has two nationwide television news programmes linked to the two national networks: Channels 1 and 2. Channel 2's 7:30 p.m. newscast, "Rapport," which is featured in this study, attracts between 20 and 30 per cent of the population daily (between 1.5 and 2 million viewers). Through spillover into adjacent countries, it also picks up followers in Oslo (Norway) and Copenhagen (Denmark) who can generally understand the Swedish version of Scandinavian.

It should be emphasized that for those who are not satisfied with the amount of foreign news on the broadcast media, there is another alternative – print journalism (though you sometimes have to wait till the next day to read about distant events). Opportunities vary of course from country to country and from city to city.

In a recent speech to mass communication experts in Gothenburg, Sweden, Professor Jeremy Tunstall (author of such works as *The Media Are American* (Tunstall 1977) and *Journalists at Work* (Tunstall 1971)), warned his European audience not to assume that the press is dead. He argued,

> Statements that the press (print) is no longer the main American source of news have been misunderstood in Europe; most such "data" derives from the commercial television industry's propaganda arm. In fact the "new media" (e.g., satellites and computers) offer many new opportunities to the plain old press, even in the USA. (Tunstall 1986)

Tunstall's thoughts are echoed in part in a special report on "Covering Foreign News" by Marcia Ruth in *Presstime* (Ruth

April 1986). She suggests that the ability to cover international events is one specific competence which newspapers are seeking to develop as a competitive edge against the broadcast media. Ruth quotes a UNESCO study from 1985 which found that the Washington *Post* devotes 41 per cent of its general news space to international affairs. The figures for the New York *Times*, Minneapolis *Star and Tribune*, and the Los Angeles *Times* were 39, 30 and 30 per cent respectively. These, of course, are fairly atypical newspapers in the US. The New York *Daily News* devotes only 19 per cent of its space to foreign news. *USA Today*, having the single largest circulation of any paper in America, is owned by Gannett – a company priding itself on not having any foreign correspondents at all. This newspaper's policy is geared towards relating events abroad to their effect on a US reader. Thus coverage of elections in the Philippines might include a sizeable section on the thoughts of Filipinos living in New York. This orientation led the paper to undertake "JetCapade," a group of travelling *USA Today* journalists who visited thirty countries by jet in six months in 1988 for the purpose of "help(ing) the USA better understand its friends – and adversaries – around the world." The 1 July report from Paris is indicative of their approach: "Food and fashion are big. . . . But back to the basics of the good life here – wine, women, song, sex. In daytime, dusk, and darkness, love is in the air everywhere."

A somewhat similar distinction between the popular press and the more "serious" newspapers can be made in Great Britain. In 1970, Stuart Hall wrote an article in *New Society* (Hall 18 June 1970: 1056-8) entitled "A World At One With Itself," alluding to the title of one of the many news magazine programmes on BBC radio. His thoughts on the popular/quality press follow the posing of this question: "Do/can the media help us to understand these significant real events in the real world? Do the media clarify them or mystify us about them?"

He continued,

Actuality versus depth is not a simple technical choice. The distinction is already built into the structure of the national press. In the arena of news and foreign affairs, popular journalism does not permit systematic exploration in depth. In the quality press, some measure of background interpretation and background is more regularly provided. Both these things are legitimated by the professional folk-wisdom. Thus, for the

11

populars, "The Great British Public is not interested in foreign news," though how the regular reader of the *Mirror*, the *Express* or the *News of the World* (Britain's circulation frontrunners) could develop an intelligent interest in foreign affairs is a matter for speculation. And for the "quality press," there is the rigid separation of "hard" news from comment. Distinctions of format and depth of treatment are hardened and institutionalized in the social structure of the national press.

James Deakin (Deakin 1984: 104), writing of the American press in his book, *Straight Stuff*, made the same observation. He said, "When . . . it is realized that issues are interwoven . . . that a thing in the present was caused by other things in the past and will cause other things in the future – then explanation begins. Understanding begins. Comprehension begins." In other words, it may sometimes be very difficult to meet the elephant at any point other than his ear, but we might overcome this problem as long as it is explained how that ear fits the rest of the beast.

A similar argument could well be applied to the development of local television news and its coverage of international affairs. Local programmes provide the attractive tabloids of the television news industry, featuring very large print, and dramatic pictures but very little depth or background data.

But in most democratic nations, the quality press is still there waging a battle for survival, a battle against corporate accountants whose interest is mainly limited to red and black ink. The Washington *Post* in the USA, the *Guardian* in the UK, *Dagens Nyheter* (Daily News) in Sweden, and many others give us an opportunity to read about, if not *all*, at least *some* international news. Britain, too, has witnessed the recent birth of the *Independent*, a quality newspaper that has met with both early journalistic and early financial success, apparently without damaging the rest of the country's "quality press."

Radio, too has its "quality" equivalents (for those who use radio for purposes other than receiving a background of music interspersed by traffic announcements). National Public Radio (NPR) in America is constantly struggling to keep its financial head above water after years of a Reagan Administration totally faithful to "market forces." NPR produces some of the best news programmes in the world ("Morning Edition" and "All Things

Considered," for example). Relatively few people in America, however, seem to know about such informative gems. The ratings people tell us that at any moment no more than 850,000 of the 241 million people (0.35 per cent) can be expected to be listening to what is virtually the only comprehensive, nationwide, afternoon news and current affairs programme on US radio.

The BBC and Swedish Radio can also be justifiably proud of their output, particularly in the spoken word channels – but even here, the listeners do not exactly flock to in-depth news and current affairs programmes. Television, with its access to dramatic moving pictures, has the attraction. But television, too, presents some brilliant exceptions in this field. "60 Minutes" on CBS, "20/20" on ABC, "Panorama" on BBC or "The World In Action" from Granada TV (UK), and similar features on Swedish television show what this audio-visual medium can produce, when time and financial resources are made available. But the fact remains that most people rely on short, snappy television and radio newscasts for their impressions of events at home and abroad.

An unavoidable question, of course, has to be posed. How can a television generation composed of individuals who watch 16,000 flickering hours of the tube (at least in America) before leaving high school be given the motivation and the critical abilities needed to discover, devour and digest deeper analyses of important issues in the broadcast media or the serious press?

According to at least one television industry whizz-kid, this question is either incorrectly posed or irrelevant. In April 1986, Robert W. Pittman, who had created the MTV music video channel five years earlier, addressed a group of newspaper publishers on the subject of the television generation and its relationship to the world. The "TV babies," according to Pittman, view the medium

as replacement for other forms of information and entertainment. ... They don't require a narrative line to take in information or entertainment. They readily respond to more elusive sense impressions communicated through feelings, mood and emotion. ... It's even possible to have movies in which images and sounds have taken the foreground and made words almost irrelevant. (R. Pittman, quoted in Stein 1986:16).

His words proved prophetic. In the early months of 1987, MTV (the music video cable channel) ran a video by the band Genesis

13

in heavy rotation (several times a day) which presented the song "Land of Confusion." In it, Ronald Reagan – and Nancy – are portrayed as grotesque, incompetent power factors. Disproportionately sized puppets from the British television show "Spitting Image" are used to create that effect. "Too many people causing too many problems" in the "land of confusion" are the phrases that dominate the tune. Otherwise there is very little logical narrative. The video ends with an out-of-contact Ronald Reagan in bed with Nancy. He has two buttons at his side: one labelled "Nurse," the other, "Nuke." He presses the latter and says afterwards, "What a bang!"

When kids are asked what the message of this visual experience might be, they will no doubt answer, "Ronald Reagan is over the hill" or something of that ilk. Follow that up with another reasonable question, namely what conclusions can be drawn from that observation, the answer would no doubt equal the depth of the response to the first query.

Can MTV's style – quickly moving images and sounds – replace the spoken and written word when informing the "TV babies" about the problems of the modern world? Can even the short, dramatic visual clips which are so popular with television news producers suffice to explain complex issues such as the need to conserve energy and the effects of burning too much fossil fuel, the significance of the US becoming the biggest debtor nation in the world, or the reasons for (and not only the visually dramatic existence of) starvation, poverty, or crime? A series of pictures depicting murders, rapes, and accidents certainly communicates "feelings, mood, and emotion," but is something more necessary in nations where government is theoretically dependent on an informed and enlightened public?

Without a narrative, without a debate which exposes and evaluates the underlying reasons for such events (which Deakin called "connexity"), the resulting impressions can surely contribute little towards public understanding.

What results from the exclusion of reports from important meetings of nations in Central America (where representatives of the US government wield the power of the strongest nation in the world) because of a lack of impressive visuals? Information about such events could be the vital cog in the mechanism that allows the general public to more fully and critically appraise the actions of those whom it has elected, thereby decreasing the likelihood that catastrophic mistakes are made without the approval of the people. Might we have avoided "Contragate?" Former US Senator J. William Fulbright stated the paradox this way, in detailing the distinction between "factual and philosophical truth, or between truth in the sense of disclosure and truth in the sense of insight." He wrote in *The Columbia Journalism Review*, "The media have thus acquired an unwholesome fascination with the singer to the neglect of the song. The result is not only an excess of emphasis on personalities but short shrift for significant policy questions" (Fulbright 1975: 41–2).

Despite sharing these reasonable fears, we are not total doomsday prophets of an ineffective, shallow news-media world. Developments in local radio and television, for example, present exciting possibilities for significant gains in the media's ability to cover and deliver the news. The combination of these news organizations earning large profits *and* an increasingly competitive journalistic and economic environment could well foster the desire to venture into new, informative pastures.

Consider that a single local independent American television news division can generate annual revenues equal to the budget of a national Swedish television channel's entire news operation, one that maintains a staff of permanent foreign correspondents. Relatively low-cost technology can also provide interesting alternatives in news gathering, allowing these smaller operators to generate their own, unique material. Might we see a return to the romantic image of the lone journalist with pad and pen, albeit now with miniature sound recorder and light-sensitive camera, travelling more widely and flexibly than the big operators in search of news, better able to thwart governments' inherent tendencies toward censorship?

Is this an impossible dream? What follows is our analysis of what exists today and what sits over the horizon.

2

Broadcast news in the USA:
turmoil, realignment, and restructuring of the traditional operators

Cable News Network dedicated over 300 people to gavel-to-gavel coverage of the 1988 Democratic National Convention in Atlanta. The cable public affairs service, C-SPAN, also offered full coverage to its viewers. The big three traditional commercial networks, on the other hand, sent smaller armies than they had in 1984 and presented extensive, but not complete coverage of the event. Additional reporting was provided by crews from local television stations, using satellite hook-ups to beam home from the convention floor images of their local anchorpeople.

The frenzy of these technology-spawned media amoeba reached ludicrous proportions as "news teams" finally had to resort to interviewing members of other "news teams" in order to have something, anything at all to transmit back home (and to justify the expense of the satellite hook-up). Philip Weiss (Weiss 1988: 31) described the scene in a 1988 *Columbia Journalism Review* article:

> The local TV people made up about a third of the press corps – one reporter I had met came from Jonesboro, Arkansas, a city of 30,000 – and I often saw the two-person crews traipsing around looking for visuals. The reporter – usually a well-fed, middle-aged man – went ahead; then, lagging a few steps behind, came the cameraman, leaner, with the camera in one hand and a tripod over his shoulder, maybe a hat on his head. From a distance they looked like a banker and his caddie who had lost their way on a par-six hole. Their stories were not always penetrating.

16

CBS's Dan Rather put it this way when interviewed in *Time Magazine*, "Seldom have so many with so much covered so little." CNN? C-SPAN? Local stations with satellite hook-ups? National broadcast networks scaling back crews and coverage? In fact, technological, economic, and political changes in all three of our sample countries are operating to dramatically alter "the news" as we've come to know it. There are more players now; financial and other resources are no longer centred with the big, traditional news gatherers; deregulation of broadcasting is a reality in the US and a fast developing one in Sweden and Great Britain. The business of broadcast news is indeed topsy-turvy, but before we can look at what we know of the world brought to us by that business, we need to meet those who give us that news.

Flagships under siege – the US network news divisions

Torrents of fame and blame have been poured over the three major commercial television networks, CBS, NBC, and ABC, and their news operations. While the Roper Polls which annually summarize US viewing habits, show more and more Americans relying on television for their access to news, the news people themselves have seen their fortunes follow a roller-coaster course.

In the days of pre-war radio, the networks' news function was clear; their role was unambiguous. Max Wylie wrote in his 1939 book, *Radio Writing*, "The networks bring to the public at large all those developments, both domestic and foreign, which affect the public at large as one great body of common people." (Wylie 1939: 511).

The past three decades, however, have produced a cavalcade of doubts and despair, interrupted by intermissions of joy or sorrow, as the ratings have gone up or down.

Edward R. Murrow, the father of the CBS investigative television series "See it Now," gave this warning to news directors in 1958:

Future historians looking at TV will find recorded in black and white or colour, evidence of decadence, escapism and insulation from the realities of the world in which we live. . . . If we go on as we are, history will take its revenge.

Ten years later, amidst concerns over an apparent waning of

17

1 Av Westin in his office at ABC television warns colleagues in the News Division of impending days of penury

interest in foreign news, Reuven Frank, then Head of NBC News, made this statement of intent: "I gather Americans are tired of TV forcing them to look at the world they live in. I refuse to consider that we can do anything else" (both quoted in Gates' 1978 history of CBS News, *Airtime: The Inside Story of CBS News*).

As the years went by, news budgets rocketed only to be hit with draconian cuts. What went wrong? ABC News' Av Westin has no doubts. He told us in July 1988,

> Too many resources, too much money, has undone network news, leaving it vulnerable to indiscriminate cost-cutting from above and unable editorially, creatively and distinctly to meet the fierce competition from increasingly aggressive and inventive news operations at local stations. . . . The traditional network news as we know it is going to go the way of the dinosaurs.

Are budget reductions a response to too many years of opulence or are they a threat to essential resources for an essential public service? Dan Rather, CBS's star anchor, commanding the highest salary in the business, sees a wider threat.

Commenting on budget cuts at CBS News, Rather wrote in a 1986 New York *Times* article, "What's at stake is the feeling that, if you can't keep a high standard of excellence at CBS news, then you may not be able to keep it anywhere in broadcast journalism." The network news boat, it would seem, is suffering from instability. From Max Wylie's 1930s through the Ed Murrows to Walter Chronkites in the 70s, CBS news was *the* news authority in the US. Since then, competition, internal problems, and new types of financial pressures have created a volatile situation full of confusion and uncertainty. All the same, each weekday evening forty million Americans, including most decision-makers in Washington, rely on half an hour of Dan, Tom, or Peter (on CBS, NBC, or ABC) to tell them what they need to know. Have Dan, Tom, and Peter become Tom, Dick, and Harry, providing essentially the same glossy package with very little substance? Will network news at dinnertime continue to play an important informative role, developing its own unique specific competence? The only way to answer such questions is to consider the effects of the many technological, financial, and political/legal factors that have revolutionized the network news environment over the past, post-Chronkite decade in American television.

New technology spelling out the rules of the game

Technological developments have radically changed the processes of acquiring, editing, packaging, and presenting broadcast news. The establishment and subsequent deregulation of satellite techniques have made it possible for news broadcasters to get pictures and sound from far-away places in a matter of hours or even minutes of an event taking place. In the days of filmed reports, one might have to wait two days. The change has also allowed new operators to enter the audio-visual distribution business, offering their satellite link services to other news broadcasters, primarily affiliates or independent television stations, thus breaking up the traditional dominance of the networks.

These enhanced news opportunities also tend to increase the role of technology in the news gathering process, as newscasters battle "to be first" with the stories. The engineer with the ground station and the task of establishing a link becomes the first person at an event, not the correspondent with the task of asking questions about what's happened. With constant feeds from news processing centres to news purchasers, and non-stop news programmes from companies such as CNN, *speed* assumes top priority, sometimes even over *investigation*. The primary goal becomes to complete the circuit; in effect, to simply appear on the air from the location of an event, not to investigate and digest the facts of a story before transmission. It is not unknown for a television reporter, having arrived at an event after the satellite link to base has been established, to start reporting to the camera with an editor back in New York or Atlanta briefing him on what to say via the return sound-feed through an earpiece.

Speedy distribution via satellite links available to all has cut a large hole in the networks' monopoly of access to material. Technology has also affected the production process in the studio. Expensive editing equipment shortens production time even more. Video graphics techniques offer not only new approaches to illustrating situations and presenting information, but also new means of cosmetically altering the packaging of the product. During the van Sauter/Joyce management era at CBS News in the early 1980s, large amounts of time, energy, and money were devoted to revamping the visual environment of the CBS Network News programme through new graphic displays. The change was partly in response to a competitor's use of new technology, as Ed Joyce (Joyce 1988: 84) recalls in his CBS memoirs when describing innovations at the news division in 1981:

> Television had entered the age of electronic graphics as well. We had the technology to create an array of special effects for illustrating breaking news stories. Electronic wipes, simple animation and other techniques were used regularly by ABC News, but had generally been ignored at CBS.

The technology was there. Competition regarding "style" probably promoted its use more than competition in "substance." And, it cost money.

As *technology* provided the opportunity for other would-be news operators to enter the business, often on a "use it because it's there" basis, *money* became a larger and larger factor in the gathering and reporting of news. The CBS news budget grew from 89 million dollars in 1978 to 157 million in 1980. Two years later the figure was 212 million dollars. The network news division budgets are now set at around 300 million dollars. The estimated net profit CBS made from sales of commercials in its evening news programme in 1979, 28 million dollars, became a deficit of 65 million dollars by 1987.

In that period of budget expansion the number of various news projects CBS and the other network divisions engaged in grew. The Sunday evening magazine programme "60 Minutes," providing a series of segments of investigational or simply human interest reporting, became a financial success. The CBS news people tried other, similar versions during weekday evenings, particularly during those prime time periods where the rival Entertainment Division was not enjoying much luck in the ratings. A late night news service, running several hours, was tried for a few years, the idea being to provide CBS's owned stations and those affiliated with it (those that take the network's materials) a cheap form of programming to fill the early morning hours. Different forms of breakfast television emanated from the CBS news division, but enjoyed little success against NBC and ABC. The morning finally became the responsibility of the Entertainment Division (as was the case with "Good Morning America" at ABC).

CBS's huge news gathering operation continues to function now, with thirty to forty correspondents' reports coming in to New York from around the world each day. Only one or two foreign reports ever get aired on the flagship "Evening News," but almost all these international stories, according to CBS, are used in some form or another in other programmes, or by affiliates and other users who take them off the CBS satellite feed.

By 1987 all three commercial network news divisions were feeling financial pressures. Management consultants were called in to carry out sophisticated time and motion studies of CBS and NBC. ABC's Head of News, Roone Arledge, spoke of the need for fiscal responsibility if news divisions were to become profit centres. CBS's new "owner," Laurance Tisch, is quoted in the 26 March 1987 San Jose *Mercury News* as giving the following assurance shortly after cutting the news budget by 34 million dollars, firing 200 people and closing two foreign bureaus: "I don't think the news division at CBS will ever make a profit. I've never said that it should. The news division is the crown jewel of this company. Without it, what is CBS?"

The star cost spiral

The pecuniary pressures on the networks can be traced to three different areas. The cost of staff has rocketed, as have variable costs in news gathering. At the same time, parent organizations have been the targets of friendly or less-friendly takeovers, which in a climate of deregulation have led to fewer and fewer areas of broadcasting being protected from "profit centre ideology."

The 1980s have also given the world the star reporter/anchorman with a seven-figure salary. Dan Rather's second anchorman contract with CBS (re-negotiated in 1984/5) gave him an annual salary of four million dollars, a deal which guaranteed Rather in excess of 36 million dollars over a ten-year period. By the mid-1980s, almost half of the 1,500 news people who worked for CBS were on contracts negotiated by agents and their salaries represented a full third of the total news budget. In 1986, CBS star reporter from "60 Minutes," Diane Sawyer, received a new contract worth 1.2 million dollars per annum. It took the Hollywood film "Broadcast News" to question these salary levels a year later. In this movie, staff at a major television news division are laid off and one of the old hands meekly suggests to the star anchor that some of his friends over whose departure he was so saddened could have kept their jobs if he knocked a million or two off his own salary. The suggestion is immediately rescinded in a torrent of apologies in the face of a disapproving glare. This is probably an accurate description of the feeling among CBS rank and file where the axe falls repeatedly.

The "star" system has had an effect on foreign news gathering, at least as regards the motivation of those out in the field. Expensive stars at home have to be used, otherwise what's the point of paying them so much money? Martin Bell, BBC Washington correspondent, gave us this observation in a July 1988 interview:

> There's less original reporting, less going out finding what's happening. It's much more bought in and voiced over in New York. It must be a very frustrating life being a foreign correspondent for a US network. You don't get on the air very often, and when something does happen in your patch, it may be your story for a day, and then they'll fly out one of their big name reporters who will take over from you. I don't think they lead much of a life.

Broadcast news in the USA

Av Westin, ABC's Vice President of News, who wrote an interesting practitioner's account of network news in 1982 called *Newswatch: How TV Decides the News*, sees no way out of the star spiral apart from moving into "days of penury" partly through cutting resources abroad. "What you will have," he said in a 1988 interview, "is a highly paid commentator, highly paid because that's what the market will demand. You'll also have a highly paid reporter at the White House and at the Pentagon. Round the world, it's going to break down."

In a historic sense, the skyrocketing of on-air news reporters salaries is somewhat bizarre. In the 1950s, with television news in its infancy and resembling a film newsreel, presenters were paid very low salaries. Instead, they received a percentage of advertising revenue. Gates (Gates 1978: 54) in his writings on CBS News notes that "only a journalist with an exceptionally pure heart was apt to complain about having his newscast interrupted by a sales pitch for toothpaste or deodorant when he personally was getting a bit of the action." This system was abolished to increase the integrity of the news presenters. Now, though, the networks have found themselves with a system of star contracts and bickering agents all playing a financial game that could endanger the existence of the goose that provides their golden eggs. Meanwhile, the direct sponsorship of news programmes, as we shall see later, has moved over to the nominally non-commercial, Public Broadcasting sector.

The running cost spiral

Staff and star salaries are one financial burden. A second pecuniary pressure on news gathering has come from running costs. These include the bills for hours of satellite time and other new technologies, increasing costs of travel, and expanding costs of maintaining foreign and domestic bureaus. Incomes, too, have been hit as the networks' main "customers," their affiliated local stations, have shown less interest in taking special news programmes from the network news divisions as they have become more technically competent to cover events themselves or more able to buy news from other sources. NBC's Ed Newman, speaking at San Jose State University in California in 1987, offered this warning:

More and more decisions about news are being taken by people outside the news divisions. The power of the affiliates is rising. Network news divisions can go on putting out worthy programmes until they are blue in the face. How long can this go on if large numbers of affiliates refuse to run them?

With the change in the "favored position" *vis-à-vis* the affiliates affecting the income side for television news, a third form of financial pressure has emerged. It involves Wall Street scrutiny and "bottom-line" management.

The attempted and successful takeover spiral

The 1980s have seen ABC acquired by Capital Cities and NBC bought by General Electric. A number of attempts to buy control of CBS Broadcasting were made, ultimately leading to a transfer of power at the network from Founding Father William Paley to entrepreneur Laurance Tisch. NBC saw a further change when its radio news operations were sold to a smaller news syndicator, Mutual Radio. NBC radio stringers now provide reports for both NBC and Mutual Radio news. Permanent radio correspondents located at the NBC television bureau in London have been done away with. CBS television and radio news are still closely co-ordinated, with Dan Rather even reading the radio headlines once every afternoon, but CBS Broadcasting has experienced a series of financial attacks. They are documented at length in Ed Joyce's *Prime Times, Bad Times* and Peter Boyer's *Who Killed CBS?*, two chunky volumes which found their way to bookshelves in 1988.

There are a number of defences against takeover bids. One is to keep Wall Street happy with current management while predicting and turning in regular increases in revenue (a difficult task if a broadcast organization is simultaneously committed to the notion that a news division does not have to make a large profit). Another is to make sure that the company is so heavily laden with debts (e.g., by borrowing cash to buy up the company's own stock) that a hostile takeover becomes too expensive a proposition. CBS has used both strategies. The second was utilized to thwart Ted Turner, when the Cable News king from Atlanta wanted to join CNN and CBS.

Another onslaught on CBS simply faded out. US Senator Jesse Helms, a conservative Republican, started a "Fairness In Media" group which expressed concern about what they saw as CBS

News taking an anti-Reagan stance. The group advised conservatives to buy CBS stock and take the company over. This was only one of many attacks by right-wingers over the years against what they have regarded as liberal thinking (socialist thinking in European terms) at CBS News. Oddly enough, the head of the News Division at the time, Gordon van Sauter, was an outspoken right-winger. Van Sauter, however, was a firm believer in television news "capturing moments." The main effect of his presence was to make the news lighter rather than more overtly right-wing.

Another suitor for CBS was Coca Cola, the drinks manufacturer, realizing the potential of media control for propagating its beverage. CBS chose Laurance A. Tisch, who had already amassed a sizeable amount of the network's stock. It then sold off its lucrative Record Company (to Japanese Sony) and a number of other assets as well. On 20 December 1987 the Wall Street *Journal* wrote, "CBS has been stripped in one year of much of what it built in 60, largely at Mr. Tisch's initiative." The 950 million dollars he paid for 25 per cent of the CBS stock was worth 1,600 million dollars at the time.

The competitive environment – independence and streamlining

Autonomous news gathering is still the institutional *raison d'être* of the Network News Divisions. "We are an independent organization," said Don DeCesare, CBS Foreign News Editor, in a 1988 interview. "From time to time that annoys the people in Washington. They complain. That's the traditional American respectful antagonism between the media and the government."

Yet, even the most independent desire can be transformed into mutual dependency in this fairly friendly battle. Consider this recollection from NBC's Ed Newman of the first years of the Reagan administration, detailed in his San Jose public address:

President Reagan got into the habit of holding so-called impromptu press conferences, when there was something he wanted to say, and I guess when he did not want to face prepared questions. The networks usually interrupted their programmes to put these press conferences on. At one of them, almost the only development was that a birthday cake was wheeled on. So there you are. You've broken into your programming for this and you've been made a fool of. What do you do next time?

Independence too is affected by a combination of technical, financial, and organizational/legal constraints. Sometimes independence seems to get mixed up with prestige, as in the case of the Reagan/Gorbachev summit in Iceland in 1986. Ed Newman recalls that

> the overall coverage was grotesque. Of course there was a big story to report. News organizations use stories of this kind to show that they are important – the larger the team, the more elaborate the arrangements, the more money they spend. . . . Money and people are assigned to these sort of things in a way which is grossly excessive. Money and people that could be employed in reporting elsewhere. Now what were the facts about the Iceland meeting? We still don't know. It's possible that the Administration does not know. The main result emerged in the form of a question: is the president of the United States capable to undertake such a meeting? That is not a very comfortable story to deal with.

Our final chapters will delve deeper into this issue of the media's independence in the face of events in the world around them. Suffice it to say that, even if the claim of independence vis-à-vis the government can occasionally be argued, *dependence* on the competition is unquestionable.

It is significant that Fox Broadcasting, Rupert Murdoch's attempt to start a fourth national network in the USA, does *not* carry news from an independent news division. Maybe one reason for this network to eschew news is what Av Westin terms "the unmistakable similarity" in the big three network evening news broadcasts, a similarity that has been repeatedly documented. Why should the fledgling Fourth Network quadruplicate its three sisters if it has nothing new to say?

The Big Three most definitely are not delivering three substantially different versions of the day's events. Consider, for instance, this "day in the life of the world" as seen by the three US network news programmes. This comparison makes the point that competition, market forces or whatever term is used does not guarantee diversity.

Table 2.1 shows that the only differences in subject choice

Broadcast news in the USA

Table 2.1 *Stories in the network news, 12 November 1986*

Network/Time	CBS	NBC	ABC
Item			
Iran arms scandal	2' 50"	1' 52"	3' 15'
Affirmative action/Reagan	2' 00"	1' 52"	—
Catholic Bishops meeting	1' 52"	1' 50"	1' 30'
Alzheimer's disease clues	1' 20"	1' 52"	1' 20'
Cold Weather hits East USA	1' 18"	0' 30"	0' 18'
Red Wolf back again	1' 52"	2' 08"	—
Rare photos of Churchill	—	—	2' 10'
Pregnant mums & drugs	1' 38"	—	—
San Francisco Bridge 50	—	—	1' 40'
Surrogate mothers	—	4' 00"	—
Suicides among elderly	3' 55"	—	—
Migrant workers' children	—	—	4' 00"

Times based on CBS logs for own output and the "opposition"

come late in the programmes in the form of sequences with a "human" or "social" angle. An even more dramatic picture of the follow-my-leader results of inter-network competition emerges when charting breaking big stories. The period we tracked during our empirical studies covered the first three weeks of the Iran–Contra scandal, from the first announcement of arms sales to Iran to the admission that some of the cash had, in fact, gone to the Contras fighting in Nicaragua. If one network had relatively less on Iran–Contra one night, it almost invariably had more the next night to make up for the difference. The converse was true as well. This is dramatically illustrated in 2.1.

The Iran–Contra story also provided an example of the type of saturation coverage to which the networks are prone. Martin Bell, BBC TV's man in Washington, believes this can undermine the whole value of television news, even to the extent of harming foreign policy. He said in an interview in 1988,

> Some of the worst foreign policy decisions made by the Carter and Reagan administrations were over their relationships with Iran in which they were unduly swayed from a useful policy by the situations of hostages, first in Iran and then in Beirut, a situation that was dramatized on the networks. Wherever

27

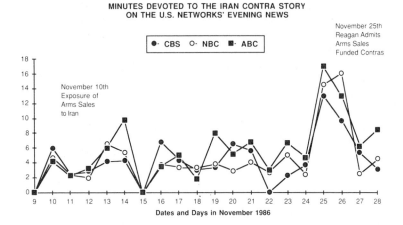

MINUTES DEVOTED TO THE IRAN CONTRA STORY
ON THE U.S. NETWORKS' EVENING NEWS

●- CBS   O- NBC   ■- ABC

2.1 Percentage of network newscasts' time devoted to Iran–Contra,
10 to 30 November 1986

Jimmy Carter went during his last year in office, the networks would ask him, "what are you going to do with the hostages?" There were a lot of other things going on in the world at the time, and probably a policy of benign neglect would have served the purposes of the hostages better. These things are dramatized by television, the plight of the hostages makes good television as does the plight of the families with tearful interviews. I just think it makes lousy foreign policy.

The dilemma of individuals in jeopardy and their situations' relation to larger interests of foreign policy is one that the networks have not really been able to solve. It's not even certain there is a solution, bearing in mind their special competitive relationship and the public's apparent fascination for dramatic situations involving individuals, a fascination which television news has nurtured over the years. Ed Newman gives two alternative views of the networks' handling of the TWA highjack in Beirut in 1985:

The view got out that TV was playing into the highjackers' hands. There is something to this. Technology and money were running riot. It was showing off, boasting, duelling. Competition for competition's sake. All sense of proportion had gone. Maybe if the press and TV had given the hijackers less attention, then the affair would not have dragged on for so long. It's just as likely, however, that the attention kept the hostages alive. . . . The story was highly educational. The education was not entirely welcome, but some reality was made clear and some aspects of American foreign policy as well. Hatred of the USA in some parts of the world is a fact. It's better that we know it. The news business, however, does not generally work in a way that systematically brings that education about. There seems to be no substantial public demand that it does so. It's the big splashy stories that somewhat erratically provide the occasion.

The inherent conflicts in a news philosophy which dictates the need to inform and explain *and* to entertain (grab and maintain), or at least not tire the audience are responsible for many of the unresolved problems of the news media. Competition occasionally helps lift a news programme to new heights, providing it with a scoop. It also can lead to streamlining, and a hesitation to carry something the opposition has missed or turned down. In such an environment, it's not surprising that the lighter, more emotional, or dramatic side flourishes with a concentration on the cosmetics of presentation. This latter situation need not be the case.

Historically much of the commercial thinking in the US news divisions can be traced to various directives from the federal authorities, especially the Federal Communication Commission (FCC), an organization which has been active over the years both *regulating* and *deregulating* broadcast media.

"Competition" and "diversity" were long seen as magic, mutually compatible routes to protecting the public interest and right to be informed. The birth, in 1943, of the independent ABC radio network, formerly a second network to NBC, was a result of this thinking. The fact that for decades ABC trailed in third place in a system where income depends on ratings led the network, then television as well as radio, to seek an image that would attract the sort of viewers commercial sponsors wished to reach. ABC thus became the first television network, according to Ron Powers (Powers 1977: 46), "to hire outside consultants for large-scale advice on the appearance and, to a degree, the content of its evening news show."

The concentration primarily on style rather than substance in quest of a competitive edge is probably a reflection of the belief

29

that "irrelevancies that stir the emotions work better that relevancies that don't," to quote NPR commentator Daniel Schorr (uttered after a televised debate between Michael Dukakis and George Bush during the 1988 US Presidential campaign).

Nowhere has this trend reached such a degree of sophistication as in local television news in the States. Even the networks are into style, and this too has its problems. CBS news presenter, Dan Rather, apparently worth his weight in gold, has to be constantly humoured. His somewhat erratic behaviour at times, such as walking off the set when a sports match ran overtime into his news slot, has to be handled with tact and "good PR."

Dan and his anchor colleagues on NBC and ABC are undoubtedly important figures in American life and public opinion. According to the 1975 People and the Press Survey of 3,000 Americans, about 90 per cent found Dan Rather to be "believable" or even "highly believable," yet fewer than half of the sample, however, could identify him in a photograph. The believability figures for Peter Jennings (ABC) and Tom Brokaw (NBC) were almost the same.

The demise of public affairs programmes and documentaries

By 1993, the news documentary will long be gone from all of the big three networks. The broadcasts that had ranged down through the decades, from Edward R. Murrow's halfhour "See It Now" programmes on Senator McCarthy to two-hour broadcasts on American POWs in Vietnam; all these will have disappeared from the networks schedules. They cost too much to produce and returned too little.

So wrote Ernest Leiser (Leiser 1986: 3C), former CBS newsman.

The production of one-subject programmes, or documentaries, has allowed broadcasters to get a bit nearer the traditional areas of investigational journalism and non-fiction writing. Often an in-depth television study can require up to a year's preparation. The results are often a source of pride and problems. The news organizations can show their true journalistic capabilities. But because the aim of most documentaries is often to create a debate about some controversial issue, inevitably there those with vested interests do not appreciate the attention bestowed upon them.

The production of documentaries, or "public affairs programmes" as the networks sometimes call them, has been closely integrated within the news divisions all along. There has been a fairly high degree of mobility between regular news and special programmes. Here, the US networks differ from the European tradition of dividing current affairs from news, a division from which the BBC, as we shall note, has formally departed of late. Documentaries, for the networks, as for any other broadcaster that claims to "tell the facts," have been a tough test of independence over the years. It must have required quite a bit of confidence for Ed Murrow to question the sincerity and honesty of Senator McCarthy; those who dare to question the inquisition need strength and support. Other documentaries have backfired. In 1982, CBS made the documentary "The Uncounted Enemy – a Vietnam Deception," accusing General William Westmorland and some of his colleagues of falsifying estimates of enemy strength during the Vietnam War. The after-shock of this was immense with the General's lawyers claiming that CBS reporters had manipulated inter-viewees and used unfair technical practices to paint the picture they wanted. A libel suit dragged on through to 1985. It was finally settled out of court with the General accepting a vague statement from CBS that he had fulfilled his patriotic duties. It didn't encourage the making of sensitive documentaries at CBS.

Money has clearly also been an issue in the fate of the documentary. According to Gaye Tuchman in *The TV Establishment* (Tuchman 1974), documentaries in 1974 could still make a modest profit. The prerequisite was that a documentary could replace a more expensive entertainment show. But because of rising costs, among other things, by 1976 documentaries had become endangered species (Powers 1977: 53). Fifteen were aired on CBS, 13 on NBC, and 8 on ABC as opposed to 28, 18 and 15 respectively in the previous year.

Documentaries were also once able to generate money for network news divisions from sales abroad, but even that option has disappeared, but not for a lack of foreign buyers if we are to believe a 1987 article in the Swedish Broadcasting Corporation's in-house magazine *Antennan*. In 1983, 54 per cent of the public affairs programmes the Swedish Second television channel bought came from the USA; ABC was one of the most respected suppliers. In 1984/5, the figure had dropped to 21 per cent and by 1986 it was as low as 12 per cent. Swedish television's senior purchasing editor noted that "documentaries are (now) regarded as a luxury in the major TV companies... ABC, which used to make good political programmes only makes one or two a year." The problem of finding sponsors has now become a major preoccupation of those still wishing to make documentaries for American television. ABC's major documentary on illiteracy in 1986 relied on heavy support from IBM. The transmission was interspersed with segments advertising IBM's different computers and learning aids.

Despite the financial and related ethical problems facing would-be documentary makers of today, there is no doubt of the historical importance of the US network documentary. Edward Jay Epstein's book, *News From Nowhere*, quotes former CBS News Director, William Small:

> When TV covered its "first war" in Vietnam, it showed a terrible truth of war in a manner new to a mass audience. A case can be made that this was cardinal to the disillusionment of Americans with the war, the cynicism of many young people towards America, and the destruction of Lyndon Johnson's tenure of office. (Epstein 1973: 9)

Television's role in the USA during the Vietnam war certainly made an impression on one British politician. Margaret Thatcher is quoted by a former BBC Director General of chastising the BBC for its coverage of the Falklands campaign and "quoting as a parallel what she described as American television losing the Vietnam War". (Milne 1988: 123)

Foreign news in the US networks, today and tomorrow

Martin Bell, with ten years' experience of watching the world in Washington for the BBC, is not impressed by the development of foreign news coverage in the US networks. He told us in 1988,

> There's less foreign news than there used to be and it's less original. They have a more insular view of the world. It's unusual to get a foreign story receiving much attention that does not have a direct American connection. That is, Saudi Arabia will only matter if the American Secretary of Defense is there. Nicaragua will matter if it throws out an American ambassador. Africa is more or less a totally forgotten continent. There was more before. CBS was much more the bulletin of record than it is now. It has localized itself, it has trivialized

2 Head of Foreign News at CBS, Don DeCesare, surveys his section of
the circular network news studio

itself, it has personalized itself round the dominant personality
of an anchor. There was an occasion during a summit meeting
in Moscow when the whole thing was voiced by the anchor
man. He talked to a few correspondents at the end. The rest of
the world just did not exist that day. There are new concepts of
what is news.

At CBS News in New York, foreign news editor, Don
DeCesare, was more positive. "I'm fairly aggressive in believing
that the future is there for us to take," he said in 1988.

And foreign news is the one thing we can do better than the
affiliates. We produce huge quantities of material every day.
We can package it better. There are more programmes we can
produce. For instance, we don't have a weekend round up of the
world. We can produce more programmes that don't go on the
regular network, now that the distribution problem has been
solved. We can use DBS, cable, cassette. You may even end up
using a narrow-cast approach, rather like magazines went
through in the 50s, aiming for a specific kind of audience. We'll

have a general overall bulletin a couple of times a day, and then a number of other different packages. The stakes are so high on networks, you're into the ratings thing. Maybe we can make programmes that aren't even advertiser-supported. . . . Suppose CBS News produced a weekly review of the world for schools. Most of them now have satellite dishes on their roofs. Suppose we produced that for American high schools, distributing it at midnight on Sundays, when satellite time is cheap, and it's ready at seven in the morning for the schools. I don't know that that wouldn't work. . . I do think you will always have an audience for an evening and morning news of the network type. People in the United States like to know what's going on.

The question Don DeCesare does not answer here is how does a network or other organization develop a unique competence in foreign news packaging without continued expansion of its foreign news gathering capabilities. If the sources of that news are a small number of correspondents in Washington, Jerusalem, London, and Moscow, how dependent can such an organization become on international visuals suppliers like Visnews, WTN, or even CNN and still claim to be independent gatherers and reporters of foreign news?

The strategies adopted have been twofold. First, an organization cuts costs by sharing resources with others, and second, it tries to increase income and control by either buying into major news distributors or providing subscription services (feeds) to other purchasers.

Two of the US networks, NBC and ABC, have increased their respective ownership stakes in the news wholesalers Visnews and WTN, hoping thereby to hedge their corporate bets. Visnews and WTN, to quote one of their executives, feel that they "have almost got the market sewn up." CBS has struck a deal with WTN for the latter to supply international material, enabling the network to save the cost of camera crews in some parts of the world, notably in Central America. But this has caused some friction because its competitor, ABC, holds corporate ownership interest in WTN.

CBS is the only American network which does not have an ownership stake in the Visnews/WTN duopoly. But it does maintain some news distribution activities of its own, with a feed which is taken by some local stations at home in the States and a daily Asian feed to subscribers (a similar service for Latin America was recently cancelled).

All three networks are trying to find different ways of cutting news-gathering costs. NBC will rely on Visnews taking over some of their own traditional bureau work. CBS still has bureaus in London, Paris, Moscow, Tel Aviv, Johannesburg, Hong Kong, Tokyo, and Bangok, as well as staff camera crews in Bonn, Athens, and Dubai. The search for alternatives must surely be high on the company's priorities. A marriage partner in the form of CNN or one of the facilities providers such as the satellite news gathering firm, CONUS, could be a strategic alternative for CBS.

Whether interlocking relationships with the international television news agencies will be a saviour for the traditional American network news divisions is another matter. Another national broadcaster, the BBC in London, has been addressing the same question, but has been producing some very different answers, as we shall see a few pages hence.

Other traditional national radio and television news in the United States: public sponsored and private commercial alternatives

All three networks have their radio news, though NBC radio, as we mentioned earlier, has been sold off by General Electric to Mutual. National radio newscasts are distributed on the hour by satellite to owned and affiliated radio stations. Radio in the US has been described by Jeremy Tunstall (Tunstall 1985: 152) as "the most pervasive dispenser of news... this phenomenon is perhaps 700 million times a day broad but less than five minutes deep." Even if a majority of Americans tell the Roper Poll they rely mainly on television for their news, radio is part of their daily sound environment. Radio produces short bursts of news, along with the weather, traffic information, and lots of music. CBS claims that its 7:00 a.m. bulletin is listened to by twice as many people as the total number of viewers of CNN cable news. The normal format is a couple of headline bursts followed by advertisements and then another story. Foreign reports are seldom longer than thirty-five or forty seconds, regardless of the nature of the story. Standard practice for a foreign correspondent delivering voice pieces to a US radio network is to produce three slightly different versions, all the same length, so that they can be distributed to different types of users, competitors, or used once an hour to maintain a slight element of variation.

With the FCC removing some of its minimum broadcast-time regulations for "non-entertainment" and other current affairs content as a part of the Reagan deregulation, the pressure on broadcasters to programme news on FM stations has decreased. Music programming is cheaper to produce and garners more profits. In fact, in 1986 alone over 2,000 full-time radio news jobs were eliminated, to be replaced by 700 part-time jobs. Even the all-news stations that grew up in the 60s and 70s (mainly on AM) are losing numbers. Three survived in Washington ten years ago; now there is only one. The Associated Press, AP, has a broadcast service providing news and spoken word spots via satellite to 1,000 stations. The numbers here, too, are decreasing. According to an AP spokesman quoted in the New York *Times* on 28 December 1986, "Most people who program music today feel news is a turn-off. . . all our emphasis goes into packaging and next to none into news gathering."

The US "public" programme suppliers, PBS, NPR, and APR, provide the non-commercial national news alternatives on both radio and television. Their output is distributed mainly from Washington via satellite to member stations. This mixture of satellite and terrestrial distribution is funded by a combination of subscriptions, federal grants, and donations from philanthropists and sponsors. These figures for KTEH-TV in San Jose, California should offer some indication of the usual budget breakdown for a small public (non-commercial) television station:

	$
Federal grant	450,000
Local county educational comittee	450,000
Grants from companies (sponsorship)	400,000
Subscriptions from viewers	2,000,000

Of a total budget of 3.4 million dollars, about half a million would be spent on broadcasting rights. Only 1 per cent of its budget would be spent on original production. An hourly news and current affairs programme from PBS would typically cost the station about $50,000 a year. With a large reliance on subscriptions, the 15 to 20,000 viewers are subjected to regular requests for more money, often via "pledge weeks" over the air.

Dependence on sponsorship has grown rapidly in recent years

as a result of a) cuts in grants from the Administration and b) the realization that public radio and television can deliver corporate image PR directly to certain attractive elite groups who prefer the PBS/NPR output to network fare. An evening with a local public television station in the San Francisco Bay area in 1986 included sponsorship plugs as follows:

Table 2.2 *Sponsors' time during six hours of public television (Based on monitoring of Channel 60, California, 24 October 1986)*

Programme	Type	Sponsor	Duration
American Interests	public affairs	Tahoe Seasons Resort	40″
		Blackwell Corporation	2″
		IBM/Exon/Avis/Pfizer	16″
The McLaughlin Group	culture	General Electric	8′
Washington Week	politics	Tahoe Seasons Resort	40″
		Ford	12′
Stock Market Review	finance	Warner Computers	14″
		McGregor Sporting Goods	12″
Wall Street Week	finance	Hilton Htl/Prudential Insurance/Sperry Corp	18″
The Computer Chronicle	technical	McGraw Hill/ Leading Edge	8″
European Journal	foreign news	Lufthansa	3″
McNiel/Lehrer Hour	news/interviews	AT&T	12″
I Claudius	drama(ex BBC)	Tahoe Season's Resort	40″

The sponsors' presentation on public television can be anything from a simple name on the screen to a traditional animated logo, verging on standard commercial format, as is the case of the AT&T spot on the McNeil/Lehrer programme. So prevalent has the role of sponsors become in US non-commercial broadcasting that Martin Bell commented, "I'm just waiting for the day when one of their presenters turns up on the screen holding a packet of Daz." If this were to happen, PBS would be exactly at the point from which the commercial networks departed in the 1950s in order to improve their independence and integrity.

Public broadcasters say they have little choice since the cuts in federal funding during the years of Reagan. Mr Reagan maintained a constant battle with Congress over funds for non-commercial broadcasting. For example, Congress proposed giving the Corporation for Public Broadcasting (CPB) $200 million in 1982; the President felt that $120 million was more than enough. His final projection for federal funds to the CPB in 1990 was even less, only $80 million, or half of what the CPB actually received in 1982 (without allowing for inflation).

CPB distributes funds both to local stations and to programme suppliers; therefore, these cuts have spread ripples all through the world of public broadcasting. For example, one of the larger public radio stations, KQED-FM in San Francisco, saw its federal grant dropped from $500,000 to $200,000 during the first half of the 1980s while its annual outlay to National Public Radio for news programmes increased from $50,000 to $200,000. Here we can note one of the important differences between the financial/competitive crunch as felt by the commercial networks as opposed to the public alternative. The networks see themselves as being threatened by local sttions which make their own newscasts. This process has not occurred in the public broadcasting arena – news programmes are still produced primarily in New York or Washington.

During NPR's first years, in the early 1970s, there was a conscious move to shift programme decision-making to local stations. The Nixon Administration fiddled with the structure, trying to decrease the central authority of the fledgling (and supposedly "liberal") NPR.

The repeat happened during the last years of the Reagan Administration, as his appointees on the CPB Board developed new ways for financing centrally produced programmes. Before the change, programming funds were approved for a two-year period, providing a shield against immediate or politically motivated cuts. Some of this cash made its way directly to NPR. As of October 1987 however, CPB money must go to individual stations which then purchase news and other programmes from NPR. NPR, no longer having the stability of a base grant, has started to generate its own funds. This is both a curse and a blessing. It means that NPR, with a Board consisting of representatives from member stations, does not have the CPB (with administration appointees) breathing so heavily down its neck. On the other hand, it has to keep some 300 local customers happy (and paying for its programmes), a fact which can make NPR more careful not to offend local potentates.

Cuts and changes in the way federal moneys are paid out have thus affected both suppliers and users, encouraging the move towards alternative sources of revenue instead of the assumed Reagan intention of localizing production, thereby removing the power of the Washington-based public broadcasters.

McNeil/Lehrer – the public television showcase

The flagship public television alternative news programme is the "McNeil/Lehrer NewsHour," a news reporting programme that includes a number of interview segments and special reports. Three to four million Americans see the show each evening, as compared to approximately twelve million for a typical network evening news presentation. McNeil/Lehrer is an interesting television news programme in that it also functions as radio, and indeed is put out as sound only on some Public Radio stations. The pace is not too fast and the pauses for television's camera moves and zooms makes it rather quaint, even humorous by contemporary radio standards. Nonetheless, it *is* relaxing.

The news programmes put out by both Public Radio and Television have what people in the business refer to as an "up-market" profile, offering an analytical approach to the news aimed at an educated audience. The 1983 "Simmons Survey of Media and Markets," quoted frequently by NPR in its publicity material, describes their typical listeners as

educated, successful, active and young. . . . The percentage who are managers and professionals is nearly twice the percentage in the US population as a whole. They are 81 per cent more likely to read the Wall Street *Journal* than the average American. They are decision-makers on the job; they invest; and they vote.

Such summaries explain why corporate sponsorship has found public broadcasting attractive. They also make clear that Public Broadcasting in the USA is hardly aimed at helping those people lower down on the socio-economic scale gain access to information not readily available through commercial alternatives. It can be questioned whether this development is compatible with public broadcasting's mission as envisioned in its founding "blue print," the 1967 Carnegie Commission Report. This plan called for, "a well financed and well directed system, substantially larger and far more pervasive and effective than that which now exists in the United States," one that "must be brought into being if the full needs of the American public are to be met" (Killian 1967: 3).

The two flagship radio news programmes emanating from NPR are "Morning Edition" and the afternoon news magazine, "All Things Considered" (ATC). Some four million Americans tune into these programmes at least once a week. Daily audience numbers average around 900,000 listeners, a figure that increased by 4½ per cent from 1987 to 1988. "Morning Edition" and "ATC" comprise the nearest one can find in the USA to a traditional European news and current affairs radio programme. They last from one-and-a-half to two hours, are divided into segments with a news summary (including occasional one-minute spots from correspondents and a series of reports and features lasting from two to ten or more minutes). Subject matter covers not only politics but science, the arts, and sports. News gathering is done by the staff in Washington in conjunction with own bureaus in Washington DC, Chicago, Los Angeles, and London (where the NPR correspondent has an office at the BBC World Service headquarters on the Strand). NPR often turns to BBC correspondents and stringers for additional foreign reports. Domestic items are frequently covered by staff from individual member stations.

Financial constraints and the competitive environment (regarding both audience and sponsors) have tended to make the public alternatives as ratings conscious as anyone else in American broadcasting. For example, one truth about radio in the US is that it is frequently "on" when people are driving their cars (in fact, by 1990, over 60 per cent of all radio listening there will be "out of home"). Traffic reports thus assume paramount importance in radio programming, so much so that many reporters have risked their lives in helicopters trying to provide the best information on jammed-up roads. A station with no traffic reports, regardless of the quality of its programming, is at a considerable disadvantage. When NPR station KQED-FM in San Francisco finally did introduce traffic reports in the mid-1980s, their audience for "Morning Edition" grew from 38,000 to 68,000 listeners. Was public broadcasting traffic news any better than that available on commercial radio? The agency that provided the reports was exactly the same one that fed traffic news to the local CBS radio station, using the same on-air voices but a different name.

NPR, as we have indicated, is a co-ordinating body which produces or commissions programmes mainly in the news area and organizes distribution to well over 300 local radio stations, many of which are based at the universities and colleges. A transponder on the Weststar 4 satellite provides public radio stations with sixteen sound channels. Twenty uplinks and over 300 downlinks allow programmes to be distributed to member stations. One channel is used exclusively for data on programme times and content. Via DACS (Direct Access Communication System), data appear automatically on printers at each station and tape recorders can be cued for recording and playback. Spare capacity on the satellite is rented out to other programme distributors, notably the BBC and the West German government-sponsored, "Deutsche Welle."

APR (American Public Radio), based in St Paul, Minnesota, is another organization which commissions and distributes pro- grammes or makes agreements with other broadcasters for the use of their material. The network receives no funds from the CPB, but relies on programme dues from affiliated stations and grants, notably from the Ford Foundation. APR now offers the BBC World Service via satellite to public stations in the USA. When the sound of London actually emerges over the local airwaves, however, it is usually linked closely to a local sponsor (who has paid at least part of the fee for the World Service). Little did the vehemently non-commercial BBC-broadcasters back at Bush House on the Strand in London know that listeners to the satellite feed of the fifteen-minute "Radio Newsreel" on US public stations throughout 1987 were informed by the APR announcer that the programme "had been made possible by a grant from the Capital Group, a money management firm investing throughout the world for American individuals and institutions."

APR also offers a news programme, "Monitoradio," supplied by the *Christian Science Monitor*, and even distributes a business programme produced by CBS. The latter is a good example of the strange interlocking arrangements which emerge within the complex competitive media environment of the USA.

Not only money makes life tougher...

We have already seen how public radio and television in the States is battling with the universal problem of non-commercial broadcasting, that is, how to remain non-commercial when funds are tight. As a programme director of a small PBS station told us during the last year of the Reagan Presidency: "With this Administration, you can't criticise it one day, as part of your

41

duty to critically appraise and inform, and then go and ask for more federal funding the next." When the cuts in aid to non-commercial broadcasters during the 80s are compared to the increase in spending on the Voice of America, for example, there is a lingering suspicion in American public broadcasting circles that independent, critical media have not enjoyed a high degree of respect or admiration among those whom Ronald Reagan chose to lead the land.

While CBS was warding off an array of "fairness in, truth in" and/or "accuracy in media" groups, the American political right wing was not yet satisfied at the level of pecuniary blood that was flowing in the public broadcasting world. Reed Irvine, writing in the Wall Street *Journal* on 28 March 1986, expressed his concern that "five years into the Reagan administration, the conservative revolution has barely touched the public broad-casting establishment." Mr Irvine, Chairman of Accuracy in Media, was shocked that "it took Ronald Reagan nearly four years to appoint a majority of the members of the board" of the CPB. "The time is ripe to follow the old advice of the Reagan transition team and defund the left-wing bureaucracy that has made public broadcasting its private playpen," he said. The fact that such right-wing heroes as free-market economist Milton Friedman were regularly given access to the public airwaves to spread their ideas, and that conservative opinion is often sought on the McNeil/Lehrer Newshour, is dismissed by Irvine as "tokens that can be cited to disarm critics."

That it's hard for broadcast news to satisfy extreme views at either end of a political scale is hardly surprising. The selection process tends to centre around middle-class values, which include liberal thinking on a number of issues and support, nominally at least, libertarian traditions. What is strange is the fact that a broadcasting service which attracts young, successful people from business and the academic world could also awaken such wrath and anger amongst an extreme right, hiding under the wing of one of America's most popular Presidents. What is even more interesting is that similar processes are observable in Britain. There, those representing the mercantile, free-market brand of right-wing thought aimed their weapons at Public Broadcasting (the BBC), replacing board members, criticizing individual broadcasters, in short doing much the same as their conservative brethren in the States. The on-going restructuring of news organization in the BBC that we are about to describe is clearly related to those pressures. That does not mean, however, that independence has been replaced by tacit acquiescence to power centres in society who do not like analytical and questioning broadcast journalism.

3

The traditional news broadcasters in Britain:
new establishments fighting older institutions

The broadcasting system of Great Britain is widely acknow-
ledged to be the most stable and yet the most dynamic in the
Western world. The British found a way to create an enormous
diversity of programmes, to encourage extremely high degrees
of professionalism. . . .Although the British system has become
the focus of discontent within the industry and certain sectors
of society, it still retains an international glamour among
broadcasting systems. (Smith 1974: 14)

Since 1974, when Anthony Smith summed up the achievements of British broadcasting with these lines, and even though
most of the world maintains that exalted opinion of the BBC,
much has happened. The great sixty-odd-years-old institution,
the BBC, has been rocked, not so much by demands on savings or
run-away costs, but by conflicts with other parts of the British
establishment. In terms of verbal intensity, attacks from the
right have dominated. The left, via observers such as the
Glasgow Media Group, have also been persistent critics, claiming
that ordinary people, strikers, peace activists, or indeed anyone
questioning the status quo, are not welcome contributors, nor
are they seen as worthy of coverage.

It may be that the BBC, in trying to tread the tightrope of
independence, has produced a vague image for itself at home. As
Jeremy Tunstall (Tunstall 1983: 158) reported in *The Media in
Britain*,

People in other countries may have an image of the BBC as a
bastion of public service broadcasting and political indepen-

dence. The BBC's image seems to be getting worse, with only 55% of Britons thinking they can always trust it and only a similar percentage believing the BBC to be in touch with ordinary people. About as many thought that it is controlled by the government (30%) as thought it independent of government (34%) while 36% did not know or would not say.

Over its six decades of institutionalization, the BBC has had to adjust to some major changes. Two of the biggest, including its creation, came about as conscious political decisions aimed in part at avoiding the American situation of free market commercialization. The monopoly, created back in the early 1920s, resulted from a fear of the free-for-all that was developing on the other side of the Atlantic, as well as no small amount of pressure from the newspaper lobby (which feared the loss of advertising). Some early commentators also linked the Corporation's birth to the desire to make things easy for the manufacturers of radio sets, via the regulation of scarce wavelengths.

Beginning as a monopoly, the British system evolved into a duopoly, with the BBC funded through a licence fee and a commercial alternative funded by the sale of advertising time. Once again, this was the British solution for adapting to commercial media developments in the States. Both sides of the duopoly are heavily regulated, with monopoly franchises guaranteeing profits to commercial television companies but providing public service obligations in the form of current affairs, educational and minority programming. The system even eventually allowed for the formation of a second commercial television channel (Channel 4), providing programming for widely diverse audience groups (including Great Britain's 500,000 Welsh speakers) but funded in part by profits from the established, protected commercial companies. Michael Grade, who left the BBC in the turmoil of 1987 to become head of Channel 4, explained the Fourth Channel's existence in a 1989 Swedish Television interview in terms of

> one of these funny British ways of doing things. We have the best of two worlds. We can accept advertising but we have a guaranteed revenue. Hopefully we can continue to be commercial, but make programmes which different groups enjoy watching, not which certain advertisers would like to be shown.

The result is an extraordinary range, from avant-garde drama to Japanese Sumo wrestling, from soaps set in immigrant settings to a daily hour-long analytical news programme somewhat similar to the McNeil/Lehrer show on US public television. Channel 4 also has an unusual organizational structure, with a small central bureaucracy commissioning most progammes from outside producers and production companies (over 60 per cent of these commissions, however, go to the established, regional commercial TV companies). Channel 4 has led the march towards fragmentation of the audience and away from the traditional notion in national scheduling of always trying to attract the largest audience from the entire population.

Few can doubt the values of the British system in terms of quality programming; the inbuilt stability allows for investments that would never be made if short-term criteria of bottom-line management ruled. But technological, political, and economic developments have moved at a rate seemingly too rapid for the traditional British broadcasters to adjust to. The licence fee, paid directly by citizens through the Post Office, may work out at less than the cost of a newspaper a day (for two BBC television channels and four national and scores of local radio stations). The payment of the licence, however, because it is made directly by individuals, is more obviously an expense than the billion pounds a year people pay for commercial television hidden in the price of their detergent or cornflakes packets. But because the level of the licence fee is a debatable quantity fixed in Parliament, and because the funds generated by licences are tied to the number of households having television sets, when people stop buying sets (as when they all have colour receivers, for example), it provides politicians with a way of putting leverage on broadcasters. In a Granada TV documentary, "The Taming of the BEEB," broadcast on 29 February 1988, a BBC official reminisced how, in 1978, a Labour Party politician threatened, "Hell will freeze over before you get a licence fee increase unless we get a better deal out of you."

British broadcasters, although supposedly a "protected species" because of their public service role, have all been subjected to the same sort of political pressures and manipulations as public broadcasters in the USA. As in the States, Britain is now witnessing a mercantile ideology most simply stated: if the public wants it, it will buy it. This has replaced the paternalism of traditional cultural conservatism, causing tremors among the broadcasting system, with not only Channel 4, but satellites, video-cassettes, and possibly more cable is accelerating the pace of audience fragmentation. The effects are similar to those felt by the networks in the USA in the wake of localization and increased independence of their affiliates.

News and current affairs on the BBC

"The function of BBC News is fairly and clearly, and absolutely without angling, to summarize the most important items of interest in the world." So said the *BBC Year Book* in 1947. Yet, the worldwide image of the BBC, and particularly that of the World Service, has hardly been enhanced by the more overt government involvement experienced during the Thatcher years.

The task of reporting independently on the Falklands conflict was almost impossible, for example. Any mention on the BBC of dissident opinion was noisily declared to be treachery. The BBC and the rest of the media were often caught between the conflicting interests of the government (keen to announce victories) and the military (keen to retain military secrets). At the same time, the traditional civil service spokesman (often of the same reportorial breed as the BBC staff) who gave correct but limited information, was being replaced by a new type of public relations spokesman whose prime duty it was to exercise news management. A statement by Mrs Thatcher in Parliament that "the case for our country is not being put with sufficient vigour on certain programmes of the BBC," (Granada TV 1988) might seem fairly innocuous to an American network news producer (considering what Washington was saying about US television news during the Vietnam war). But in the British system, it was seen as signalling what former head of News and Current Affairs, Alan Protheroe, called on Granada TV a "concerted attack to discredit and damage the BBC."

Northern Ireland has also been another problem story, regularly digging holes in the independent image of the BBC. The October 1988 order, "The Home Secretary's Notice on Nothern Ireland," forbidding the BBC to run interviews with suspected terrorists, or to even quote anyone who makes a supporting statement about their organizations, has been one of the harshest intrusions on the notion that the BBC is capable of exercising journalistic responsibility. As a result, BBC correspondents abroad have been treated with an attitude of "if you can't report on your own dissidents, don't start talking about human rights abuses here." Making matters even more uncertain is the issue of secrecy and what exactly constitutes "the national interest" (as opposed to the citizens' right to know).

A number of interesting parallels to the United States can be drawn. The Westmorland documentary, "The Uncounted Enemy," involved CBS News in lengthy and expensive court hearings. In addition, many observers have linked this event with the growth of various "fairness in media" groups and the Jesse Helms bid to take over that network. The BBC had a similar experience. Its flagship investigative programme, "Panorama," produced "Maggie's Militant Tendency," detailing the activities of far-right members of the Conservative Party. The story was based on a report produced by the Young Conservatives. Broadcast in January of 1984, it led to a series of libel suits, which were ultimately settled expensively for the BBC. In fact, the last one was finalized only two days before the full court hearing was due to start. What seemed to be a "rock solid" case became much less sure as a number of witnesses suffered changes of heart; 100 Conservative MPs were moved to call for the "restoration of standards at the BBC" (Milne 1988: 182-189). Standards, of course, are in the eye of the beholder.

While the Reagan Administration was seating its own people on the Board of the CPB and preparing rule changes for programme funding, the Thatcher government was moving to strengthen its control over the BBC by changing the complexion of the Board of Governors. With both the Chairman and Vice-Chairman being Conservatives, and Conservatives replacing Liberals on the Board, the traditional "hands-off" style of management began to change. Former news and current affairs boss, Alan Protheroe, recalled in the 1988 Granada programme on the BBC that "one did get rather tired of being involved in rather ritualistic crucifixions when one appeared before the Board of Governors at the BBC. It became sadly a less happy organization."

One senior CBS news executive told us that he regarded the BBC as a quasi-governmental organization. His view is understandable yet not entirely correct. Even in the wake of unprecedented turmoil, however, it is not easy to "undo" the BBC, to turn such an established institution (and its values) topsy-turvy, to bring it to heel to others with strong views about what the media may or may not say.

Traditional news broadcasters in Britain

The next NCA Meeting will
be held at 11.30 a.m. on
Tuesday 14 July 1987 in
The Sixth Floor Suite, TVC

Week 27
(367 - 377)

NEWS AND CURRENT AFFAIRS MEETING

Tuesday 7 July 1987, 11.30 am
The Board Room, Broadcasting House

Present: CA to DG (in the Chair), CCNS, Ed R N, EXSN, Political
Editor, CA to DP Tel, HTDR, HESCAP, HJT, Dep Ed RN, AHCAG Tel,
DHCA(WS), H Morn Seq R, Ed "Newsbeat", E(W) NCA, AHCAMP,
Ed NPMS, AHDF Tel, HNCA (Midlands), EN(SW), NE (Radio York),
Data Protection Officer, Deputy Solicitor, CA Inf Div

Secretariat: Nadine Grieve

---

367   PRELIMINARIES

CA to DG welcomed David Sizer (Data Protection Officer),
Chris Cook (EN[SW]), David Miller (NE [Radio York]) and
Stephen Claypole in his new role as EXSN.

PREVIOUS MINUTES

368   SOUTH AFRICA (353)

CA to DG said ADG had a busy schedule of meetings in
South Africa and it was to be hoped he would return with
some good news.

369   CORRECTION TO PREVIOUS MINUTES

Minute 366. John Cole (Political Editor) said Television
News was employing a Russian-speaking researcher, rather
than a presenter, as minuted.

370   WOODLANDS PARK CONFERENCE (353)

Summary

CA to DG said the conference had been useful and
stimulating. She valued the opportunity the creation of
a new directorate gave to reassessing methods of working
and deployment of staff and resources. DDG had opened
the conference by giving his overview of coverage and had
looked at:

3.1 Minutes from a BBC News and Current Affairs Meeting demonstrate
the organization's myriad of titles, abbreviations, and rituals

49

"Auntie," or the BEEB, as the BBC is still affectionately known, is a sturdy and at times sluggish organization, the internal ways of which are protected from the outside by an amazing bureaucracy replete with a jungle of titles and regulations, a wealth of professional knowledge, and an ability to make quality programmes.

The reputation for truth rather than propaganda that the BBC established during World War II lives on in many quarters despite discontent among politicians and increased "freedom of choice" from commercial alternatives. When there's a big story, the public turns primarily to the BBC rather than to sources such as ITV or IRN (the commercial television and radio news alternatives respectively). On the 1:00 p.m. television news the day after a Pan Am jet crashed over Lockerbie (21 December 1988), the number of viewers for the BBC rose from a normal four to an all-time high of seven million. This is the only time of day when BBC television and commercial ITN run parallel network newscasts. ITN's figures showed no comparable increase.

When news first appeared on British radio it was with the somewhat unwilling co-operation of the newspaper proprietors. They had had their way over advertising and controlled news reporting by delivering a bulletin to be read at 7:00 p.m., well after the papers had enjoyed most of their sales. Now, news is everywhere on radio, once an hour on BBC national and local radio, as well as on local commercial radio at different times on different channels. As a percentage of output, however, news programming on BBC Radio has remained constant at around 6 per cent ever since the 1930s. Television statistics show a somewhat different picture. Though BBC television has doubled its news time since 1953, as a proportion of total output, news programming has dropped from 13 to 4 per cent. Current affairs programmes account for another 15 or so per cent on both radio and television.

There is little information in the various annual *Yearbooks* regarding the relative importance of foreign and domestic news other than occasional references to appointments of new correspondents. The only time the foreign/domestic division seems to have led to a debate was during the immediate post-World War II period. The *BBC Yearbook* for 1947, under the heading "Problems of News Broadcasts in the First Year of Peace," notes some of the difficulties in turning away from war reporting:

The problem of the news desks was faithfully to report what

Table 3.1 *Hours of news and percentage of total output*

| Year | Radio News | | TV News | |
	hrs/annum	%	hrs/annum	%
1936		6		
1953/54	1019	7	247	13
1986/87	1877	6	454	4

Source: *BBC Annual Handbooks.* Note that current affairs/documentaries accounted for an additional 1400 hours on television (1986) and 4770 hours on radio. The 1953 television figure is for "newsreel and documentary films" but does not include "documentary programmes."

was happening at home in a land striving under a new government to set its house in order and what was happening in the grim tangled realm of foreign affairs. . . . Foreign affairs competed with domestic.

Then, as now, there was no rule of thumb designating the relative importance of foreign and home news items. "BBC editors are controlled only by their own sense of truth of balance and of public appetite," concluded the 1947 summary.

Forty years ago, news production for domestic and international transmissions was far more integrated than it is now. One news division produced forty-eight hours a week of news and current affairs programming for listeners abroad as well as selected items for the home bulletins. Now, with the increase in size and complexity of operations, there are growing differences in home and international news' structure and aims. Of course, the means of financing the output have always been different: the licence fee for domestic operations, and government grants drawn from tax moneys for international transmissions (BBC World Service).

Access to each other's news sources and various forms of co-operation regarding foreign correspondents are important features though not always used as much as one would expect. The editorial question of what is of interest to a home audience and what is of interest and importance for an international audience in practice do lead to different answers. The BBC World Service, in fact, often becomes less ethnocentrically British than does the domestic news despite its financing from the Foreign Office, whose charge is, in part, presenting Britain to the world.

A recent example illustrates the different ways of thinking that have evolved in BBC External News and Home News selection. In November of 1988, Chancellor Kohl of West

3 Staff compiling television news bulletins at the BBC's television centre in London work in a maze of monitors, video display terminals, and telecommunications equipment

4 The view from the BBC television news presenter's desk. Prompters (providing text to be read) are perched on cameras, all of which are remote-controlled

Germany visited President Reagan in part to say goodbye, but primarily to discuss important trade and currency issues. The next day Mrs Thatcher arrived in Washington on what turned out to be mainly a ritual/ceremonial visit during which the British Prime Minister used many superlatives to express her admiration for Mr Reagan. At a main editorial meeting at Bush House senior editors engaged in a lively discussion about the relative importance one should attach to the two different visits in their news transmissions to the rest of the world from Britain. The issue was put bluntly by one specialist correspondent who, after recognizing the economic importance of West Germany to the US, suggested that, "It's more important for the world to know about an arm-twister than an ****-licker." For home news, the issue was simpler. "Anywhere Mrs Thatcher goes is an important news story, and we covered the Kohl visit anyway," was the Head of Domestic Radio News' evaluation. BBC Television re-ran generous portions of Mrs Thatcher's public speech in Washington praising Mr Reagan's special qualities. The World Service presented extensive analysis of West Germany's importance to the United States, given the strength of the Deutschmark.

It is interesting to note that the BBC World Service, since it made its programmes available throughout Britain on an AM–Medium Wave frequency during the day and on Long Wave at night, has attracted a home audience of about a million (cumulative over a week) without advertising its wares at all at home. In fact, the BBC's own International Broadcasting and Research Unit produced an audience analysis in May 1986 that dismissed the notion that this increase in British listeners was due to "elderly insomniacs." The report concluded, "The evidence points rather to the conclusion that the World Service provides programming, particularly a global view of news and current affairs, which its listeners often find lacking in domestic services." We will return to the activities of international broadcasters such as the BBC World Service in chapter 6.

The competitive news environment in Britain

With no commercial radio network operating in Britain as yet, the BBC's only radio competition comes from the local commercial radio stations who are fed national and international news by their central IRN (Independent Radio News) agency. Internally,

BBC Radio does have a certain amount of "quasi-competition." The regions have their own news and magazine programmes (BBC Radio Scotland, Wales, Northern Ireland, and the Welsh language Radio Cymru). The four national radio news networks all air news, the majority of it broadcast on the spoken-word channel, Radio 4. Radio 4's 6:00 p.m. halfhour newscast attracts an audience of around one million listeners. The pop/rock music channel, Radio 1, carries short bursts of news half-past the hour as well as longer, up-tempo newscasts known as "Newsbeat." These are an attempt to present the main news stories of the day (as well as quite a few human-interest items) for a mass audience by embedding them in an environment of popular music. The fifteen-minute "Newsbeat" show usually ends with an item from the music business, thereby facilitating the return to normal music format programming.

This reporting of the news in various styles requires that incoming material be presented in different ways for different channels. A story about dead birds floating ashore off the Scandinavian coastline is presented in a graver, more sedate fashion for Radio 4. The urgency of the issue is marked by a quickened tempo for "Newsbeat" (and the instruction to this book's first author as he filed his report to "imagine a record-player spinning in front of you when reading your piece"). The result is similar to the sound picture on newscasts on most US radio stations, with the obvious exception of National Public Radio. The BBC's "Newsbeat" claims an average daily audience of approximately four million people and, as such, is regarded as being of great significance by BBC Radio News.

The competitive television news environment in the UK

Television news in Britain produces national and regional output as well. The flagship programmes are the BBC's "9 O'clock News" on BBC 1 and the ITN "News at Ten," broadcast over the entire first commercial channel, ITV.

ITN is an organization created in 1955 for the sole purpose of providing news for commercial television. It is non-profit-making and is owned by the regional commercial television franchise holders. It also provides network news for Channel 4. Regional ITV stations also provide their own local newscasts.

Here, once again we can note parallels between this essentially public service environment and the free-market, US model. The two main evening newscasts usually attract the same average size of audience as is the case in US network news; however, there are fairly large fluctuations from day to day. Most observers agree that content, in terms of choice of news subjects, is relatively similar on the two British programmes: 3 March 1987 can serve as an example. The two UK blockbuster news programmes concurred in the choice of no less than nine major stories. The BBC aired three stories about the Royal Family: the Queen Mother phoning her grandson on the HMS Ark Royal; Prince Philip talking about pandas; and Princess Anne making a "Save The Children Fund" award. ITN carried two of the three, including instead of the last a short spot on US spy John Pollard and the soccer results.

The same streamlining effects so noticeable in the States are evident in Britain as well. The two news organizations watch each other very closely – both hunt the same mass audience.

For years, we have had tremendously similar news values. ITN bulletins have matched ours at the BBC story for story. We're the same type of people with the same middle-aged, middle-class values that have dominated the industry for years,

one BBC foreign news editor told us in 1988. Now however, a policy change can be discerned. "There's a policy on our side to become more serious. It appears to us that ITN, faced with Murdoch's Sky Channel round the corner is going the other way for the tabloid style" he added.

Streamlining of story selection among the "majors" is not merely a consequence of more than similar people with similar values making similar choices. The complicated interlocking arrangements in supply patterns have just as much, if not more, influence (though even these developments in the organizational structure may be related to similarities in norms of newsworthiness). NBC, Reuters, and the BBC all own Visnews which sells to virtually anyone who will pay for news material (including local stations in the States, via INN, and the new Sky satellite news channel in Europe). ABC, Australia's Channel 9, and ITN own the other primary news agency, WTN, supplying material not only to ABC in the States, but also to the McNeil/Lehrer hour on PBS. WTN claims to serve some 1,200 television stations worldwide with international news. Their contracts include a multi-million dollar deal signed in the autumn of 1988 with the Japanese national broadcaster, NHK.

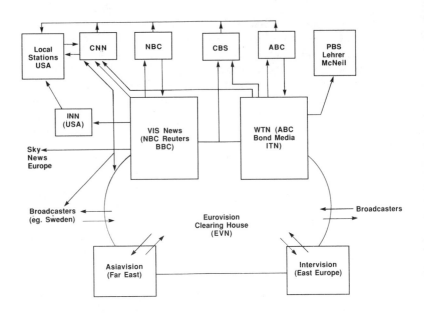

3.2 The interlocked system for international distribution of television news material (Bond Media is essentially the same as Channel 9 Australia).

The activities of Visnews and WTN are matched carefully through the Eurovision clearing house (EVN) via a complicated, archaic system of bidding and points. At a daily conference, the two agencies can offer material for the Eurovision Pool (to which most major Western broadcasters are affiliated, including the three US commercial networks and CNN). If Visnews develops a story which WTN also has available, WTN shouts "Match!" A points system based on previous "matches" determines whether Visnews supplies that story or if that right rotates to WTN. Once in the pool, however, material is available to all who are associated with the pool including Visnews and WTN's own commercial customers. Thus, WTN material can also end up on a Visnews feed to the States. This extraordinary self-regulating system assures that everyone is happy, provides interesting opportunities for Visnews and WTN to play poker at the Eurovision table, and adds to the general streamlining and homogenizing effects readily evident when comparing the different television news programmes.

Many writers commenting on the similarity of news selection within the network families have referred to an explanatory consensus model. In other words, the people who make the selections think the same way. Organizational entrenchment as illustrated above is probably just as important a factor. One of the reasons that NBC bought a 37 per cent share in Visnews in November of 1988 was purely functional – to cut costs by avoiding overlap in coverage. Ed Planter, NBC's bureau chief in London, confirmed the trend when he told us, "The cost of news gathering has become so prohibitive that we will rely more and more on Visnews, just as ABC relies on WTN. We will also rely more and more on outside providers of resources, such as camera crews."

CBS may be the only kid on the American network television block not to buy into an international agency, but it has signed an agreement with WTN (part-owned by ABC) which gives it access to WTN materials excluding those supplied by ABC, allowing it to cut its own costs for news gathering. What could rock this tightly knit set-up for international news distribution is the possibility of ITN (and WTN) losing the special monopoly position *vis-à-vis* commercial television in Great Britain, a change proposed by the Thatcher government as part of its "Broadcasting in the '90s" deregulation package. For now, though, Visnews and WTN are jostling for position, carving up the market, and trying to make sure that no competition moves in. The US facilities provider, CONUS, is already hovering on the edge, waiting for further deregulation of European satellite services before moving in and offering its expertise in the field of SNG (Satellite News Gathering). In fact, a number of licences have been granted by the British government for satellite up-links. This weakening of the traditional monopolies of the large, national telecommunications organizations (PTTs) is going on throughout Europe. None the less, satellite links still account for one of the largest agency costs in news gathering and distribution.

There exist other possibilities for expanding the international exchange of news. Intervision, representing television operations in Eastern Europe, does have an exchange with Eurovision. The flow, however, has traditionally been somewhat one-way. The number of news stories fed from the West to the East increased from approximately 700 during the first year of the agreement (1966) to almost 7,000 by 1982. The counter-flow from eastern Europe to Eurovision numbered only around 500 items in 1982.

This situation has and will continue to change as the full effects of *glasnost* increase interest in the West for news from the USSR and other Intervision countries.

The ratings game in Britain

Seven to ten million nightly viewers is the usually accepted average for each of the major BBC and ITN newscasts, but the figures do increase significantly when a major news story breaks. Nightly variations too, are considerable, as the following figures from a relatively quiet week (as seen by news editors) and the week of the Pan Am Lockerbie crash indicate:

Table 3.2 *Fluctuating audience figures for main TV evening newscasts on BBC TV and ITV*

The Quiet Week (28 November to 3 December 1988)						
Programme	28/11	29/11	30/11	1/12	2/12	3/12
BBC 9 O'clock News (in millions)	9.4	7.9	6.5	5.9	7.4	7.4
ITN News at Ten (in millions)	5.4	8.8	8.1	8.6	6.6	7.5

The Not Quiet Week (19 December to 24 December 1988)						
Programme	19/12	20/12	21/12	22/12	23/12	24/12
BBC 9 O'clock News (in millions)	13.1	9.0	13.0	10.0	9.7	11.0
ITN News at Ten (in millions)	5.0	8.4	13.0	9.9	7.9	8.8

Source: BBC Audience Research/News

The fluctuations in Table 3.2 above suggest that the decision that twenty million viewers each day make is more a question of scheduling vagaries than absolute programme loyalty. A series of low Monday night audiences for the ITN news coincided with the running of a lead-in dramatic series which enjoyed the critics' but not the public's acclaim. The Pan Am crash on 21 December attracted maximum audiences, with additional millions watching both news programmes.

An interesting question is raised by these observations. The BBC has opted to create a specific competence or profile by "going more serious," hoping thereby to capture a larger share of the available audience in the face of increasing competition. Can such changes of format and style outweigh the effects of scheduling, for example, lead-in programming, the quality of programmes airing opposite the news, striking news events? A revamped "9 O'clock News" was launched in November 1988 with new and rather expensive graphics and more individual sequences offering in-depth analyses by topic specialists. Audience figures for the following month did not indicate that the "rebirth" could compensate for scheduling factors. At the time, though, it was simply too early to draw definite conclusions; the process could well take time and will certainly be related, in part, to positioning and re-positioning among the competitors.

Heading for the 1990s

In November 1988 the British government published a White Paper entitled "Broadcasting in the '90s: Competition, Choice and Quality." While recognizing the "special role" of the BBC as a "cornerstone of broadcasting," the general tone was one of deregulatory ideology based on the belief that free market-forces and a multiplicity of channels would guarantee a wide freedom of choice to listeners and viewers. The report contained a number of specifics.

Remaining commercial, but with funding guaranteed in the event of advertising revenue shortfalls, Channel 4 would continue to be protected. The argument for public service broadcasting funded by a licence fee was not given strong support. By the mid-90s, in fact, the BBC will have to look for other means of finance, notably audience subscription and sponsorship. Until then, at least until 1991, the licence fee would be linked to the Retail Price Index.

The report was vague regarding the financing of radio in the UK. An earlier document, the 1985 Peacock Report, had recommended selling off the BBC's two popular music network radio channels (Radios 1 and 2), a proposal that raised protests even from the record industry. British record companies saw the national public service networks as the best guarantee for the continued airing of a wide range of music. The traditional networks were seen as more in their interests than the possibility of an American-style, narrowly "formatted" form of radio. The new report merely noted that "account will need to be taken in due course of the implications for funding radio." It is difficult to imagine any system of paying for radio listening via subscription to individual channels or programmes other than the existing licence fee and commercial support methods.

The proposal for the BBC to move, at least in part, towards sponsorship is also surprising, as recent events demonstrate. In the same White Paper that calls for a new funding formula, the British government expresses its commitment to a Council of Europe plan to regulate transborder television (essentially all television in Europe). Yet one clause in this convention of which Britain was an inaugural signatory in Strasbourg in May 1989 deals specifically with limitations on sponsorship. The text of the agreement includes the statement, "Sponsored programmes shall not encourage the purchase or rental of the products or services of the sponsor or a third party, in particular by making special promotional references to those programmes or services in such programmes." All twenty-three member nations of the Council of Europe, even those who had not signed as of May 1989, have agreed to this principle.

If the BBC is "safe" in terms of licence moneys for at least the next few years, the ITV situation could change radically if plans to open new national commercial channels become a reality. ITN will lose its privileged position within the commercial television family since other news producers will be able to bid for franchises. The government decribes the aim of the proposed expansion as seeking to create "a flexible framework that allows entrepreneurs and viewers to decide in the marketplace, subject to minimum necessary regulation, which technologies should play the most significant roles." On news supplies to the "new" ITV (renamed Channel 3), the government plans to do away with the system of a non-profit-making ITN, owned collectively by the contracting programme companies. "Adequate competition to the BBC" is another aim of the new structure. Therefore, the supply of news, states the White Paper (1988: 21-22), "would, unlike the funding of ITN at present, include a profit element to establish the organization's commercial value."

Reactions to the heralding of such radical changes have been varied. The nature of the response has depended on whether those venturing an opinion regard the Market Economy as a civilized or an uncivilized instrument for regulating broadcasting as well as whether they have an attitude of faith in or distaste for non-commercial public service media.

Brian Wenham, once Director of Programmes at BBC Television, wrote in the 13 November 1988 edition of the *Observer*, "In future, everything is to be up for grabs." A reply could be couched in the words, admittedly written two years earlier by David

Elstein in *The BBC and Public Service Broadcasting* (Elstein in MacCabe/Stewart 1986: 83). He articulated much of the thinking inherent in the "Broadcasting in the '90s" master plan:

> Of course, programme makers – largely recruited from the educated class – welcome [the present] arrangement, and educated foreigners applaud it. The "historic compromise" further includes workers and trade unions deriving high incomes from a stable structure and, of course, the politicians and mandarins who know they can control or browbeat broadcasters within the regulated system those broadcasters so enthusiastically embrace.

What is surprising in the British context is that those conservatives with more traditional cultural tastes have remained quiet on the issue despite a future where they stand to lose their classical concerts and sedate news magazine programmes that, for now at least, are uninterrupted by commercial breaks. Some six months after the publication of the White Paper, there began to emerge signs of a revolt, even by some of those very individuals whom the Conservative government had put in to run broadcasting. The IBA (Independent Broadcasting Authority), which oversees commercial broadcasters, complained that government plans to auction off future commercial TV franchises to the highest bidders would divert too much money from programme-making, at the expense of quality, since current incumbents would be tempted to stockpile funds to guarantee winning the next round of auctions, rather than gambling in expensive productions. Such views are reported in a *Sunday Times* article of 19 March 1989: "Hurd's hand-picked ITV chiefs rebel".

So, with the BBC assured of possibly another half decade of solid licence fee financing pegged to the Retail Price Index, what strategy has the Corporation adopted? The "Birt Revolution," affecting news more than any other type of programming, holds several clues.

The 1988 Birt Revolution

Adoption of new policies does not necessarily produce actual changes in an organization's operations. Mr John Birt, appointed Deputy Director General of the BBC in 1987 (from commercial London Weekend Television), did, however, introduce a measure of confusion into the system (maybe a necessary tactic when trying to effect change in a very stable institution). His boss, Mr Michael Checkland, promoted to BBC Director General from a position as a corporate accountant, gave Birt overall responsibility for news and current affairs, that sensitive area which had brought the BBC into conflict with Mrs Thatcher. Many observers inside and outside the BEEB assumed that Birt was moved in to tame the BBC in accordance with the pleasures of a strong Government. Several of his decisions regarding a number of "Panorama" episodes, faithfully reported in the London-based satirical paper, *Private Eye*, and confirmed internally, suggest that this may in fact have been his mission.

Such suspicions led many to the feeling that the Birt era was a preamble to the dismantling of the BBC, one of the more conspicuous remaining non-privatized entities in Great Britain. Others, less conspiratorially inclined, believed simply that Birt holds a passionate belief in his favourite phrase, "The Mission to Explain," and that he seeks to improve what he regarded as sinking standards of accuracy and impartiality at the BBC. As he declared in a speech entitled "Decent Media," the keynote address at the April 1988 meeting of the Royal Television Society,

> There are too many stitch-ups and stick-ups in our studios and in our films, too many contributors who vow never to return. . . . The pursuit of accurate, impartial, fair and enquiring journalism of quality on television and elsewhere comes easiest to those who have open minds. . . . It comes hardest to those imbued with a disdain for, and not just a healthy suspicion of, established centres of power.

Making public such criticism of a sixty-year old institution that thoroughly believes in its own impartiality led, not surprisingly, to upheaval, discontent, and damage to organization morale. This does not mean that turmoil was not a necessity; other considerations will have to be weighed and more time will have to pass before a more accurate judgement can be made.

Changes at the BBC resulting from changes in leadership are not unknown. Philip Schlesinger recounted another series of upsets at Radio News in the early 1970s when a new Editor, Mr Peter Woon, was brought in. He, too, had passionate beliefs, but in the value of what the BBC terms "actuality," actual recordings of voices or sounds which can add to the authenticity of a report. It was difficult for journalists used to writing well thought-out pieces to adjust to this technique, leading Schlesinger (1987: 266) to write, "There was a tremendous upheaval. A lot of pedantic, old-style people were retired early or received paper promotions." Soon, though, business was back more or less to normal apart from elements of a generation change.

Schlesinger recounts these events in a chapter of his 1987 book, *Putting Reality Together*, called "The Limits of Change." In it he also refers to a series of articles called "The Bias Against Understanding" by John Birt and Peter Jay which first appeared in 1981 in *The Times* of London and later in a book of essays edited by Mr Jay, called *The Crisis for Western Political Economy and Other Essays* (Jay 1984).

Messrs Jay and Birt have featured prominently in the British broadcasting debate ever since that series of *Times* articles. Peter Jay looked to be a technical futurist in the 1985 Peacock Committee study on broadcasting. He presented a vision of a society of individuals wired via fibre-optics to an ever-increasing range of electronic choices. He also argued that the notion of a traditional broadcasting corporation was irrevelant in such a media environment.

The original Birt–Jay *Times* articles are important. They constitute one of the few attempts in the UK to conceive a different way of organizing radio and television news (even if its component parts are not novel). They also explain much of the recent organizational change at BBC News and Current Affairs.

The Birt approach includes two important elements. The first is structural, seeing news as consisting of events which trigger initial reports which lead to a series of analyses at different levels of depth. These are then linked temporally to output. For example, a train crash would be immediateiy reported as hard news. Later in the day, an initial analysis would list possible causes, relations with other, similar events, and the like. Within a week, a longer piece might delve into larger questions of travel safety, communications, investments, and so on. The more typical "hard facts followed by the human suffering" approach does not marry well with the Birt–Jay model.

Given this view of how news should be covered and reported, Birt and Jay also concluded that the traditional division between News and Current Affairs divisions in the BBC made little sense.

An overriding assumption of their perspective is that news production is a routine and fairly predictable operation, inter-

The Known World of Broadcast News

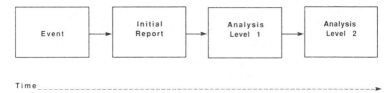

3.3 The Birt–Jay model of logical news reporting

rupted only occasionally by the unexpected. Life, however, is not as simple as this. The world is neither unchanging nor totally predictable; who can foretell what news events may or may not happen in the time span from the occurrence of the original news item to Analysis Level 2? Other events can, and often do intervene to halt the analytical process envisioned in this model.

The second change recommended by Birt–Jay concerned the criteria of competencies which they felt should characterize the people who produce and present the news. Should it be media people or topic specialists? Television, particularly, has traditionally utilized reporters whose first area of competence is the medium itself, often based on the techniques of film, even if they are usually supported by a small number of specialist correspondents (politics, environment, economics, etc).

We have already noted how the "star" reporters, the charismatic fillers of the little screen, monopolize the big stories on the US networks. Expertise is introduced to viewers through interviews with outsiders. This is the way television news has developed universally, producing criticism from a number of observers. Former BBC Governor Francis Williams, writing on foreign news gathering, has deplored this trend toward media suitability in lieu of access to knowledge. "Even less satisfactory as a means of illumination are those overseas forays by air-borne reporters," he wrote (1969: 269),

> All are conditioned by the necessity to interview in front of the camera only those who can discuss the situation, whatever the situation may be, in the language of the viewer at home, so that faculty in a foreign language and a readiness to be questioned in it are more important than depth of knowledge.

A coarser way of saying this, is that television news tends to be so audio-visually as opposed to informationally orientated, that it prefers a pretty face that can speak English to a homely one that says something interesting and requires subtitles.

The BBC, relying on Visnews and the Eurovision exchange system for much of its foreign video material, has not maintained a large number of its own foreign bureaus housing linguistically qualified correspondents. Instead, a team of well-known, home-based faces act as "firemen," rushing off everywhere to report on anything. Technology, too, has extended the demands on the professional media reporter. As John Mahony, BBC Television foreign news editor, told us in 1988, "Sometimes a correspondent who is sent off to cover a subject has to spend more time on the logistics of getting the material home quickly than on the item itself."

Jay and Birt claimed that this type of professionalization produces a "bias against understanding." Their recipe is to combine an integrated news and current affairs organization with the employment of journalists who are specialists in different fields of knowledge.

The Birt–Jay formula of integration plus specialization produces a large, strong news organization but tends to ignore the realities of a competitive environment the effects of which are so obvious in the US television networks. It ignores, too, the trend towards fragmentation of the audience as the number of channels increases, a trend which Peter Jay so warmly embraced during his performances in front of the Peacock committee. Integration (current affairs/news) coupled with the replacement of a small group of "jack of all subjects" media reporters with a large group of specialists, requires a bigger organization, with a longer hierarchy, which costs money. But in an atmosphere of deregulation, where new competitors will lean towards a populist approach (delivering mass audiences to advertisers), can a strategy which involves filling a newscast with specialized segments continue to attract the necessary millions of viewers the BBC needs to justify its existence as a national broadcast service?

Organizationally, at least, the integration of news and current affairs programming has been carried out. One effect has been that a flagship programme such as "Panorama" is now more closely integrated into the general news output of the Corporation. It becomes harder for "Panorama," via a small staff of journalists with good contacts, to produce films which might annoy the establishment (or the government), embarrass the BBC or even pull it into the libel courts. The loss, of course, is that element of risk-taking which is an essential ingredient of editorial independence.

The extended BBC news/current affairs hierarchy

John Birt moved into a BBC post which the ousted Director General, Alisdair Milne, had created to "protect news standards and be my right hand in that often contentious area." Birt then recreated another organizational entity which Milne had abolished, namely a News Directorate in charge of all radio and television news and current affairs. Milne had concluded that such a Directorate removes "at a stroke a large segment of Television and Radio's responsibilities and carries within it the seeds of dissension and disharmony over scheduling and expenditure" (Milne 1988: 73). The News Directorate was re-instated in 1987 and was filled with both outside and inside recruits. The argument for having a Directorate operating above the now-combined news and current affairs organization was presumably that new financial and editorial directions had to be formulated by a special body. Inevitably, the size of the hierarchy increased. Foreign correspondents, in particular, found themselves further removed from the top of the news hierarchy. Decisions previously taken at the Home or Foreign News Editor level had to be referred upwards. One is reminded of the traditional principles of good administration formulated by classical theorists such as Fayol and Parkinson: administration should be simple and the right to make decisions should be delegated as far as possible down the organization.

The increased levels of hierarchy function as a strengthened filter against sensitive issues being treated in an unsatisfactory (i.e., for the BBC) fashion. Extra-sensitive programmes, after being dealt with in the News Directorate, can then get yet another vetting in the office of the Deputy Director General. At least this is the theory. As students of bureaucracy know too well, the increased number of decision-makers means increased opportunities to hear "No" as well as greater risks for inefficiency and lack of flexibility (especially if the aims and goals of the organization are not clearly articulated and shared at all levels).

Specialist journalism for radio and television

The specialist journalism highlighted by Birt–Jay in the early 80s is being slowly extended, mainly in relation to television output through the establishment of three units, covering foreign affairs and defence, social affairs, and business and economics.

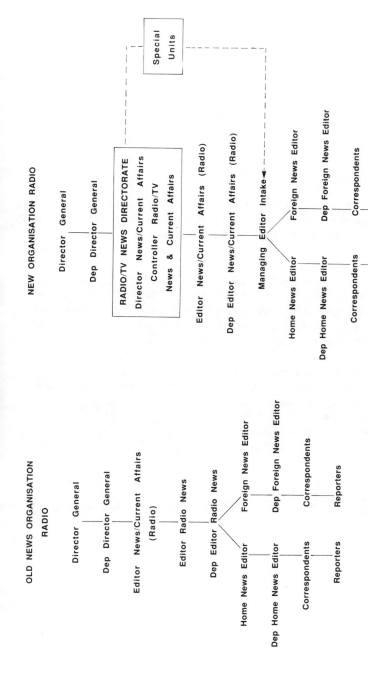

OLD NEWS ORGANISATION RADIO

Director General

Dep Director General

Editor News/Current Affairs (Radio)

Editor Radio News

Dep Editor Radio News

Foreign News Editor — Home News Editor

Dep Foreign News Editor

Correspondents

Reporters

Dep Home News Editor

Correspondents

Reporters

NEW ORGANISATION RADIO

Director General

Dep Director General

RADIO/TV NEWS DIRECTORATE
Director News/Current Affairs
Controller Radio/TV
News & Current Affairs

Special Units

Editor News/Current Affairs (Radio)

Dep Editor News/Current Affairs (Radio)

Managing Editor Intake

Home News Editor — Foreign News Editor

Dep Home News Editor

Correspondents

Reporters

Dep Foreign News Editor

Correspondents

Reporters

3.4 New levels of hierarchy in the organization of BBC Radio News with the integration of news/current affairs and the introduction of a News Directorate with specialist journalist units

The foreign affairs and defence unit includes international and diplomatic expertise as well as additional foreign correspondents based in London (one for Africa and another for an area loosely termed "the developing world"). This unit will be closely related to an expansion of BBC Television's network of foreign correspondents to be stationed in locations as yet undetermined.

Contracting specialists costs money; without a planned injection of money into news of around ten to fifteen million pounds a year for the next four years, this will be impossible to accomplish in a meaningful way. The strategy, however, is clear – the specialists' presence and knowledge should allow the BBC to move "up market," providing more authoritative news and thereby higher status and a measure of safety (vis-à-vis its critics).

What is less clear is the exact organizational role of the new specialist groups. In traditional administrative theory terms, are they "line" (producing and presenting news) or "staff" (advising those with media competence) or both? A bit of both is probably the answer. A wealth of organizational literature has dealt with the line–staff dichotomy over the past decades. Lack of clarity in that relationship theoretically will lead to confusion, misunderstanding, conflicts, and inefficiency (for example, Urwick 1953). The Birt–Jay postulates do not deal with this issue, they merely state that specialist journalism is preferable to journalism based on proficiency in handling media techniques and norms.

The introduction of the new specialist units has not been without its practical problems. In the words of one television reporter well known to BBC viewers, "You can't put a quart in a pint bottle." Correspondents have been employed in considerable numbers (often with salaries far higher than those of existing staff) without a corresponding increase in output of either news or special programmes. Frustration has expressed itself in the number of dissenting internal memoranda that have found their way into the outside press. It can also be argued that the series of strikes that disrupted BBC News operations throughout 1989 were not only related to a wage dispute; they also reflected general dissatisfaction within the organization. This supports the contention regarding the reorganization of news that a clear initial line–staff division, with the specialist groups performing the roles of researchers as opposed to competing with existing production groups for on-air time, might have been a wiser introductory policy.

The overall BBC news strategy of "going serious", however, is

68

not illogical. Competition from at least two new satellite news services, Sky News and the BSB "Now" Channel, mandates a definition of specific competencies. The move should be "up market" and the BBC feels that this is part of the public service ethos. This quote from a 1989 letter from a News Directorate member, Richard Ayre, illustrates the thinking:

> My guess is that satellite broadcasters will provide a good and popular mix of picture stories and event coverage, but little journalism. That is not necessarily a pejorative assessment. But the BBC believes that people want journalism as an integral part of a public service news operation. And, by the way, we think that strategy will help us hold onto audience share, not surrender it.

A cynic might argue that a preponderance of specialists pedagogically spelling out the facts through in-depth analyses on the "9 O'clock News" will make the BBC so boring that people will tune out. A *Financial Times* writer, Christopher Dunkley, under the heading, "The Nine O'Clock News Goes Serious," commented in November of 1988 on the new, revamped newscast by observing,

> It is now more solemn, more austere, more didactic, drier than ever and even narrower in scope. "News" under the new regime seems to mean, above all, politics and human affairs... but however demotic the language may be, the tone is not that of a friend passing on information. There is, rather, the sense that the tablets are being handed down from some superior to the hoi poloi."

Spending and saving: expanding and holding back

Putting not only news and current affairs, but also radio and television under the same organizational lid has triggered the search for joint savings, usually by means of sharing the same staff. The term "bimedia" has become a BBC buzzword. A bimedia office will be opened in Tokyo, meaning that the correspondent there will work both for radio and television. On the face of it, this might seem a wise economic organizational solution. Some doubts, however, have been raised simply because television news reporting is so technologically driven. With logistics so crucial to television reporting, would a journalist involved in preparing a visual piece, editing, organizing satellite transfer, and so on, be able to set all that aside and attend to the needs of BBC Domestic National News, BBC World Service, BBC Scotland, and on and on? Swedish Broadcasting, for instance, had a similar system before reorganization of the Corporation in the late 1970s. Many radio and television journalists as well as managers there testify to the value of separate, "unimedia" groups.

The Chairman of the Board of Governors at the BBC, Marmaduke Hussey, is a man who battled with the rigid print unions at *The Times* (London) after the year-long closure of that paper over the introduction of new technology. The former accountant, Michael Checkland, is his Director General. Tougher cost accounting has thus come as no greater a surprise than bureau closures and firings at CBS after the coming of Mr Tisch. Even staff who are doubtful about other organizational changes admit that better control of spending was necessary. As Ann Sloman, a BBC current affairs editor, told us,

> There's been a growing desire to become more managerially efficient. Two or three years ago, I as an editor could wander around without really worrying too much about budgets. That's all changed with an accountant as Director General. Now, if we want a new filing cabinet, I have to ask what does it cost, which budget will it come from, where do we make a saving? Some of the changes have been good, weeding out hopeless people and making the place more streamlined. The trouble is that this has got muddled up with a preoccupation with structures. Hierarchical structures are not the answer, standards supported by good strong editors with the right staff are.

Even cost accounting can go too far, however, leading to unexpected consequences. For example, a proposed system of "actual costs" whereby every service provided from one unit or department to another is subject to internal debiting might appear reasonable. But this is not an unimaginable scenario: If BBC Radio Scotland must pay BBC Radio News in London for the use of national and international news, then this might well encourage a localization of international news gathering similar to that witnessed in the USA, thereby weakening the economic base for the BBC's news gathering at the national level as the "locals" spend their money elsewhere.

Both domestic and foreign news operations at the BBC are in the midst of adjusting to new budget controls and routines. The foreign news sector is both expanding *and* looking for ways to save money, two directions of movement which must be balanced carefully if chaos is not to ensue. Even telephone calls abroad have a budget limit at both the Domestic and World Service operations in an attempt to limit excessive expenses in what is an otherwise essential service. Satellite costs, which run approximately £1,200 for a minimum booking of ten minutes (of which only one-and-a-half may actually be used), are a major cost which can rarely be predicted in advance other than very roughly. Permanent audio hi-fi quality links to Washington, Brussels or other news centres cost thousands of pounds monthly. All such costs should and are being questioned. Yet, at the same time, new correspondents are taking up positions in locales deemed to be strategically important, thereby expanding the budget and committing future resources. We will return to the thinking behind the details of this expansion in the next chapter.

Religiously following principles of "actual cost" accounting assumes that a broadcasting corporation can be equated with a manufacturing concern that turns physical raw materials into physically refined products. Broadcasting is essentially an extant bureaucracy through which information flows and is processed and in which human experiences are documented using audio or audio-visual technology. Waste must be countered via sense, not nonsense. The administrators and accountants should meet the production staff on a sensible middle ground, a necessary and sometimes painful process for institutions such as the staid BBC. Once again, returning to traditional administrative theory, if overall goals are not clear and shared by all (or at least most) members of the organization, then the process of achieving its aims will be confusing and doomed to failure.

We will return to the issue of the Birt Revolution and its relevance for news availability and selection in a later chapter. Its stated aim of going serious in a news environment characterized by a movement toward the popular, tabloid approach makes the changes sketched in these pages some of the most significant happenings in the history of BBC News. It's something that future media historians will wish to have chronicled from as many different perspectives as possible. Maybe they will discuss it as a passing phase, overtaken by "economic realities". The major expansion of news announced in 1988 called for an extra injection of some fifteen million pounds per annum from 1990–3. In January 1990, however, the Phillips report on overall savings within the BBC was published (Ariel 1990:2–8). As a result, management recommended that News and Current Affairs should achieve annual savings of five million pounds by 1993.

4

Medium-sized traditional operators in Europe:
the example of broadcast news in Sweden

A comparison of the development of broadcasting in Sweden and Britain produces an interesting catalogue of similarities and differences. When faced with the possibility of a commercial free-for-all back in the early 1920s, Sweden opted for a BBC type of solution with a single organization being entrusted with a monopoly on the right to transmit radio programmes.

While the franchises in both nations have established the principle of the State not meddling in programme policy, the BBC's obligations to the State are monitored by a Board of Governors, a selection of the "good and the wise" (chosen, though, by the Government). Sweden, however, opted to organize the broadcasting monopoly as a limited company. For its first thirty years shares in the Swedish radio company were divided between the press and industrial interests involved in the manufacture and sale of receivers. In the 1950s, with the introduction of television, ownership was expanded to include a selection of Sweden's influential *popular movements* (the Churches, Trade Unions, the Co-operative Movement, the Agrarian interests, and so on). Ownership of shares in the broadcasting organization meant, in reality, little more than membership in a total of one-third of the seats on the Board and a 6 per cent return on each group's nominal investment in shares. The government nominated the remaining two-thirds of the board members, selecting them from across the parliamentary political spectrum. The principle was established that broadcasting was to be non-commercial and funded by a licence fee. The directors were not to meddle in the programme-making functions as long as output was factual and satisfied demands of impartiality.

This very special Swedish structure has survived for almost 65 years. A significant change did occur, however, in 1978, two years after a non-socialist coalition temporarily ousted the ruling Social Democrats who had been in power for decades. The radio and television organization was allowed to retain its monopoly, but was divided up into four different programme-producing companies (national radio, local radio, television and educational radio, and television). All four were subsidiaries to a parent company which retained the old name of the Corporation, "Sveriges Radio." Each had Boards of Directors composed of a majority of politicians from different political parties with a mandate to oversee the operations of the company *without* making decisions about programme policy.

With the number of politicians involved in the various broadcasting companies dramatically increased by the creation of these separate Boards, the boardrooms became battle grounds for skirmishes between different vested interests rather than a means of providing firm leadership and support to Sveriges Radio. It would prove to be a guarantee for the confusion which was to ensue when the companies' monopoly was *de facto* broken by the satellite and cable revolution of the mid-1980s (Hadenius and Weibull 1985: 159–62). The monopoly was further weakened about this time through the establishment of community radio and cable television services completely outside the control of Sveriges Radio.

As trans-border satellite transmissions were beginning to gain wide acceptance among Swedish viewers, the political desire to expand domestic broadcasting also grew. There was major disagreement, however, on how to fund such a system. With the television-set market saturated, one could not rely on an increase in the number of receivers (i.e., new licences) to pay for additional channels as had been the case in the 1960s and 1970s. Some saw the introduction of advertising as the solution to Sveriges Radio's problems. Others regarded a reliance on commercial revenue as the greatest possible threat to public service broadcasting. By mid-1989, Sweden was the last country in Western Europe not to formally allow national or local *commercial* radio and television, even though her Nordic neighbours, Norway, Denmark, and Finland, all allowed advertisers to finance television transmissions from their own soil (terrestrial transmissions as opposed to satellite transmissions). At the same time, advertisement-supported television, arriving from abroad via satellites, was a fact in Sweden, encouraged by a somewhat vague cable legislation which permitted the distribution of programmes with commercials as long as the advertising was, to quote, "not specifically directed at Sweden". A word or two of Norwegian – which is almost the same language – was sufficient to circumnavigate the law! And with politicians unwilling to allow major increases in the licence fee, even non-commercial Swedish radio and television was allowing and even encouraging a measure of "back door" commercial support through "sponsored" programmes. That financial problems led to unconventional solutions is hardly surprising, considering that Sveriges Radio and its subsidiaries run three national radio channels, twenty-five local radio stations, and two television channels. This represents almost the same number of channels as the BBC, but based on a licence fee that is only slightly higher, and is paid by a population of eight million as opposed to fifty-five million.

Despite ambitious attempts to find alternative, legal sources of funding and drastic cuts in staffing, the 1980s have been characterized by a severe limit on investments in the more costly segments of Swedish television production, particularly drama and big budget entertainment shows. The axe has not fallen as heavily on news operations. For some 250 million kronor per annum (forty million US dollars or twenty-five million pounds), Swedish broadcasting runs two separate television news organizations, one per channel, as well as both a news and a current affairs division within the national radio company. All twenty-five local radio stations also run their own news departments.

Despite the penury for the organization as a whole, foreign news gathering has received high priority. Swedish television news runs a dozen foreign bureaus (more than BBC-TV) and Swedish Radio has thirteen foreign correspondents stationed abroad.

News in Swedish radio and television

Just as with the BBC, the development of radio news was viewed with concern, and was hindered by press interests in the early years of the Swedish radio monopoly. The Swedish news agency, TT, which is owned by the Swedish press, had a formal monopoly on radio news summaries up until 1956. Although the first news and current affairs programme did go on the air in 1937, it was required that a bulletin from TT had to precede any commentary or report which was compiled by the radio staff. Moreover, these broadcasts could not deal with any item not previously included in the TT bulletin. The clause in the Swedish radio franchise requiring it to base its news on material from TT was not formally removed until 1966, and then only despite considerable opposition from the press. Bulletins compiled by TT and read by their own staff can still be heard in the Swedish broadcast media on both national and local radio. In 1988, TT started selling its radio news services to those with the necessary financial resources who transmit via Sweden's fast growing network of small "neighbourhood" radio transmitters.

In the 1950s, the process of building up independent news resources was under way. Just as the BBC stood firm against the Government of Anthony Eden regarding publicity for those opposed to the Suez invasion in 1956, so too did Swedish Radio stand firm when ruling Social Democrats complained about certain items on the news. Allowing Communist MPs to comment over the airwaves (even though they had been elected to Parliament) was one such issue. The head of the news division, Per Persson, made his policy patently clear in a 1956 memo to the director of the radio company. He wrote that those working with radio news "should not have to ignore important news items, merely for fear of having to deal with highly-explosive material" (Elgemyr 1987: 35). That principle has survived to this day.

Another interesting British–Swedish parallel concerns the effects of pirate radio. The unlicensed off-shore radio pirates that took over British radio waves and listeners in the mid-1960s led to the creation of BBC Radio 1, a service and entertainment channel presenting pop music shows interspersed with news, weather, traffic, and the like. The pirates were effectively banned by the British government making advertising on their stations a criminal offence.

This was the same method used previously by Sweden to come to terms with two very popular radio pirates, Radio Syd (South) and Radio Nord (North), both taking to the air in 1961. Swedish radio tried to counter this competition by increasing its output of news summaries, something the pirates were not good at. Finally, however, the Swedish pirates were banned by making advertising on them illegal, and Swedish Radio started a third national radio channel, with light music and news every hour from 5:00 a.m. to 11:00 p.m.

It was not until 1986 that radio news became a twenty-four-hour operation, and then only as a result of the confusion that ensued when the Prime Minister, Olof Palme, was assassinated in central Stockholm late on Friday 28 February. While the BBC midnight news was carrying a voice report of the shooting from Stockholm, Sweden's Programme 3 was still playing rock music. Its newsroom was not staffed after 11:00 p.m. A confused duty announcer did receive a news flash from the TT agency confirming the murder, but could not reach senior news personnel by phone for instructions because the emergency phone number list had not been updated for some time.

Whereas when American President John Kennedy was killed in Dallas in 1963, 90 per cent of the public knew of the assassination within sixty minutes, it took nine hours in 1986 for 90 per cent of the Swedes to find out that their Prime Minister was dead (Weibull *et al.* 1987: 143). This muddle in the face of a national disaster made it clear to broadcast management that neither domestic nor foreign news stops when Sweden goes to bed. Round-the-clock staffing of the radio newsroom and bulletins were quickly introduced.

Swedish Radio now produces three thirty-minute and three fifteen-minute news and actuality programmes daily, as well as hourly bulletins. The radio news department also produces a number of current affairs segments for different magazine programmes in the national speech network, Programme 1.

The department also works closely with a current and social affairs unit which produces hourly weekday programmes with subject matter often related to the top stories in the news. These programmes can be compared to "All Things Considered" on NPR in the States or a programme such as "PM," broadcast at the same time each weekday on BBC Radio 4, adjacent to the main 6:00 p.m. news.

News on Swedish television started in the format of a cinema-type newsreel when the medium was first introduced in the mid-50s. This style survived until the late 1960s when a second channel was started. The two-channel television structure was based on a concept promoted by Olof Palme who was minister in charge of Education and Media at the time. Instead of following the British solution of a non-commercial and a commercial organization in competition with each other, Palme suggested the possibility of two separate channels within the same broadcasting company but each with a brief to cover a full range of programmes and thereby compete. There was also a code governing the types of unfair competition which were to be avoided. As a result, a scheduler, out of fairness, would see that "Perry Mason" was not regularly scheduled on one channel against the news on the other.

The two channels developed two fairly independent news departments, with Channel 1 producing the daily programme "Aktuellt" (actuality) transmitted at 9:00 p.m., and Channel 2 news producing "Rapport", on at 7:30 p.m. Independence, however, was limited by a number of factors. The regional bureaus had as a rule (and still have) only one local reporter providing material to both Channels. The same applied to most foreign correspondents. What's more, a form of enforced "bimediality" had existed since 1958 when a central news office, feeding both radio and television, was created. Some foreign correspondents had to work for both media. One reason for this was the desire to save money by pooling resources as the number of broadcast channels and the demands on news output expanded. Here one can note a parallel to management thinking at the BBC thirty years later with the arrival of John Birt as Deputy Director General in 1987 and the upgrading of the term "bimedia" to buzzword status.

There is also another interesting BBC–Swedish parallel. During the late 1950s period of Swedish Radio's fight for independence from both the Government and the press, the then Director General, Olof Rydbeck, saw the news as the most contentious area of operations, one inevitably leading to controversy. He felt that a central news desk, responsible for all bulletins, would simplify co-ordination, especially in the case of sensitive news stories where questions might be raised about the company's adherence to the terms of its monopoly franchise with the Swedish State. Thus the top management could control matters involving problem issues as well as provide a unified institutional stance against criticism from outside. Top management would not be caught unaware by "unsuitable" subjects turning up in the news. If the go-ahead was given, then any ensuing fuss would ensure management's total support for decisions made lower down the organization. To accomplish this in a hands-on fashion, the Director General attended a daily meeting with all senior news editors at which he was informed of the day's major stories and the intended approach. This routine continued through to 1969. Rydbeck would even go as far as to commission outside, academic "objectivity studies" to strengthen his security should a conflict with the Establishment arise.

Once again, almost thirty years later, we find similar tactics employed at the BBC following a period of political turmoil. The introduction of a news directorate, a lengthening of the hierarchy, and a decrease in the delegation of responsibility in the news organization has been combined with the integration of radio and television news and current affairs, thus tightening control from above. The difference is, of course, that the Swedish development in the 1950s was part of its evolution towards independence, as news programmes "came to be taken over completely by journalists with a background in the press" (Westerståhl and Johansson 1986: 137). A generous interpretation of what is happening at the BBC is that the Corporation is trying to recover from a series of attacks on the institutional independence it won in previous decades, warding off future onslaughts through tighter managerial control. A more cynical interpretation would see the new BBC modes of managerial control as primarily intended to appease a disgruntled government via the imposition of heavier supervision and a tighter lid on journalistic activities in areas deemed to be sensitive.

The organization of news on national radio in Sweden

Charting the respective organizations for radio news in the BBC and Swedish broadcasting produces very different results. Size, of

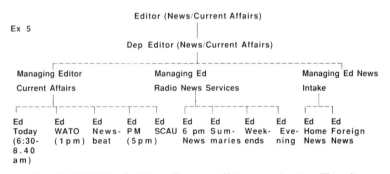

4.1 The 1989 BBC Radio News/Current affairs organization. The editors on the left run specific news analysis programmes. SCAU = Special Current Affairs Unit (for documentaries). WATO = "The World at One" (lunchtime current affairs programme). The editors on the right are in charge of specific newscasts as well as newsflow. The new Specialist Units are absent (their hierarchical position is unclear)

course, is an important factor. Current Affairs and Radio News have not as yet been integrated in Sweden. For the BBC, the integration has produced a broad, horizontal layer in the hierarchy at the level of "home" and "foreign news editor." The functions performed by the editors on this level range from responsibility for daily current affairs programmes and bulletins to responsibility for the flow of incoming news; a mixed bag, in other words.

An equivalent chart for Swedish Radio produces a very different picture. The broad base includes a mixture of subject specialist and media specialist units. Editors (or "producers") are not tied to one specific programme, but rotate.

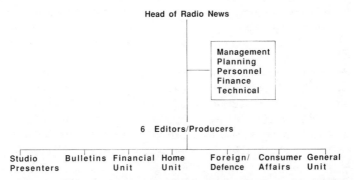

4.2 The organization of Radio News at Swedish Radio (1989). Executive producers (editors) rotate between different news programmes. In-depth coverage is provided by specialist groups. This chart is a construction based on interviews with staff

Just as with the BBC, this Swedish organizational chart shows a mixture of line and staff functions. A team of studio reporters is available for interviews and for presentation of programmes. The bulletin group produces news bulletins and shorter summaries based on incoming material from news agencies (Swedish TT, including Reuters, and AP) as well as material from the other specialist groups. The financial unit produces its own daily business programmes as well as feeding other parts of the news ouput with financial news.

The home unit covers parliamentary affairs and labour market issues. Defence is lumped together with foreign affairs; thirteen foreign-based correspondents report to the Head of the Foreign Affairs Unit.

The *Consumer Affairs* Unit is unusual in radio terms. It is intended to be the broadcast equivalent of a magazine such as *Which?* in Britain or *Consumer Reports* in the US. In other words, it looks at what the consumer is offered in the market and covers areas such as price and quality, unfair trading practices, and fraud. The group consists of four full-time reporters and has a very generous budget for freelancers. The group has its own segments in a mid-morning magazine programme on the speech channel (Programme 1) and it also provides reports for regular news programmes.

The general unit covers a number of specialist areas: environment, legal, social welfare, immigrants, and so on. A number of senior correspondents are attached to this group.

Management is administered through the Head of Radio News (who reports directly to the managing director of the radio company) and a management team covering four areas of responsibility. The Head of Planning is in charge of computer services and the task of building up a quick-access, institutional memory. The second area consists of a technical adviser whose main concern is the improvement of sound quality or, as Eric Fichtelius, the Head of News put it, "to prepare for the digital age, when reporters have digital recorders, when digital tape can be fed home over the telephone or by a portable satellite up-link, and when editing is done digitally."

Six senior producers ("editors" in BBC terminology) rotate production functions on different days and different programmes.

Specialist co-ordination and competence problems

Eric Fichtelius told us in 1989, "If you specialize too much, you have no general reporters left. They are the ones who discover new areas, covering stories which otherwise would get lost in between the different specialist groups." At that time the Swedish Radio News department was undertaking an overhaul of the relationship between the general, financial, and consumer specialist units. The emergence of certain large stories had highlighted the need for cross-fertilization between the groups. Covering the development of the European Community (EC) and its relevance for neutral Sweden involved many aspects: foreign policy, defence, financial, labour market, domestic, political, and so on.

An *ad hoc* solution to the problem of rigidity arising from the specialist structure had been the construction of temporary, cross-functional groups to cover particular subjects. For instance, in the summer of 1988 when 60 per cent of the seals in the North Sea were dying from a form of distemper virus, and poisonous algae in the Kattegat Sea were killing off all marine life down to a certain depth, such groups were formed combining environmental, scientific, and foreign news expertise.

Another example of a major story which required an improvised solution was the crash of a prototype Swedish military jet fighter (JAS Gripen) on its second flight in early 1989. JAS is one of the biggest industrial projects ever undertaken by Sweden, a major investment for the taxpayer, with the aim of producing an independent contribution to the Swedish defence effort (at a cost far higher than if Sweden had purchased jet fighters from abroad). The crash was a major set-back and led some politicians to suggest that the mammoth project should be abandoned. Doubts were raised in the Armed Forces. Aeronautic experts expressed concern about the design of the plane. Thorough coverage of such a news item required a journalistic effort which would not only take time, but which would require a combination of different specialist competencies. Aspects relating to foreign, defence, industrial, and labour market policy would have to be weighed together. A temporary group would need time to dig up all the facts without running the risk of being pulled off the story as soon as some other major news item turned up. Here we can witness a move towards a looser type of specialist structure, where particular combinations of expertise can be created according to the nature of specific stories which happen to break. A prerequisite for this, of course, is *sufficient journalist resources*, so that such groups can be moved away from daily routine.

Overlap with other departments in the radio company

Increased specialization in the news department is bound to lead to problems of overlap with separate current affairs departments. The BBC has tried to solve this by merely joining the two together in one organization, placing them under one hierarchy. Even so, quite a bit of overlap exists between a programme such as "PM," for example, from 5:00 to 6:00 p.m. on BBC Radio 4, and the "6 O'clock News" which immediately follows. The same applies to Swedish Radio in the late afternoon segment on the speech channel:

4:45 – 5:00 p.m.	fifteen-minute news programme (News Department)
5:00 – 6:00 p.m.	sixty minutes of in-depth coverage (Current Affairs Department)
6:00 – 6:30 p.m.	main thirty-minute news (bulletin/reports; News Department)
6:30 – 6:35 p.m.	Weather from Meteorological Office
6:35 – 6:45 p.m.	Business News (News Department, Financial Unit)
6:45 – 7:00 p.m.	Arts News in Brief (Cultural Department and News Department)

Sometimes the departments cover the same stories. Sometimes the Current Affairs hour covers some special topic which is not related at all to the top stories of the day. What may appear to be redundancy and/or inefficiency may, in fact, be a benefit. It can be argued that an analytical process under way simultaneously within two separate departments increases overall independence, making it harder for outside vested interests to manipulate the organization. The same argument, as we shall see later, has been put forward for retaining two independent news departments within the television company.

While *specialization* raises interesting questions regarding the Radio News department's relationship to the existing Current Affairs department, opportunities for overlap and conflict have come from another direction within the radio company. There has been a tendency for light entertainment programmes to become more "newsy." Disc jockeys/presenters, keen to depart from their rather boring traditional role of putting pieces of plastic on a turntable and taking them off again at the end of the song, have been looking for subjects other than music to talk about. This brings them into the field of magazine programmes, and even news (soft or hard). One such programme, "Efter Tre" (After Three), runs from 3:00 p.m. to 6:00 p.m. on the light music channel (Programme 3), competing directly during its final hour with the current affairs programme on the speech channel (Programme 1). It has become extremely popular. Not everyone in the news division, however, is happy with such a development.

Eric Fichtelius, Head of the News Department, said,

What has happened is that we have got a group applying tabloid paper news values in the building. Bjorn Borg taking

82

too many pills, murders, scandals. etc. are their staple fare. We try to maintain a more serious approach. We should always be at the scene when something happens. We should be quick, but we must retain the criterion of seriousness in everything we do.

The "After Three" team, in fact, had access to the same wire services as the news department, but after an unfortunate incident regarding a false news flash of a nuclear accident, an agreement was made that such matters would be handled only by the news department.

There is not only a division of responsibilities between News and "After Three," there also exists a give-and-take relationship. If in the course of a chat with the presenter of the afternoon show, for example, an interviewee makes a newsworthy statement, it can be and often is picked up by the news department and may appear again in the context of the 6:00 p.m. thirty-minute bulletin. This sort of co-operation between those with entertainment and news responsibilities is somewhat unusual in large broadcasting organizations. The divisions elsewhere tend to be watertight, with relationships characterized by disdain rather than admiration.

These examples show that just as in-depth analysis and comment is no longer the prerogative of current affairs departments, neither are hard or soft news the monopoly of the news department, regardless of the level of mutual admiration. In Britain, for example, there is popular radio presenter Jimmy Young on BBC's MOR (middle of the road) music network, Radio 2. Some of the most newsworthy people regularly take part in his music programmes, talking about news topics and even making news. For many news-makers, media access via a popular talk/music show host can be even more attractive (and safer) than putting their points to a trained journalist from a serious news programme.

This observation applies equally well to both radio and television. Magazine programmes presented by competent personalities who are often journalists have provided the Entertainment Department at Swedish Television with a means of providing attractive programmes without incurring the costs usually associated with flashy, glittery shows. Often younger staff contribute with experiments in the form of such programmes. "Soft news" items, sometimes from abroad, are not unusual.

These frequently encompass a departure from the traditional mode of television reporting – a departure from the "this is your correspondent standing by a local landmark, followed by an interview with a local potentate interspersed with the obligatory cut-ins of your correspondent listening and nodding attentively although filmed afterwards" style. In April 1989 for example, "Svepet" (The Sweep) devoted most of one of its transmissions to "entertainment" in the Baltic Republic, Estonia. The filmed segments from the Estonian capital, Tallin, offered amazing insight into everything from high-brow culture, post-*glasnost* relaxation of censorship, and night-club shows to black market dealers and prostitution (as well as reactions from locals to the fact that for the first time these issues were becoming subjects of public debate). Of course, without *perestroika* and the Baltic nationalism movements, the sequence would have been unthinkable. Even so, few viewers would have expected to see such a report on a typical television news programme. In the "Svepet" story, the people in the report are the "stars," not the news correspondent working hard to create or polish a profile.

From the USA we can similarly note the way in which "breakfast television" has moved from the News Divisions of the networks over to their Entertainment Divisions. When ABC's "Good Morning America" spent a week transmitting from Sweden in June of 1988, Americans were given the opportunity to learn more about all aspects of Swedish life than they would have in scores of years watching every evening network newscast.

Foreign news on Swedish radio

In April 1988 the Swedish National Radio Company's policy statement, "National Radio in the '90s," proclaimed boldly,

> Foreign news coverage will continue to be a particular responsibility for national radio. Knowledge about the world does not increase merely because Sky Channel finds its way into more Swedish homes. New foreign correspondents are needed in Southern Europe, Asia and Central America.

One-third of the radio news budget goes to maintaining a net of thirteen foreign correspondents. Their brief, according to news Head Eric Fichtelius, is to provide "our own voices from around the world. Wherever there is a relevance, we should be able to describe events via our own staff who live in the region and speak the language." ·

The existing operational bases follow an historically established pattern, with radio bureaus in London, Paris, Bonn, New York, Washington and Moscow. The Nordic nations are covered by bureaus in Oslo and Helsinki; a district office in the south of Sweden monitors Copenhagen and Denmark. More recent additions are the Middle East (moved from Beirut to Cyprus), Hong Kong (with responsibility for all of Asia), Buenos Aires (Central and South America), and Harare in Zimbabwe. The Harare correspondent, however, in the past was regularly refused permission by the authorities in Pretoria to work in South Africa. This was related to the Swedish government's policy of condemning apartheid, banning trade with South Africa, and giving aid to the Frontline States. *Glasnost*, South-Africa-style, as of February 1990, has improved this situation.

The general argument for maintaining an expensive network of international reporters is that they can develop personal profiles, reporting back in a way which has relevance for Swedish interests and knowledge. Access to international news services with sound and/or vision helps this development. With CNN offering block coverage of important news conferences, a Swedish radio correspondent does not have to concentrate on getting the same basic sound, but can hunt other commentaries and audio illustrations.

A regularly cited example concerns the 1988 summit in the USSR between US Secretary of State George Schultz and his Soviet equivalent, Eduard Shevardnadze. When they emerged after a meeting to give a statement, it would have been inefficient for the Swedish Radio's Moscow correspondent to battle to get his microphone near the two statesmen. CNN gave the statement block coverage, so sound was lifted back in Stockholm from that coverage. The correspondent on the spot, meanwhile, concentrated on getting comments from other sources and analysing what was said. A similar principle applies, as we shall see shortly, in the running of Swedish Television's foreign news operations.

The organization of television news at Sveriges radio

In formal terms, the two Swedish television news departments live autonomous lives. In practice, though, they share certain technical and correspondent resources and have some measure of mutual dependence. Together they produce about eleven hours of news programmes a week. On top of this, both channels offer a number of current and social affairs programmes, the standard format being a film/video segment followed by a debate. Current affairs and news, in other words, have been integrated in Swedish Television.

As with the Radio Company, foreign news receives high priority. Each television news department has (or is in the process of acquiring) five correspondents. Washington, however, is the only place where each will maintain its own correspondent. Miami, Hong Kong, and Moscow have shared correspondents, and by 1990, each department hopes to have three additional exclusive correspondents, covering Brussels, Vienna, Bonn, Jerusalem, Tokyo and Harare. The Harare correspondent will cover Africa south of the Sahara.

One interesting development is that Swedish television news intends to close its London bureau in favour of Brussels, which is seen as a better vantage point for covering central Europe (Radio is closing its Paris office and moving to Brussels as well). In Brussels a reporter has access to television from France, Germany, and the Benelux countries, as well as Britain. The European Community is headquartered in the Belgian capital, and transportation to neighbouring countries is fast and regular.

Having a small number of exclusive correspondents in different locations leaves each news department with several geographical gaps. Would it not be more logical to share them all, for example, having only one in Washington? Swedish television says "No." Exclusive correspondents, even in small numbers, mean that each channel's news programmes can develop their own profile. When one channel cannot acquire its own coverage, pictures can always be purchased or otherwise received via the Eurovision network. Both departments also have a small team of home-based correspondents who can travel to different places. As TV1's foreign news editor, Malcolm Dixelius, put it, "Eighty per cent of all foreign news is predictable. You know this war is going on, or that that summit meeting is going to take place. If it's important, you can plan your own coverage or request material."

Small can be beautiful: rules of the game for medium-sized players

Swedish national television news provides a fine example of how smaller television news organizations try to survive on limited budgets in an environment dominated by a few major actors. A number of its "secrets" can be discerned:

1 Don't compete on the same terms as the Big Boys. Swedish television's news budget cannot encompass the quantity of satellite links which the major news agencies (or even the US networks) utilize. On the other hand, most material collected by Visnews, WTN, or the US networks and the BBC can usually be acquired via the Eurovision news exchange system. This exchange system requires, of course, that Swedish television honours its obligation to provide Eurovision with hard news when such material turns up and is covered in Sweden.

2 Acquire basic material from Eurovision or purchase from other global suppliers. CNN is one of the main sources. In 1989 Swedish television paid CNN approximately one million kronor (100,000 pounds or 160,000 dollars) for the right to take up to sixty minutes of its material per day. Its own correspondents do not have to worry about filming important press conferences or events when CNN provides block coverage. The larger actors (the main agencies and networks), however, are almost required to provide their own coverage, since they obviously cannot sell CNN material to their many subscribers. Moreover, if CNN should fail to have coverage, the medium-sized Swedish television organization can buy from one of these majors.

Swedish television can also take material straight off the Soviet television satellite which provides basic material from events in the USSR.

3 Give the highest priority to exclusive material from your own correspondents. Correspondents and their camera crews do not have to devote their effort into getting that picture, for the 800th time, of the president getting out of a helicopter. Nor are they required to supply a regular two minutes a day. Instead, they are encouraged to spend more time at the site of a news event than is possible for a Visnews crew, for example, for whom speed is a priority. Correspondents concentrate more

on producing mini-documentaries, with more background material.

A consequence of this principle is that correspondents often look for other aspects of an event to cover than those chosen by the Big Boys like the American networks or Visnews. The 1988 Israeli elections offer a good example. On election day, the US networks, Visnews and WTN, each sent teams to cover the Labour and Likud party vigils. Knowing that that material would be available elsewhere via Eurovision or direct purchase, Swedish television's man in Jerusalem tracked down the extreme religious parties who enjoyed some election success. He garnered unique material that went out over Eurovision and was seen universally. Dixelius told us, "We were the only people who had those corkscrew guys dancing and drinking vodka; that was fun!"

4 Co-operate with other medium and small television organizations, pooling resources where possible. This co-operation can be short or long-term.

While Sweden's foreign policy of neutrality creates political problems for its integration with EC Europe, it has little effect on its ability to co-operate with other European television companies. Swedish television news is opening a bureau in Vienna together with a West German television organization. The aim is to provide a joint vantage point for monitoring and covering developments in Eastern Europe, an important source area for news over the next few years. By pooling cameras, crews, and editing equipment, costs can be cut radically. Competition is not a problem since the co-operating news organizations have totally different audiences, speaking different languages in different countries.

Short-term co-operation between the smaller players can be on an *ad hoc* basis. Malcolm Dixelius explained how this works. "When (in 1988) there was a general strike on the West Bank," he said,

> four or five news teams from smaller companies would sit down in the morning and divide up things or places which were thought to be worth covering. Our man worked with ARD from West Germany and TF1 from France. They did this several times. In fact, when I was in France over the New Year, I was very proud to see that two bits of film we had taken were shown on TF1's summary of the past year.

5 Utilize the flexibility that goes with being small. Larger organizations with complicated working structures and union relationships often find it harder to adjust to the introduction of new technologies than do smaller ones. Two-man ENG (electronic news gathering) camera teams were common in Swedish television some time before they were introduced in the BBC or ITN. New, small, light-weight cameras can be used by single reporters, covering stories where a three or four person film team could never operate.

Smaller organizations enjoy another kind of flexibility. A major outlay for all television news gathering operations is satellite costs. Swedish television places a priority on the *exclusivity* of its correspondents' reports rather than on the speed at which they are brought home. When a satellite link has been established by a major operator, there are often small amounts of free time on either side of the booking. The link is up, but no material is being carried. Swedish television can therefore ask for a so-called "sequential," at a special rate, to transmit a short piece of news video.

6 Sell unique material back to the major players. The second principle, let the major international agencies satisfy the demands of speed, allows Swedish television correspondents to spend more time covering stories. Frequently they can reach areas and cover some types of events better than the majors.

Historically, Swedish Television news has an extensive track record in this field. In the late 1960s and early 1970s, Sweden pursued an active foreign policy of supporting independence movements around the world, often openly criticizing Super Power involvement in smaller nations. The result was that Swedish film teams were welcome almost everywhere (with the obvious exceptions of South Africa and Chile after its 1971 military coup). Its most obvious successes can be seen in Vietnam.

On Midsummer's Day 1972, Swedish journalist Eric Ericsson and photographer Bjorn Henriksson filmed the US bombing of a system of irrigation dams in northern Vietnam. The footage was sold for a small fee to CBS while the Nixon Administration continued to deny that such attacks had taken place. When a Nixon spokesman repeated these denials on the CBS "Evening News," Walter Chronkite confronted him with the filmed evidence. A total of twenty-three countries bought that footage. Eventually, a series of later trips to North Vietnam were underwritten by CBS and NBC.

Several modes of operations developed during this period are still applied by Swedish television when gathering news abroad today. One is the use of a small team (one or two people) that can stay on the scene of an event longer, producing not only news spots but also mini-documentaries. Since it is so expensive for a large organization (Visnews, CBS, BBC, etc.) to keep a crew on location, the tendency is to pull them out as quickly as possible. The type of material that a slightly longer sojourn can produce becomes attractive in the international news market.

For Swedish television, however, the sale of its news is not a money-making exercise. ITN in Britain often purchases its reportage material. The price is low, a mere 150 dollar administration fee and 200 dollars per minute. Sales such as this have an important prestige value for Swedish television. But because it buys more than it sells, Swedish television has no interest in upping the prices; if that were to happen, the Big Boys would reciprocate and the Swedes would not be able to afford anything from them.

Organizational and bimedial integration: advantages and limits

While Swedish Radio has separate news and current affairs departments, Sweden's national, licence-financed television company has two news departments which both combine news and current affairs. Separating news and in-depth analysis (as in Swedish Radio) or running two parallel organizations which attempt to do both (as in the case of Television), are regarded by staff journalists as effective means of making it harder for vested interests, political parties or others to manipulate the news. Two entities analysing the same news phenomena from different angles are harder to "newsmanage" than one.

Bimediality as a means of improving cost efficiency is rejected by the news departments at both Swedish Radio and Television. The objection is based not on fear of diminished empires, but on past experience. "Prior to 1978, when Radio became a separate company, we had to share correspondents with TV," Eric Fichtelius recalled.

Our painful experience was that radio always suffered. Correspondents want to get on air; that's how they measure their value. And television news carries much more prestige than radio. Also, if you're working on TV news, you have a film team, you have to edit the material, arrange for transmission links. Half the time goes to administration, because the technology is so demanding. One man and a mobile phone is often all we (in radio) need to get the story back and on the air, while events are still happening.

Staff at Swedish television agree.

We are totally against the concept of bimedia correspondents. We want our correspondents to stay longer and to concentrate on one thing at a time. This is incompatible with Radio's demands. We are different types of media. If a correspondent had a brief to *combine* radio and TV, say, by producing a short daily two minute voice piece illustrated by pictures, then bimediality might work. But that's not the way we use our correspondents. We want them to produce not only news items but also longer pieces, mini-documentaries.

This from television's Dixelius.

The future for radio and television news in Sweden

The Management of both radio and television news agree that a number of pressures have been mounting throughout the latter half of the 80s.

— With politicians unwilling to allow for major licence fee increases, and even demanding 2 per cent annual savings within the Swedish broadcasting organization, salaries have stagnated. Many qualified personnel have left to work either for the press or for the industrial sector. Others, willing to gamble on success in the open market, have accepted generous redundancy offers (called Golden Handshakes in the US) and have started their own independent production companies. Many of these companies then end up selling their services back to Swedish Television.

— One of the fastest growing employment areas in Sweden has been the field of information. Both private and public sector organizations have been employing journalists and PR staff to handle and manage the flow of information to the media. Broadcast news staff "get the answers even before we've asked

91

the questions" as one radio journalist put it. Many more want to use or even manipulate media channels.

— The assassination of Olof Palme in 1986 and the ensuing years of confusion, as well as a number of other major "affairs" or scandals, have dominated domestic and foreign news gathering throughout the decade. Swedish arms exports to forbidden nations have provided major and difficult news stories. In 1986, Sweden's Bofors company won its biggest industrial deal ever for the delivery of field artillery to India. At the same time, sums of money had been transferred to anonymous numbered accounts in Swiss banks. Swedish law prohibits bribery in connection with business deals. Olof Palme had personally promised Rhajiv Ghandi that no bribes would be paid to middle-men for the Indian contract. The Government was embarrassed. The Head of the Official Weapons' Export Inspectorate mysteriously fell from a platform in front of a train in the Stockholm underground. Other major pending arms orders could be at stake if the media were to expose too much of the workings of the international arms trade.

As this thriller developed, the broadcasters suddenly found themselves under siege from numerous groups wishing to affect news flow. Peace groups produced regular exposés, the substance of which the journalists found hard to judge via independent confirmation. The Government had its own interests, as did the police and others involved in the many official investigations – investigations which seemed to get nowhere.

While all this was happening, another investigation, that of the Olof Palme murder, was also going from bad to worse, with Heads of Police being fired and Justice Ministers resigning. Knowing that 52 per cent of all Swedes listen to at least one radio bulletin a day and that 28 per cent watch television news daily, it is not surprising that thoughts about the responsibilities and limitations of the broadcast news media came to overshadow the workings of these organizations.

While scandals were causing upheavals in Swedish society, the competitive environment in the media was changing, as were news values among the Swedish broadcasters. To understand the extent of this change we have to look back at the early 1970s.

From affordable radicalism to enforced adaptation

When Swedish television was divided into two channels in 1969, the second channel (TV2) became known as the Red Channel. Its news programme, "Rapport," reflected the radical background of many of its employees. A study reported in 1972 by Sveriges Radio's Audience Research Unit showed that 45 per cent of all foreign news on "Rapport" dealt with events in Asia, mainly the Indo-China war. Comparing those broadcast journalists with the early founding fathers of Sweden's public service broadcasting, Professors Jorgen Westerståhl and Folke Johansson of Gothenburg University concluded, "If the old men, in the paternalistic era, knew what was right, the newcomers knew what was wrong" (Westerståhl and Johansson 1986: 137).

They also noted that subjects such as violent crime, royalty, religion, and other items in the "human interest" category were taboo at this time. But as the 1970s and 1980s progressed, change became discernible. On 15 April 1989, one of Sweden's more prominent television critics wrote in the largest Swedish morning paper, *Dagens Nyheter*,

> Rapport has learned from US news programmes, successful in terms of audience figures, to mix important items with amusing lighter fare. In TV jargon this is referred to as the "mix." Hard news should be mixed with human interest stories so that we who are the less serious or rather "thick" viewers won't get disappointed and press the remote control button. So it was that Rapport on Monday went straight from a story from an international catastrophe into a report on whether or not golf caddies should wear safety helmets. Then on Tuesday we were shown how Liza Minelli's pet dog was put on board a private plane to be extradited from Sweden.

This critic's comments emphasize an important point. Such a mix would have been unthinkable during Channel 2's more radical days. The same article also noted that Channel 1 had scheduled a highly attractive drama series for the summer season to be transmitted at 7:30 each evening (competing with "Rapport," Channel 2's primary evening newscast and a time usually reserved for educational or special interest programmes). Although no new policies had formally been announced, this, in effect, marked a major loosening-up of the former rules governing scheduling between the two channels.

There is more than inter-Channel competition in Sweden's broadcast future. A number of significant elements are already observable.

1 Although Sveriges Radio still has a monopoly on terrestrial television transmissions in Sweden, satellite programmes offering news are available on cable systems. According to the National Cable Board, 700,000 Swedish homes (equivalent to 25 per cent of the population) could receive satellite television in February of 1989 (an increase of 60 per cent over the 1988 figure). Several of these new channels offer news. One, Scansat TV3, provides bulletins of international and Swedish news presented by Scandinavian speakers. Scansat's own figures from January 1990 claim a reach of 1,077,000 homes (32.4 per cent of all Swedish television households).

2 Local radio is technically organized as a subsidiary to Sveriges Radio, but there exist strong elements of both internationalization and localization. The local radio station in Stockholm, for instance, relays BBC World Service international bulletins taken off a satellite.

Third Tier Radio (neighbourhood or community radio) has seen an enormous expansion since its introduction in 1979. Ostensibly non-profit-making organizations can rent time on small local radio transmitters. Some of these try to sound like US commercial radio stations (though without commercials other than those promoting the transmitting organization). They provide a mix of pop music, traffic reports, weather, and news. One such station, in Sweden's second city, Gothenburg, even relayed the Voice of America for a time.

3 Sweden put its own Tele-X direct broadcasting satellite into orbit in April 1989. At the time of this writing, the Swedish Space Agency (which manages Tele-X) was still not sure to whom it will rent the satellite's three television channels (though neighbouring Norway has an option on one of them).

4 With satellites making commercial television a reality, Sweden's politicians opposed to broadcast advertising are being forced to come to terms with the situation. Sweden does have room in the frequency spectrum allotted to it for a third terrestrial television channel. A home-based, advertising-supported channel is seen by many as a preferable alternative to signals coming in from space via European commercial satellites. Such a channel would not only be easier to control nationally, it would diffuse throughout the country more quickly than cable or satellite, and would almost certainly take away much advertising revenue from those operators.

5

Challenging the traditional broadcasters:
new players in the news game

Big and small, we have looked at the national broadcasters in the United States, Great Britain, and Sweden. Throughout those discussions we could not help but mention the growth of both local news gatherers and presenters as well as the effects of satellite technology on access to news from afar. These developments warrant further inspection.

Local and independent stations: which news from where?

A Thursday afternoon in March 1987. The producer of the day at KTVU, Channel 2, Oakland, California is planning the 10:00 p.m. sixty-minute evening newscast. KTVU claims to be the fastest growing station in local television news in America, attracting approximately 17 per cent of the viewers in the San Francisco Bay Area nightly, or almost 300,000 people. It offers local, national, and international news. Owned by Cox Broadcasting, it has access to material from Cox's Washington bureau and, if necessary, from Cox's other affiliated stations in various cities. Local news coverage relies heavily on the constant monitoring of emergency services (fire, ambulance and police). Access to foreign news, however, comes from four main sources:

— CNN, a barter deal ensures that KTVU has access to CNN material as long as CNN can use KTVU pictures should there be a big story in the San Francisco area. Specials can also be requested from CNN on a fixed cost basis.
— VISNEWS out of London, via the INDEX network (run by

95

5 Five TV monitors showing what competitors are offering dominate the scene in the KTVU, Channel 2 newsroom, Oakland, California

WPIX and Tribune Broadcasting). This gives about twenty-five minutes of semi-edited news stories from around the world, arriving daily on a 4:00 p.m. feed.

— The CBS regional feed in Northern California. If a big news event occurs and is covered by KTVU, the station puts it on the CBS regional feed; in return it can use any material on that feed.

— Own deals with other broadcasters (e.g., Mexican Television).

This particular Thursday in March was an interesting news day in America. For one thing, President Reagan was due to hold his first press conference on the Irangate affair in three months. So, what would the different segments of the KTVU newshour include? "I'll lead with the murder suspect (a man accused of killing a six year-old child), unless Ronnie has a heart attack or starts foaming at the mouth," instructed producer Earl Frounfelter,

The second segment will be all Reagan; I've called in an articulate Professor of International Relations from San Francisco State University, as well as Pete McClosky, a former Representative who served on the Watergate Committee. I want them to talk about the speech, because it's probably the most important one since the speech he made for Barry Goldwater.

At the final planning meeting, Frounfelter indicated that he would tell the two anchors which questions to ask these experts. "The third segment will be whatever's left over, the fourth ... international news, and the fifth, weather and some silly feature that I'm obliged to run. There will also be a segment which is a feature about vice in Oakland."

This short summary of intent from the producer of an independent newscast gives great insight into a somewhat chequered picture of news values. A generous measure of disrespect for Reagan and Washington is coupled with a feeling of necessity when it comes to analysing what the President has to say in a press conference. But the station does not do it through top reporters in Washington (as would be the case on the networks), but rather by bringing in locally known academics and politicians.

Since KTVU is on at 10:00 p.m. and therefore not scheduled adjacent to a network newscast as is the case with the local CBS, NBC and ABC affiliates' news programmes, some run-down of international news is seen as essential. The producer explains,

If we pretend that some people only watch Channel 2 News, then we have an obligation to cover national and international news. That's our charter as it were. We don't have anyone else on the same channel to tell us about DC or London. If we don't do it, the Channel 2 viewers won't see it. Those who stick to the affiliates can get it from Dan, Tom or Peter.

Here we have an indication of what might be called "schizo-phrenic" local news station behaviour. These operations provide both a localization and an internationalization of the news. The producer at this independent was clearly proud of what they produced, even if he was not entirely satisfied. There were some dissatisfactions, such as limited funds for additional reporters and travel, that he would not talk about on tape. The station, in particular the news programme, was obviously making good money for Cox broadcasting.

It would have been unthinkable for the British broadcast media not to lead with Mrs Thatcher if she spoke out after months of silence on an issue of great magnitude. The Channel 2 producer was quite convinced about his relative priorities:

They're high interest stories. A six year old kid disappears. Days go by and he turns up dead. Everybody gets interested. It's like the little girl who fell down a well all those years ago, and everybody stayed tuned, coast to coast, on radio. A little kid in trouble is a high interest story. Unless Reagan says, "I'm releasing the 7th Fleet to go after the Ayatollah," then the ongoing saga of Irangate is not considered to be as interesting. The day after the Tower Report (on President Reagan's involvement or lack of involvement in moving funds to the contras in Nicaragua) CBS put on a one-hour special. I happened to tape it, it was very good, but nobody watched it. NBC cleaned up the ratings because they stayed with Cosby. We ran an old film for the ninth time and beat out the CBS hour special. At least the people who were surveyed that night did not see the Tower Report as something they wanted to tune into.

Here, directly stated, is the local television view of the networks' dilemma regarding in-depth public affairs programmes. With ratings pulling the strings and local stations able at least to get pictures of international events and often having access to local experts, the quality journalistic output of the networks is often pushed aside. The "20/20," "60 Minutes" type of magazine programme offering a series of short segments seems to be the only type of televised current affairs programme that survives nationally. And to do even that they often are forced to resort to gossipy subjects involving film stars and the private lives of VIPs to boost ratings.

As with the networks, technological, financial, and legal/political factors have dramatically impacted the locals in the US. Deregulation has allowed for the formation of major groups of stations with the relatively new "12/12/12 Rule," permitting one owner to control twelve each of AM, FM (radio) and television stations covering up to a maximum of 25 per cent of the population. The CBS affiliate in San Francisco, for example, is owned by Westinghouse, which has no reason to be particularly fond of CBS from a corporate point of view. Thus, KTVU Channel 2 can co-operate with the local affiliate of the CBS network; their news programmes do not compete in the same time slot. The expansion of satellite-fed cable television has allowed KTVU to play the "super station" game, offering itself as far afield as the state of Oregon, over 500 miles away from the locality it is licensed to serve.

The financial rewards of local news have been increasing at the same time that the costs of the network news operations have gone sky high. The news director of the San Francisco NBC affiliate even went so far as to make this offer in a 1986 issue of the *Columbia Journalism Revue*, "If the General Manager said, 'I'll give you ten million dollars and we're going to drop the NBC Nightly News. Can we and should we?' I'd say yes" (Drummond 1986: 51).

Exact earnings from local news are closely guarded secrets. William Drummond cites 1,800 dollars as a price for a thirty-second commercial on such a station in 1986. If we assume a price of around 2,000 dollars per spot in an hour-long newscast with some fifteen minutes of advertising, 350 days a year, annual revenue should amount to around *20 million dollars*. That's roughly equal to the total budget for one Swedish Television news division which includes ten correspondents stationed around the world. With revenues such as this, relatively small local stations could do a lot more in the way of news gathering and reporting, but why bother when profits and audiences are already there?

The local television affiliates in the USA are so strong and "independent" that they now even compete with the networks for satellite links. Av Westin, Vice President at ABC New York, has seen it happening, even with stations owned by ABC. "There was recently an example where some woman went berserk just outside of Chicago, walked into a school and shot some children, went somewhere else and ultimately shot herself," he told us.

A great scandal for the night. The local ABC station is owned by us and you would think it would be loyal and responsible to the network. It told ABC News that they would have to wait in line behind twenty-seven other feeds being sent out by the local station to twenty-seven other stations around the country who switched and bought it from them.

Local stations are also now in the business of occasionally sending their own reporters abroad. Bill Drummond tells the story of a local station in Sacramento, California that sent a reporter to Angola to cover the activities of the FNLA guerrillas. "Nobody is helping them," the reporter boldly stated, showing total ignorance of the South African government's on-going involvement in support of the anti-MPLA forces. Drummond concluded, "Size means more flexibility, but it also means less quality control on what reaches the air." On the other hand, stations' desire to do their own foreign news gathering (so obviously present at KTVU but hampered by budget limitations) can be seen as a positive departure from the small town provincialism that marked most local news coverage for three decades.

It's easy to produce an intellectual attack on local news. It tries to entertain rather than inform. It can't get into investigative journalism and can become very dependent on the printed press. As a KTVU news producer related to us in 1987,

> A newspaper who's paying a reporter thirty-five thousand dollars can afford to put him on a story for two weeks and hope to get something. A television station paying twice or three times as much doesn't want to waste someone for that long on a story which might not pay off. A station our size looks at itself and says, "Gee, I've got this fire here, and that kid missing there. . . " It means that if you have limited resources you have to keep on the day's events.

But there is another way of looking at local television news, one of positive futurism. Technology will continue to provide stations with access to reports from around the world, often admittedly with a preponderance of dramatic visuals. But, through linking up, possibly with local stations at home or in other countries, these smaller outfits can conceivably produce alternative views of the world to those put forward by the network reporters who move in Washington's corridors of power. Maybe these local reports would be less ethnocentric, less geared to what someone in the Administration or at the State Department wants to say.

It is possible that these developments can help increase enlightenment. In our quantitative study of news output, KTVU appears again. Its foreign news coverage might be short on total time, but its angle is certainly different from that delivered by the big three commercial networks.

It is an interesting irony that the new communication technologies of cable and satellite that have so badly eroded the networks' share of the audience are the same technologies that have put the independents in such an enviable position in the American media environment. Before cable, there were two basic types of stations in the US. Affiliates were just that, affiliated by contract with a network. All an affiliate had to do to receive the network's prestige and programming was make its viewers available through the airing of those programmes in its market. The networks even paid them for broadcasting their shows.

The other type of station was an independent and, as the name suggests, was independent of any network. It produced its own programming or aired syndicated (or purchased) material from outside suppliers. Usually this content consisted of old network programmes in re-run, ancient movies, and local or regional sports.

The affiliates dominated for two reasons. First, they had better offerings – at least in terms of production quality – and they were almost always located in the VHF band (Channels 2 through 13). Independents were most typically located in the harder to receive UHF band (Channels 14 through 83). In fact, it was not until 1974 that a law was effected that required all sets manufactured in or imported into the US to equalize all stations by having them all "click in" on the tuner. Cable simply erased any reception or technical difference between VHF and UHF because all stations could be received with equal ease and fidelity. Moreover, cable's overwhelming array of options further blurred the distinction between network and independent programming.

Satellite added to the change because it helped bring the independents to a wider audience and it made possible the delivery of dozens of channels to the cable company for wired distribution to viewers, further fragmenting the networks' audience. Local news, cheap to produce and high in advertising dollar return, became an easy way for independents and affiliates alike to "look good" in the parade of channels. But because the affiliates already "looked good" because of their affiliation, it was the "indies" that benefited the greatest. KTVU-TV, the station that opened this section and represented independents in our quantitative analysis, is a prime example of an independent that has done remarkably well, financially and journalistically, in its news organization.

Localization/internationalization trends in other countries

The trend towards the localization of news decisions is already spreading to countries other than the United States. The BBC, for example, experienced this when Radio Leeds went on the air in 1968. This local station enjoyed a great deal of success, started its own newsroom, opting out of the main national current affairs programmes to run its own (including national and international news taken from the PA, Press Association, and other wire services). An internal BBC memo quoted an observation that "the infection spread outwards from Leeds."

Local radio stations in Britain frequently complain that national news put together in the central newsrooms is too London-centred, at times even patronizing. The most critical problem in news selection and mixing (local/national/international) occurred, according to a 1986 BBC report, when a skeleton staff opened up in the morning and had to choose lead stories. They were not always "well-informed on national and international affairs." With access to international news increasing, the opportunities for local radio stations to bypass national parent organizations increase. CNN and the BBC World Service are available in more and more newsrooms. The thrill of being the first in Europe with a juicy news-flash may even become as attractive for news organizations as being the first European DJ to play a new Top 20 hit from the States is in general music programming.

Where, then, are the checks and balances? Local and regional television in Europe cannot yet fully emulate local stations in the USA, partly because satellite costs remain too high. But as deregulation spreads, as new licences for SNG are granted, this will almost certainly change. Whether reactions to the States experience will be limited to a moral panic, or whether the opportunities provided by local television news will be sensibly debated, remains to be seen. One standard (possibly apocryphal) story from the worst side of US local television will almost certainly be told. As William Drummond tells it, a local news director and his assistant are sitting down to watch their own 11:00 p.m. newscast. The lead story is a fire at an orphanage. On a second television they're keeping an eye on a competitor's handling of the story. "Oh no," says the boss, "Their flames are higher than our flames." "It's all right, Chief," says the assistant, "Our nuns are crying harder than their nuns."

Such a caricature is only an extreme case of the possible. Decisions are made and attitudes are formed on the basis of audience size and assumptions about audience interests. News or journalistic values are often non-existent. Local stations often take on subjects they know little about and/or ignore stories of significance because of what they perceive as "audience demands."

However, a greater danger – one related to the public's access to information – is that of the streamlining effects so noticeable with the networks making their way onto local newscasts. With the competition, or "opposition," becoming the main focus of attention in local newsrooms, different news programmes start looking very similar. This applies not only to hard news, but even to features, special segments, and "soft news", as Joseph Turow observed in a 1981 study of four local stations in a mid-western American city. He wrote, "a reliance on prepackaged features and public relations sources, coupled with a desire for upbeat, visually interesting stories, results in a similarity of soft news across programs and stations, despite different programming strategies" (Turow 1983: 111). One example he cited consisted of a feature on diamond rings and bracelets manufactured by the South African-based company, De Beers. Despite the ongoing debate in the US on South Africa, sanctions, and apartheid, there was no attempt in the programme to raise the obvious issue of the propriety of publicity drives designed to sell South African diamonds. "The talkshow host (questioned later by Turow) revealed ignorance of the 'hard news' issue."

Streamlining and high profits in a competitive market economy are usually the ingredients that encourage some organizations to develop individual areas of competence. Local station revenue is clearly sufficient to cover the costs of increased news gathering, even the costs of sending local reporters abroad. Local stations can also establish new configurations of news gatherers, working together, often bypassing the traditional networks. If this seems to attract viewers, then presumably, station managements will wish to encourage and extend it. We can conceive of a future where large local stations such as KTVU strike their own deals with broadcasters in other countries, giving them, on a lucky day, access to material which even Visnews or CNN do not have. The risk in the present local station approach to gathering its own foreign news, through an occasional presence abroad, is that it typically gets done on a "rush in-rush out" basis, with very little background knowledge and preparation. On the other hand, the general public's ability to find out what's going on abroad, especially in cases involving US foreign policy, could also be equally hampered by the "star reporter" development at the networks: with one or two highly paid news correspondents who base their access to knowledge on close contacts with politicians and State Department figures, blinkers could descend even over their eyes.

Barter, satellite, and cable: the new news suppliers

Not all local independent stations have the interest or the resources to cover national/international news in the same fashion as Channel 2. They can, however, get a nightly half-hour package, "USA Tonight," from INN (Independent News Network); 115 American stations do, covering 73 per cent of the viewing public. A twenty-eight minute broadcast includes about seven minutes of advertising, half of which is sold by INN. The other half can be sold by the station carrying the programme; and it can also sell ninety seconds total before and after the programme. Thus it is a barter deal. "USA Tonight" has an estimated nightly audience of about 2,000,000 viewers. INN is owned by Tribune Broadcasting and originates out of the studios of the independent station, WPIX in New York. The INN newcast usually starts with a major story, similar to what is carried as a lead on the networks. The organization's stated intent, as a producer explained to us, is to "give people the major stories of the day at home and abroad," a wide brief, open to many interpretations.

When a major chemical spill occurred in the Rhine (November 1986), INN devoted the whole of the first few minutes to this environmental story; the networks ignored it or carried it as a short item further down. One possible explanation, apart from the producer's apparent interest in ecological issues, is that INN works closely with Visnews. Visnews, with its European base, would certainly have carried the Rhine spill at the top of its daily international news package. INN simply followed suit.

After a lead story (or stories) comes a commercial break followed by a series of short international stories, usually twenty to forty seconds long, lasting around two minutes. After another commercial break, the next segment is generally "Health Beat," dedicated to innovations in the medical field. This segment is nationally sponsored (i.e., commercial revenues go directly to INN), frequently by an aspirin manufacturer.

INN also runs a number of other regular features with special emphasis. "INN Focus" explores one issue or event. One example from 1986 was a five-part series called "America's Obsession with Sex." It examined the effects on American youth of the overtly sexual images in advertising and popular entertainment. Another regular special-emphasis segment in the INN News is "American Scrapbook," a human interest series covering phenomena such as

Veterans' Day celebrations across America. INN usually ends its newscast with a human-interest story of a fairly "respectable" ilk, such as the Pope's visit to a foreign country, the America's Cup competition, or the actions of an heroic fire fighter.

INN not only produces the nightly "USA Tonight" newscast; it also organizes the INDEX feed to a group of independent local stations. It includes twenty to thirty minutes of international news assembled by Visnews in London (37.5 per cent of which is owned by NBC) and national stories either from INN bureaus or from stations belonging to the INDEX network. Channel 2 in Oakland is a member.

CNN, Cable News Network

CNN is the nearest thing in television to the BBC World Service in radio. It is an around-the-clock service of informative programming that includes hard news, features, specialist news programmes, and block coverage of major events.

Ted Turner, the man who created CNN, has been described as a person who does exactly what he pleases. His track record includes winning the America's Cup in 1977, an attempt to take over CBS in 1985, organizing his own "Goodwill Games" for world peace in Moscow, starting two cable news networks (CNN and CNN Headline News) and buying United Artists/MGM Films.

CNN made "its historic debut," as Turner Broadcasting publicity puts it, on 1 June 1980, feeding non-stop television news to 1.7 million homes across the USA. The money came, in part, from profits Turner made in the late 1970s with his cable-television-fed "Super-Station," independent WTBS in Atlanta. He bought film rights cheaply (suppliers assumed he had a local independent station in that southern city) and then aired them to the nation via satellite and cable.

CNN now feeds fifty million cable households in the States. An international version is available to cable systems and broadcasters in Europe. In Greece, for instance, it is re-broadcast 24 hours a day. The US version is fed to Asia via satellite and is on Japanese television a few hours each day. A Latin-American feed is planned and will be available on a privately owned American satellite having a footprint that covers the southern portion of the American continent.

CNN gathers its international news through a variety of

channels. It is affiliated with both the West and East European television organizations, Eurovision and Intervision, resulting on occasion in the blacking out of specific items in its European feed in as much as they originated from European broadcasters via Eurovision. CNN also has the right to use WTN material.

Like the US networks, CNN maintains a number of foreign bureaus (Cairo, Frankfurt, Jerusalem, London, Moscow, Nairobi, Panama City, Rome and Tokyo). CNN has different arrangements with different broadcasters who use material from it, re-broadcast it, or even provide material in return. Barter exchange deals with American stations are common (the station can use CNN material as long as it guarantees to supply CNN with material when something newsworthy occurs in its area). A "small" broadcaster such as Swedish Television pays an annual subscription fee, allowing it full usage of any CNN material. This, as we have noted, is particularly advantageous when CNN runs "start to finish" coverage of major events.

Views on the full CNN news network vary. CBS' Don DeCesare admits that the CNN people "have done a brilliant job of name recognition," but adds,

> don't fall victim to the CNN-isation of the world. Their total audience for all twenty-four hours of any day is less than our morning broadcast audience alone. Their actual audience is fairly small. Our 7 o'clock hourly on radio is more than their total audience. Our evening news is quintuple. In my view, they're not really a player.

CBS however, like most other broadcasters, watches CNN closely in its own newsroom. Thinking no doubt of CBS' own costs for expensive presenters, Mr DeCesare added, "The process of cutting costs is going on everywhere. CNN has certainly pioneered low-budget anchoring."

The foreign news editor of Swedish Television's Channel 1 newscast, Malcolm Dixelius, is more positive.

> CNN is doing an incredible job. It saves us a lot of time having access to them and the right to use the material. The only problem is finding the extra time to edit out pictures when they have one hundred per cent coverage of a major event. They are also re-defining the whole concept of television news, moving it away from the standard menu of politics and disasters, and into new areas such as Third World issues.

Turner knows where he can make money in the future, at the same time being philanthropic through various other projects.

Dixelius was referring here to Ted Turner's "Better World Society" foundation in New York which seeks to discover and fund documentary programmes on issues involving ecology and conflicts in the world. With outside moneyed interests closely watching Turner and controlling some of his purse strings after the UA/MGM purchase, this venture has become somewhat limited. Despite Turner's apparent interest in environmental and peace issues, his success with CNN has been credited to a different, less "liberal" sort of attitude toward workers' organizations. Former CBSer, Ernest Leiser, wrote in the New York *Times Magazine,*

Had the new venture employed union labor, as did the Big Three, had it paid competitive salaries, had it bought expensive real estate, had it not used novices to operate its cameras and edit its tape and film. . . the Cable News Network would never have made it.

CNN headline news

Believing that a knowledgeable public is a cornerstone of the free world, Headline News strives to provide a maximum of information in a minimum of time, allowing the public access to the latest world news at any time of the day.

So touts CNN's own publicity materials. CNN "Headline News" is the ultimate television news service for "people on the move." It presents a rolling half-hour sequence which promises to take the viewer "around the world in 30 minutes." Far from all the thirty minutes are news, however, and few of the stories say much about the world outside the USA. Of the approximately twenty-one minutes that remain after eliminating the commercials, we found that, on average, less than four minutes were devoted to foreign news. Two or more minutes were devoted to sports and one minute to the activities of various Hollywood luminaries. The different segments are so tightly scheduled that local cable operators can opt out of some parts and insert their own local news stories. Headline News had a short-lived competitor, Satellite News Channel, started by ABC and Westinghouse. After losing forty million dollars, it was bought up by Turner and dropped. Headline News has the potential to reach 19.2 million people in the US, but the actual numbers of viewers at any one time in the many, fragmented cable systems that carry it is only a fraction of that.

Who pays?

CNN earns its revenue in part from subscription fees. It demands a fee per subscriber for cable networks and other users (hotels, etc.). At eleven cents per household/month in the USA (in September 1988), this amounts to fifty-seven million dollars per annum.

Other income comes from commercials in the programming itself and from deals with other users (primarily broadcasting companies). Even though the total number of viewers at any time are low, one should not underestimate the effect of CNN in setting a general news agenda, and at times even affecting the news approaches adopted by other organizations. The fact that the CNN monitor has found its way into newsrooms at radio and television stations as well as at newspapers gives it near wire-service status not unlike that enjoyed by Reuters or AP. Rather than waiting for AP to summarize a press conference for example, if CNN covers it, then the journalists can immediately choose their own quotes. It also provides opportunities to cover foreign news more quickly in this fashion. As CNN further expands its penetration – in February of 1989 it was already in seventy-five countries according to its Atlanta publicity office – so will its influence and status increase – assuming no successful competitors get into the sky. Its only real broadcast competitor as of now is the BBC World Service which is also becoming more common in more and more newsrooms. In parts of the world where broadcasters have little money for foreign news gathering of their own and where CNN is easily available on satellite, it can provide entire bulletins, or least a majority of those broadcasters' foreign news.

Satellite and cable distribution of news in the USA and Europe

Throughout the 1970s, cable and satellite have been two magic words among media entrepreneurs in the Western world, as they envisioned little wires under the ground fed by signals received from satellites by big dishes as a means of creating new markets for the distribution of electronic media. These technologies would allow new programme producing companies to compete against the established giants who controlled the available frequencies for terrestrial transmission.

In the US, cable has grown like wildfire. According to the cable industry's own 1988 *Facts* booklet, American cable penetration now exceeds 50 per cent; that is, half of all the television households are wired to cable. In those homes, loyalty to the traditional three networks has decreased. In 1978, for example, the Big Three accounted for 92 per cent of all the viewing in America. By 1988, that number had dropped to 70 per cent. Programming produced especially for cable has made the biggest inroads into network viewing, so much so, in fact, that in February of 1989 the three networks announced that they would band together to promote and advertise themselves as an alternative to the new television technologies. As a network spokesman told the New York *Times*, such an agreement would offer the networks not only a single voice, but the economy that results from joint sponsorship.

There were two main reasons for the rapid success of cable in the US. One was improved reception, an issue in rural areas where over-the-air stations tend to be sparsely situated, and in big cities, where tall buildings foul picture quality. Another was the growing availability of programmes which did not carry commercials (especially film channels such as Home Box Office). Initially, cable operators were required to carry all local programmes available in their area, called the "must carry" rule, and provide generous public access production facilities. The type of cable company that developed usually offered the networks, local stations, and possibly several "premium" stations, for which one paid an additional fee, all for a reasonably low monthly cost.

Ultimately, though, a new breed of cable operator appeared, some offering up to forty channels of basic fare, numerous premium channels, *and* scrambled "pay-per-view" capacity. Initially, cable was lucrative but was usually locally owned, with each municipality able to grant individual franchises. With deregulation, however, things changed. The green light was given for cable companies to amalgamate and grow. When GillCable, the franchise holder in San Jose in California's Silicon Valley, was sold in 1988, for example, the price was in the neighbourhood of three hundred million dollars, equivalent to a fee of 2,500 dollars for each of its subscribers.

Programming on American cable systems shows a high degree of specialization, leading to fragmentation of the audience. Specialist channels presenting exclusively business news, weather, home shopping (replacing mail order catalogues), preachers presenting numerous variations on the evangelical Christian theme, travel bargains, sports, old films, and on and on fill the output.

Most offerings come in via satellite signals to a central distribution point. Satellites, however, are used for much more than bringing fare to cable operators, e.g., the distribution of news, network, and syndicated programming, and films from point A (a distributor) to television broadcaster at point B. This has encouraged tens of thousands of Americans to erect "backyard" dishes, becoming the modern television equivalent of the shortwave radio DXer. One popular pastime involves using the dish to pick up those channels which are utilized to carry recently released films which are being distributed nationally by satellite for re-distribution over local cable television companies.

This has yet to occur in Europe, where satellites have been a government or PTT monopoly. The Continent, however, is on the threshold of a major change, as Luxembourg has launched the medium-power Astra satellite, and with licences for up- and downlinking signals being granted to private firms.

Deep pockets in the European satellite/cable business

Cable has not grown like wildfire all over Europe, even if its penetration may be high in particular countries. The countries with the highest penetration are Holland, Belgium, and Finland. Of Europe's estimated 119 million television homes, only 12.6 million were on cable as of 1987. Growth is fairly fast in Sweden where almost one million, over 30 per cent of the homes now are wired, equivalent to about 25 per cent of the population. Swedish cable operators, however, envisage a maximum reach of about 50 per cent in this sparsely populated country.

A number of reasons can be suggested for the relatively sluggish growth of cable in Europe. They relate precisely, though in an opposite fashion, to those factors that have encouraged the American cable boom: the quality of existing reception and the quality of existing programme content. The UK mixture of regulated public-service and commercial radio and television already provides a wide range of programmes. The British public as yet has not thirsted for those satellite channels which are available from space. As Brian Diamond, American Program Director of MTV Europe, told us, "When you ask the British why they don't have cable, they'll answer, 'we don't want anyone digging up our streets, thank you.'"

In addition, the plurality of European culture has provided programmers with problems. How should they deal with the different languages spoken on that continent? By running special services for different countries, by sub-titling or by assuming everyone can understand English? All these strategies have been tried with none providing a formula for pan-European market success. European national cultural interests have also reacted against allowing a free-for-all among the satellite programme companies. They dread the notion of programmes beaming across borders with little or no control over content, advertising standards, and the like. The Council of Europe's 1989 formula for a European satellite convention will, in theory, regulate satellite broadcast content. The matters with which it deals are issues of the amount of advertising, number of advertising breaks, sponsorship, and the amount of European as opposed to non-European (read US) programme material.

Since different member countries have vested interests in different projects, it seems unlikely that this convention will do more than limit the extremes in programme choice. Pornographic channels will be banned, for example, as will "obscenities." Bearing in mind that what is art to one person could be highly offensive to another, this outcome should also lead to interesting programme debates in Europe.

The reason that direct home satellite reception has not flourished in Europe is technological. Existing satellite programmes have been available on satellites such as Eutelsat F-1, Intelsat V, or in the case of the French, on Telecom 1A and 1B. These are low-power communications satellites requiring dishes between two and five metres in diameter for reception, thus limiting that reception to cable networks. Individual dishes have been few and far between, and even then mainly on the roofs of business premises or hotels.

Those entrepreneurs who have seen seen a financial eldorado in European cable have needed very deep pockets. Rupert Murdoch's Sky Channel, for instance, has been transmitting for most of the 80s continually in the red despite claiming to reach over seven million homes. Obviously, as Sky's experience indicates, the stakes, and potential losses, can be astronomic.

Even a truly "European" project, Europa TV, underwritten by the governments of Holland, Ireland, West Germany, Portugal, and Italy, which was intended to provide multi-lingual, pan-European television, collapsed after three years in 1986. Its intended financial support was to be 50 per cent public purse, 50 per cent revenue from commercials. Advertisers shunned the project and some governments were late in paying their dues. The Dutch government, which paid for the satellite transponder, reputedly lost some three-and-a-half million pounds in the Europa TV project. These experiences, however, have not deterred the EBU from announcing a new satellite news channel with content mainly from the Eurovision news exchange system. This project, at the time of writing, is still very much in the planning stage.

News output on the European satellite

The successful launch of Luxembourg's medium-power Astra satellite in December 1988 allowed Mr Murdoch to expand his European satellite television interests, though concentrating his efforts on reaching the British market.

Four Astra transponders were booked by News International and one commenced carrying the 24-hour Sky News channel in February 1989. Its target, however, will be only the British audience; in fact, even the Sky entertainment channel is to be scrambled and decoders will only be sold in Great Britain. This might seem an odd use of Astra, since its footprint was created so as to cover most of Europe. But purchasing rights for all of Europe simply costs too much, even for Murdoch, so the strategy is to opt for the British market.

Up to now, Britain has played a strange role in European satellite television. Many of satellite's programmes are British, much of its music video material is produced by the British music industry, but virtually no one can see these programmes in Britain because of the absence of cable. Sky is now attempting to manufacture and sell 60 cm dishes, persuading individuals to install this additional antenna, and to encourage those buildings with central antennae to choose the satellite alternative (SMATV, Satellite Master Antenna Television). Public response throughout 1989 has been lukewarm. In the last four months of 1989 the Sky TV operation out of London was losing £2,000,000 a week –

that's almost a fifth of the *annual* budget for one of Swedish Television's news divisions. The losses, according to the parent company, Mr Murdoch's News International, were "in accordance with its long-term business plan."

Sky News gets its foreign news from the standard sources, namely Visnews and WTN (though it may not show Visnews material produced by the BBC, which owns a percentage of that supplier). If we are to believe Bill Spencer, formerly of the BBC's "9 O'clock News," and one of the satellite channel's many new recruits, Sky will adopt a decidedly populist image. He told a reporter, "Sky News has a much wider appeal. . . it will cover the kind of stories that the BBC would never touch" (Wade 1989: 45). He offered as examples the story of a workaholic couple that wed on their lunch break and a valuable Shropshire cat that is for sale with its owner's home.

Another 24 hour news channel was planned for late 1989 – the NOW Channel – to be delivered via BSB (British Satellite Broadcasting) over a high power satellite with a small footprint covering the British Isles and Ireland. The start was delayed several times because of technical problems regarding scrambling (making sure people who don't pay can't tune in) and reception. Interestingly, the antenna for this service, known as a "squarial," is more like a pad than a dish and is therefore less costly. But receiving BSB could be just as expensive as receiving Astra. Astra transmits with the conventional European PAL system (as opposed to the NTSC system used in the US). BSB, on the other hand, will use the more advanced MAC system, requiring special receiving equipment but offering vastly superior picture quality.

Aiming for the lucrative Scandinavian market: Scansat/TV3

SCANSAT, or TV3, as it calls itself (Sweden has two national channels, TV1 and TV2) began feeding the Scandinavian cable market in 1988. It has been costing its owner, Swedish multi-millionaire Jan Stenbeck, an estimated twenty-five million pounds a year. Among its output of predominantly entertainment programmes purchased primarily from the USA, some news programmes do appear. These news shows illustrate probably the cheapest way of putting an international television news show together.

Scansat transmits four bulletins an evening varying in duration from three to fifteen minutes. These are edited in London and are composed primarily of international news voiced in different Scandinavian languages. The budget only allows for a token amount of domestic Scandinavian news. Material is bought in a "rough-edited" form from both Visnews and WTN.

A team of ten journalists and five production staff produces the bulletins. Newscasts produced in this fashion cost approximately one million pounds per annum, less than one-tenth of the annual cost of one of Sweden's two domestic television news divisions, or, as the man who set up Scansat news (Dan Damon) told us, "almost as much as the BBC spent on a new set of graphics for the 9 O'clock News".

An obvious question to Dan Damon concerned the possibility of creating a different profile or look for the news, in as much as Scansat uses the same material as other European newscasters. "The only way to get material at the price we pay is for Visnews to sell it to as many as possible, spreading the costs," he reported in 1988,

> We can hardly create our own profile at this stage. It might change in the future with satellite stations becoming bigger sources of revenue. Government support for national broadcasters all over Europe seems to be on the decrease. Unfettered competition looks like the thing of the future in Europe, not that I necessarily approve. Murdoch is spending hundreds of millions of pounds to make something different as regards British news on Sky. But with international news, there's very little chance that more than one cameraman is on the scene when the ferry goes down. That's the way it's always been, but then there weren't so many channels that it mattered.

In March 1989, Scansat announced it had acquired the services of Swedish Television Channel Two's foreign news editor who would function as both editor and anchorman. A bulletin of Scandinavian news would be introduced at 7:00 p.m. every evening (thirty minutes before the traditional transmission time for TV2's "Rapport"). Clearly news is seen by Scansat as giving a competitive advantage; alternatively, the absence of news is seen as a disadvantage in the present competitive situation.

The future for satellite radio and television in Europe

Satellite capacity over Europe is likely to expand. Of Astra's sixteen transponders, it is impossible to estimate how many will carry profitable programmes; some will certainly collapse, providing newly empty channels to new high bidders. Astra's owners, including several European banks, Thames Television, and other financial interests, will hardly want the transponders to remain unused during the satellite's ten-year life span. Other satellites are either already in orbit or are planned to enter orbit within the next year or so.

As European telecommunications develop, employing a combination of optic fibre cables and satellite links, more and more capacity will be used for telecommunications, transfer of business information and data, and so on. A buyers' market is likely to develop if Mr Murdoch's plans do not follow his predicted financial path and if the British continue to refuse to dig up their streets or put dishes on their roofs. Deregulation will certainly allow more possibilities for SNG, encouraged further if a situation of an oversupply of transponder time and an undersupply of large time-block users develops. *International Broadcasting* reported in November 1988 that "many firms are waiting on the doorstep ready with the necessary technology" to supply mobile up- and down-link facilities for business telecommunications.

Sound radio satellite channels will be plentiful; the Eurovision organization has been asking member broadcasters if they can use empty sound transponder channels. In fact, it has considered the idea of a pan-European satellite radio channel, providing music, news, weather and other service information in different languages. The plan has not moved beyond one experimental transmission in 1985.

The European scenario is not a simple one. Billions of dollars and European currencies are being invested in media projects aimed at tapping a lucrative market. "News" is seen as an important ingredient in any formula for success. Whether the news continues to inform and maybe even irritate will depend greatly on the type of competitive environment that unfolds. One prediction is that we will see low-cost technology (inexpensive one-man camera crews, for example) producing greater variety in news gathering, and high cost technology (for example, the necessary satellite links) becoming even cheaper for distribution. The operators who can adapt to the advantages that such a scenario offers will be the ones who reap the greatest audience and therefore, financial rewards. Many, however, will fall by the wayside with a large financial bang.

6

The international news broadcasters:
information, disinformation, and improvised truth

By bouncing short-wave signals on and off the ionosphere, radio programmes can theoretically be transmitted to any point on the globe. Medium Wave AM signals have a short day-time reach, but can cover far greater distances at night when waves are reflected back to earth from the lower ionosphere. Reception at a distance, however, is not always guaranteed; atmospheric disturbances, sun-spot cycles and other such factors affect dispersion of radio waves. Overcrowding of the spectrum is also a growing problem. As the number of transmissions has increased, interference has become the rule rather than the exception. Attempts to regulate, via international agreement, the plethora of short-wave broadcasters have met with some formal but little practical success. The general rule has been that the broadcaster with the strongest signal gets through, thus leading to a general increase in the number of high power transmitters and, therefore, even more interference. Both hours of broadcasting and numbers of broadcasters have increased steadily.

Exact figures for hours of broadcasting are hard to come by. Schedules can be changed at short notice. "Hours of Broadcasting" is not always the same as hours of programme production. Sweden, for instance, has an external radio service which both relays domestic Swedish radio and produces half-hour programmes in eight different languages daily. Production amounts, in other words, to four hours in all (or twenty-eight hours a week), with only news bulletins being updated in certain transmissions. The same English programme will be transmitted up to a dozen times on different frequencies beamed in different

Table 6.1 *Some of the largest international radio broadcasters*

Broadcaster	Number of hours/week			No of languages
	1950	1970	1988	1988
USA (VOA, Radio Free Europe, Radio Liberty, Radio Marti)	497	1907	2360	66
USSR (including Radio Moscow + language services)	533	1908	2223	78
China (Mainland)	66	1276	1453	44
Taiwan	NA	NA	1195	17
West Germany	0	804	831	35
Egypt	0	546	792	32
UK (BBC external)	643	719	768	36
Transworld (religious)	NA	NA	540	60
Voice of the Andes (religious)	NA	NA	493	13
East Germany	0	375	480	11
India	116	389	462	24
Albania	26	487	459	21

Sources: (1950/1970) BBC Annual Reports 87–8. (1988 estimates – VOA Annual report 1989)

directions. Published statistics show Sweden transmitting 209 hours of programmes per week, since each new transmission of the same programme is regarded as a new programme. The same applies to many of the available statistics in this area.

There is even uncertainty as regards the numbers of potential shortwave listeners, i.e., those who own radios with SW bands. A BBC report from 1987, "World Radio and Television Receivers," estimates the total number of radio sets at around 1,200 million. Almost all have an AM Medium Wave band, and varying percentages have SW circuits. A study commissioned by the Voice of America (Fortner and Durham 1988) suggests that the BBC estimate is too high, but does conclude from studies of average households in different regions of the world that there are approximately 500 million shortwave receivers, with no less than 170 million in Asia alone. Numbers, according to this report, will increase only slowly in Africa and Middle Asia, but far more rapidly in Western Europe (travellers wishing to keep in touch), Eastern Europe (a continued thirst for news from the West), Asia, and Central America. "In Central America," it read, the drug trade, which uses radio – and other consumer commodities – to launder money and provide easily liquidated goods to bypass import quotas and tariffs, will spur large increases in SW radio penetration, while in Asia the newly industrializing countries (NICs) along the Pacific rim, and the "opening" of the People's Republic of China to foreign goods and joint ventures in electronics production, will have major effects on the penetration of all consumer goods, including SW radios, in the region". (Fortner and Durnham 1988: 12)

Even if the number of receivers is increasing, the quality of reception in the new generations of receivers has not necessarily kept pace. The ability to tune to SW stations in the crowded environment of the 1980s may have even decreased "as manufacturers turn their attention to cassette players, speakers and other cosmetic features" (Elliott 1988: 2) which are such an important part of the marketing of radios in this day and age.

While there are minor differences of opinion among broadcasters regarding the number of SW sets, estimates of the numbers of actual listeners vary enormously. This is not surprising considering the difficulties involved in conducting audience research on a global scale. And it is not unlikely that estimates are sweetened to impress governments and parliaments who foot the bill for the transmissions.

A February 1987 publicity release from the Voice of America claims that "in an average week, all around the world, more than 130 million persons tune their radios to the Voice of America." The BBC claims that 125 million listen to its World Services at least once a week. The BBC, on the other hand, excludes certain countries from its estimate (where figures are regarded as too uncertain), notably China. The VOA does include China in its estimates. Exact figures are the sort of quantities that can neither be proved nor disproved. It can be said with a fair degree of certainty, however, that an awful lot of people around the world listen. One unsystematic but compelling piece of evidence that the audience is substantial comes in the form of letters to broadcasters. The BBC receives a half a million letters a year; Radio Netherlands gets 130,000; and, relatively small broadcasters such as Radio Sweden and Radio Canada International both collect 40,000 pieces of mail annually. Although these figures might sound impressive, there is no known methodology for transferring data about quantities of mail to quantities of listeners; maybe such a conversion system does not even exist. Even the BBC is wary of drawing conclusions about audience size from the size of the mailbag. Epistles from the unknown audience many leagues away are, however, an important form of feedback, affecting programme strategies, and providing for the multitude of "answer your questions" programmes that abound.

Sudden changes in the quantity and content of letters received can be used to infer interesting conclusions about political changes and sources of information in a target country. Mainland China, after the suppression of student demonstrations in June 1989, provides such a case. Up to May 1989, the BBC World Service was receiving about 3,000 letters a month from China, either direct from Peking or via Hong Kong. In June, after the government had used troops to quell the demonstrations, only 600 letters arrived. The figures were the same in July. The tone was mainly appreciative of the BBC's coverage of events in China and supportive of the so-called "pro-democracy movement". The August mailbag from China showed a further drop, to less than 500 pieces of mail. BBC staff reading and analysing those letters, however, noticed a significant change of emphasis. Several of those Chinese listeners who wrote to the BBC in August wanted to know why they were getting incorrect information about the state of affairs in their country. The BBC version, they claimed, did not tally with what they had seen with their own eyes and heard on Beijing TV. The official Chinese TV version of the truth, in other words, was gaining domestic acceptance.

The relative power of television in China, compared to external broadcasting sources of information, is also illustrated by the findings of a listener survey commissioned by the United States Information Agency in May 1989, whilst the student demonstrations were reaching a climax in the capital, but carried out in an urban area. A summary provided by the BBC department for International Broadcasting and Audience research notes:

Foreign Radio did not appear to have gained listeners in any great quantities in urban Nanning (the capital of Guangxi autonomous region in southern China) while the pro-democracy demonstrations were taking place in Beijing and elsewhere in China in May. . . under a tenth of the people interviewed had listened to any foreign stations in the past year. . . radio listening is not a popular activity in urban Nanning: about half of the adult population do not appear to listen to radio at all. (Six out of ten have a radio set at home while television ownership is almost universal). Television is by far the most important source of domestic and international news.

The speedy and thorough penetration of television into China clearly helped those in power in June 1989 create and maintain an atmosphere of stability in the nation. One can also surmise that many of those who previously listened to and wrote letters to the BBC were students and intellectuals in the big cities. The downfall of China's former ally, Romania's leader Ceausescu, in December 1989 illustrated a very different aspect of TV-media usage. As we pointed out at the beginning of this book, the first institution the revolutionary National Front took over was the country's TV studios in Bucharest. Without such access to live broadcast media, the outcome might have been very different.

Categorizing the broadcasters

Amongst the multitude of international radio transmissions, there are undoubtedly many which do not attract even a measurable audience. Some observers have even suggested that there is a type of international broadcast which is not even intended for a general audience. Ron Powers (1977: xviii) writing in the mid-1970s, and Hamid Mowlana in his fascinating, recently produced volume *Global Information And World Communication* (Mowlana 1986) both suggest that much international broadcasting is intended for government monitors in other countries. This is a means of spreading information which can affect another country's perception of the transmitting country's policies, or even the receiving nation's own foreign policy. Rather than expressing the government line in a press hand-out to the local Corps Diplomatique, an international transmission gives the message more status; it's plausible, after all, that a far greater audience might just have heard it!

One certainty is that shortwave radio provides immense opportunities to hear all sorts of different forms of "foreign" news. The range is amazing. Radio Tirana will broadcast the latest potato crop statistics from Albania. Radio Sweden will cover the Nordic area, including the story of the municipality of Pajala where the men outnumber the women so disproportionately that the town is inviting eligible spinsters from anywhere in

Europe to spend a courting week "on the local taxpayer." A frenzied outburst from Libya might have a neighbouring frequency presenting gentle persuasion from South Africa. The Radio Moscow "world service" in true post-*glasnost* fashion confesses more sins of past potentates, while not far away on the dial the BBC presents an authoritative bulletin of world news.

That programme formats on shortwave are changing as broadcasters experiment to find ways of attracting listeners is confirmed by Kim Elliot (1988: 5), Head of Audience Research at the Voice of America. He wrote,

> Two of the largest international broadcasting stations, Radio Moscow and Radio Beijing, have developed much more lively and listenable programming as the politics of those countries have changed. Radio Beijing no longer begins broadcasts with quotations from Chairman Mao, followed by acerbic commentaries; instead, it now has attractive cultural features and its newscasts with reports from correspondents overseas. Radio Moscow has become somewhat less self-righteous. . . . Many Eastern European stations, such as Radio Prague, have followed suit with imaginative programming of their own. Among Western stations, the BBC and Radio Netherlands have been experimenting with new programming approaches.

Table 6.1 on page 117 presents only a fraction of the hundreds of international broadcasters who fill the airwaves with programme material, much of which can be characterized as "international news." Intentions, methods of funding, technical resources and programme strategies cover a wide range. The same applies to their varied degrees of success in reaching a wide audience.

Funding

With the exception of most international religious broadcasters and the handful of international commercial broadcasters, operations are usually paid for by government funds, in other words by the taxpayer in most democracies. Privatization and sponsorship are not common in international radio broadcasting; but they could well be round the corner. In other words, the Voice of America (including Radio Free Europe and Radio Liberty, annually budgeted at approximately 400 million US dollars), the BBC World Service (approximately 100 million pounds), Radio Sweden (approximately three million pounds or five million dollars) all have to convince their politicians and relevant civil servants that the investment is worth while.

Choice of target audience

This varies widely. A major target for the external services of Swedish Radio are the scattered groups of Swedes living abroad (ex-patriates). Efficient re-broadcasting of domestic news programmes is therefore an important element in attaining this goal. The Voice of America, however, does not treat US citizens living abroad as an important target group. The VOA is more geared to "explaining" US foreign policy to foreigners than informing its many countrymen abroad about what's going on at home (CNN, or in the case of military personnel, AFRTS, American Forces Radio, and Television, cater far better to that need). For the BBC World Service, ex-patriates are described in the newsroom guide as "a small group, but very vocal. They may use us as their main news medium, and do not like change."

Target groups in international broadcasting can range from the vaguest possible designations (anyone who can pick us up) to the most specific. Examples of the latter are broadcasts complied by the ANC (African National Congress) beamed into South Africa from transmitters in Tanzania. Even within the more general fare provided by international broadcasters, one can find programmes intended for specific groups of recipients. Nations with significant merchant navies produce and transmit programmes specifically for seamen (e.g., the "Seven Seas" on the BBC World Service).

Technical means

Reaching different target audiences often requires different technical means that vary over time and from broadcaster to broadcaster. Without a functioning international system of sanctions for regulating the use of shortwave frequencies, one means of achieving success in reaching desired audiences has been increasing transmitter power. The 100kW transmitters that were common up to the late 60s have been upgraded to or replaced in many cases by 500kW transmitters. This not only exacerbates the problem of overcrowding of the airwaves, but it also increases the cost of running transmitting stations. A twenty-four-hour-a-day 500kW transmitter, after all, uses nearly 4.5 million kilowatt hours of power per year.

"Out of band" transmissions are also a means of circumnavigating the problems of overcrowding. Shortwave broadcasts occur via frequencies within loosely defined wave bands (25 metre, 31m, 41m, 49m, etc). These are marked on most short-wave receivers. By transmitting on the edge of one of these bands, it is possible to avoid overcrowding. If a broadcaster moves too far away from the assigned frequency range (or from the unassigned range that has become commonly known), fewer listeners will discover the signal, defeating the point of the exercise.

Still another strategy is to choose a transmission frequency which is adjacent to an established, popular broadcaster. Radio Moscow favoured this approach in the 1970s, marketing its own English-language, Radio Moscow "World Service," by occupying frequencies as near as possible to those used regularly by the traditional BBC World Service. This policy caused irritation among regular BBC World Service listeners, who had to put up with more interference and confusion among new listeners. On the positive side, it forced Radio Moscow to liven up its programmes; the contrast was otherwise too obviously negative.

"Jamming," blocking out incoming signals, is a very expensive, negative way of affecting what comes through. Frequently used by Eastern Block countries in the past, most jamming had ceased by 1988. Even the United States Information Agency's "surrogate" stations in West Germany (Radio Liberty and Radio Free Europe) were getting through to the Soviet Union without intentional interference.

The use of relay stations is presently the most popular method used for improving transmission to far-away places. The BBC has long had access to booster transmitters in the Commonwealth (in Singapore, Hong Kong, Cyprus, Ascension Island, the Seychelles, etc.), with satellite technology allowing a perfect signal to be fed to the relay station.

Relay facilities can be bought, franchised, inherited or exchanged. Examples of all these alternatives exist today. Gabon in Africa will sell transmitter time to virtually anyone who is willing to pay. Sri Lanka has provided the same service for years to American evangelists wishing to reach prospective individual clients in the Indian sub-continent. Brazil rents transmitter time to such varied broadcasting clients as Radio Surinam International and the BBC.

Big and rich broadcasters can even seek permission to erect their own transmitters on foreign territory; a sort of franchising arrangement. The VOA is completing construction of relay stations in Morocco and Israel, part of a 365 million dollar modernization plan for the VOA authorized by the Reagan Administration. The VOA also plans relay stations in Thailand, Botswana, Sri Lanka, and the little Caribbean island of Grenada, where "US forces returned the government to the people" in 1985, as a VOA comment once put it. Deutsche Welle, the West German international broadcasting organization, has also used a mixture of foreign policy activities, including donations, to improve relay facilities. In the early 1970s, Deutsche Welle gave Malta a one million pound grant for permission to erect a 600 kW Medium Wave relay for its Arabic service. Ruanda also received a transmitting station as part of a foreign aid package from the Federal Republic. This has helped Deutsche Welle gain a loud and clear signal in East and Central Africa.

The practice of exchanging transmitter resources is also gaining in popularity. A listener who picks up Radio Beijing, for example, has no way of knowing if the signal originated from a transmitter in China or from one in Mali or French Guyana (which happen to relay Chinese programmes).

As of the first week of April 1989, Austria and Canada also embarked on a direct exchange agreement, whereby Radio Canada International programmes intended for Eastern Europe are transmitted over a Radio Austria International transmitter in Moosbrun. In return, Radio Canada offers the Austrians time on its powerful transmitter in Sackville for transmission of Austrian programmes intended for North America. Canada has a similar deal with Japan.

Satellites, as we have mentioned, are already used for feeding signals to relay stations. They also allow for re-transmission with Hi-Fi quality via the resources of any broadcaster with a dish and a desire for a particular sort of programme material. The BBC World Service offers two satellite radio feeds via global communication satellites. One carries the World Service in English and the second channel relays a mixture of the other languages in which the BBC transmits. Any local station which wishes to relay parts of the output can do it for free. Thus Radio Stockholm, in the Swedish capital, can run the BBC World Service news for nine minutes every evening at 7:00 p.m. This assumes, of course, that Radio Stockholm's management continues to be convinced that BBC World Service news is of a sufficiently high standard (as regards reliability, impartiality) to warrant re-transmission. Most international broadcasters are considering options which combine modern satellite technology with a continued presence on short and medium waves.

Direct broadcasting satellites: an alternative?

The dream of many of the richer international radio broadcasters, of course, is a future where DBS can replace the uncertainties and overcrowding of shortwave terrestrial transmissions. The dream is a long way off. It assumes a) available frequencies via available satellites and b) widespread diffusion of reception equipment so that individuals, anywhere within a suitable satellite footprint, can receive signals. Both prerequisites, at present, are still in the world of fantasy. A consultant's report to the Voice of America (Fortner and Durham 1988: 3) concluded that on a frequency of 26MHz, "it would take 47 geostationary satellites or 20 satellites in 8-hour orbits to fully satisfy the voice channel requirements of the broadcast schedule provided by VOA."

This same report also refers to opinions voiced by BBC executives that their "terrestrial SW system for international services can safely be relied on at least until the year 2020" (Fortner and Durham 1988: 8). Shortwave broadcasting, in other words, is rather like the private car in Los Angeles; finding a free parking lot gets harder and harder as the number of automobiles increases, but there's really no viable alternative to getting from point A to point B. Overcrowding justs gets worse and worse. The difference between the two is that there is no functioning system of regulation, deciding who can park their signal when and where. There is definitely no system whereby sanctions can be applied to those broadcasters who park in the way of others, let alone a mechanism whereby those whose parking interferes with others can be towed away.

Operating strategies in the international airwaves

The strategies adopted by different international broadcasters cover a wide range in the content of their programmes, the groups they target as listeners and the various combinations of the two. At the extreme ends of the content spectrum there are stations offering overt propaganda ("we are the best, everyone else is lying"), or the opposite ("these are the plain facts, take it or leave it"). In between are all forms mild persuasion. Common

125

6 A statement of intent from the BBC's World Service greets passengers
waiting for their flights at London Heathrow's Terminal 4

to all is the desire to win some form of goodwill, either loosely for
a nation or more specifically for a particular ideology or policy.

Some international broadcasters: the BBC external services

A standard American textbook on the electronic media (Head
and Sterling 1987: 30) has this to say about the BBC's
international broadcasting activities:

> The BBC retains the highest credibility amongst external
> broadcasters. Throughout the world, listeners tune automati-
> cally to the BBC when in doubt about the authenticity of news
> sources. In times of local disorder, it is not uncommon for
> foreign government officials to turn to the BBC for vital
> information about the state of affairs in their own countries.

There is much truth in this accolade. The BBC's reputation is
not associated with propaganda in the same way that Radio
Moscow and the VOA are. The BBC does provide an important
source of alternative information in many countries; Lybia's
Colonel Gadaffi is said to listen daily to the BBC. It would be
naive, however, to assume that the BBC World Service exists
merely for the benefit of mankind, without a specific goodwill

7 Action twenty-four hours a day in the BBC World Service's central newsroom at Bush House, the Strand, London

creating function. Julian Hale, himself a broadcaster for many years at World Service headquarters (Bush House in London), presents this description in his excellent book *Radio Power*:

> The BBC's line is to take as much of the propaganda element out of international broadcasting as possible. . . . This does not mean that the BBC's goal, to influence foreigners' minds in favour of the political principles it represents, differs fundamentally from that of any other External service. It so happens that those principles are the minimally offensive ones of liberalism, moderation and parliamentary democracy; and that the best way to promote them is through liberal, moderate means. (Hale 1975: xv)

The BBC's ethos for international broadcasts developed partly out of experiences during World War II. A preponderance of truth, it was believed, had a far more positive psychological effect on radio listeners than the Nazi brand of propaganda transmissions. Out of this developed an interesting, and fairly stable relationship with the State or, to be more specific, with the Foreign Office in London. The British taxpayers, via the Foreign Office, pay for the operation. The "return" on the investment for Britain is considerable goodwill and an operation characterized

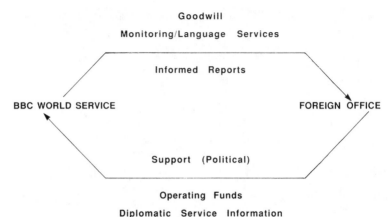

Goodwill

Monitoring/Language Services

Informed Reports

BBC WORLD SERVICE

FOREIGN OFFICE

Support (Political)

Operating Funds

Diplomatic Service Information

6.1 Demand–reward relationship between the BBC and the Foreign Office is a prerequisite for stability and the continued existence of the BBC World Service

by authoritativeness, reliability, stability and professionalism. There is a clear give and take relationship with the establishment which allows the operation to continue.

The Foreign Office requires the BBC to run a monitoring service and stipulates which language services should be carried. The BBC gathers goodwill by retaining editorial control over its output. The BBC's independence from the rest of Britain's foreign PR efforts allows for an independent production of informed reports based on its own sources, reports which provide alternatives to those coming out of standard diplomatic channels. Cases are on record of the BBC announcing details of political upheavals, coups, etc. even before local British embassies have been aware that something was afoot. The story is told of how an evacuation from Lebanon of British subjects was planned. The Foreign Office had arranged for a boat to enter one of the Lebanese harbours. The BBC's English-language World Service channel was asked to broadcast a message telling all Britons to head immediately for the harbour. A BBC contact in Lebanon, who could monitor the harbour in question from his flat, managed to get through to Bush House on the phone. He reported that the rescue vessel was anchored well out to sea and couldn't get into the harbour because a storm was raging. BBC staff recall an interesting exchange of opinions with the Foreign Office. "It ended up with us telling the Foreign Office where their boat was." The Foreign Office rewards the BBC by encouraging

Parliament to provide it funds (known as a "grant in aid") and also allows Bush House chiefs to have access to some diplomatic telegram traffic. An agreement known as the "licence" stipulates that the Foreign Office informs the BBC about "conditions in and policies of Her Majesty's Government" in countries about which it is felt the BBC should be informed.

Editorial independence, though, is a holy cow, understood certainly by the diplomatic and civil service, but not always by the British politicians. David Spaull, recently retired News Editor of the BBC World Service, gave us a story which illustrates this point. "Way back," he said,

> long before the Ayatollah, a newly appointed Foreign Office minister phoned us up and said, "you will make it clear that the sovereignty of the Gulf is Persian." We said, "Minister, if you wish to make a statement that that is official government policy, we'll carry it." That would have been a good news story, but not any other way. We're not in the business of pushing out government plugs without any intrinsic news value. . . . Successive British governments, although they would love to have the World Service presenting them favourably, have realised the value of having an independent news service. Anything else would only last 24 hours anyway.

A number of events over the past three decades have served to establish the rules of the game for politicians, civil servants, and the BBC alike.

The Suez Crisis of 1956 was a critical incident both as a test and an affirmation of the BBC External Services' (as it was known at the time) editorial independence. The Government resented the BBC airing the views of those opposed to the Suez invasion. A Foreign Office official was ordered to take up residence at Bush House to make sure that transmissions adhered to a proper government policy. The official was effectively "sent to Coventry" (isolated by those around him). The end of the fighting in Egypt saw the end of the BBC/Foreign Office conflict.

Julian Hale (1975: 57) recalls that

> in a sense, by reaching the threshold of open confrontation, and pulling back, the air was now cleared of mutual paranoia. Both sides had tested how far they could go. Compromise had seen to be a workable formula, not just a holding operation until something better could be dreamed up.

It has since been discovered that the British government secretly took over a commercial radio station in Cyprus during the Suez crisis to broadcast the "proper" explanation of British foreign policy, independently of the BBC. A similar action was taken during the Rhodesia crisis in the 1970s and again during the Falklands conflict in the early 1980s when a British Government Spanish-language station was established on Ascension Island. It is interesting to note that the BBC World Service was *refused* permission by the Foreign Office/Ministry of Defence to send its own correspondent with the task force heading for the Falklands/Malvinas Islands.

An attempt was made in 1985 to formalize the relationship between the BBC World Service (BBC–WS) and the Foreign and Commonwealth Office (FCO), as Britain's equivalent of the US State Department is known. The so-called Perry Report resulted in a statement of objectives as follows:

> The BBC External Services (the World Services) should enhance Britain's standing abroad and form among listeners a better understanding of the UK. In order to achieve this they must:
> — provide a credible, unbiased, reliable, accurate, balanced and independent news service
> — give a balanced British view of national and international developments
> — represent British life accurately and effectively
> — increase the understanding and speaking of English.

The Perry Report ends with an addendum which stipulates that decisions regarding factors such as quality, balance and impartiality are solely the responsibility of BBC–WS. At Bush House, the newsroom guidelines put this in another way: "Broadcasting in the 'national interest' means just that; it is not necessarily the same as 'in the government's interest.'"

The relationship between BBC–WS and the FCO is stable, but not in perfect equilibrium. That tensions exist is illustrated in a Swedish Government Report on international broadcasting, based in part on interviews with personnel both at the British FCO and BBC–WS. The report found differences of opinion regarding target groups for overseas broadcasts, with the FCO preferring the goal of reaching an educated elite in every region, while the BBC wanted to aim for maximizing a general audience. Another conflict lives. One BBC chief is quoted as saying, "They want us to transmit to potential enemies, we want to transmit to friends and enemies alike" (Englund 1986: 7).

Carrying out the brief

Every twenty-four hours, the BBC–WS newsroom produces 200 news broadcasts which are transmitted in English and thirty-six foreign languages. Apart from the twenty-four-hour World Service in English, there are:

— the European Services (Russian for the Soviet Union, various other Eastern and Western European languages)
— the Latin American Service (Portuguese and Spanish)
— the Three A's or the Arabic (9 hours daily), African (including an English-language African alternative to the World Service) and the Asian Service (covering a geographical area from Iran to Japan and Sri Lanka to Nepal)

The main sources of news are the international agencies, its own correspondents (staff or freelance), and monitoring reports, supplemented at times by information from British diplomatic sources. The newsroom follows the principle, wherever possible, of demanding that a news item be confirmed by two different agencies before it be carried. A confirmation or denial via one of the BBC's own correspondents carries more weight, however. The BBC maintains an impressive network of staff correspondents and/or freelancers (stringers) in most capitals of the world. Many of the stringers also have to work for other news organizations to survive, so the same voice might be heard, for example, on the BBC, Radio Sweden, Radio Canada International, and NPR in the USA. When a big news story breaks in a small country, literally scores of stations around the world chase up the local BBC correspondent for some exclusive comments. Since the BBC World Service is also carried by many other broadcasters, BBC news reporters can be heard via many transmitters in a multitude of countries.

Another BBC routine involves requesting monitoring reports from the receiving station at Caversham, England, when the focus of news turns on a particular foreign country. Caversham has played an important role in the difficult job of covering events in the Middle East during the Gulf War. From a base in Cyprus, some of the BBC Middle Eastern correspondent's material for his reports on the tanker war in the Gulf was gleaned, not from local sources, but from monitoring reports on Gulf radio stations from back at home.

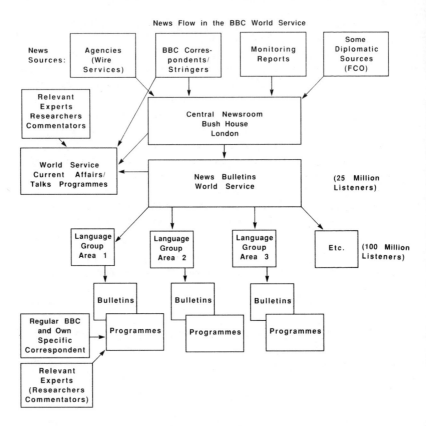

6.2 Newsflow through the BBC World Service from source to programme

Problems facing the BBC–WS news services

The aim of speedily verifying all news items via a combination of agency reports, a correspondent's confirmation as well as monitoring results, is not always a practical possibility. In some parts of French-speaking Africa, for instance, the French agency AFP has a virtual monopoly. As to monitoring, Caversham cannot listen to every corner of the world; an exchange agreement with the equivalent organization in the USA helps alleviate this problem in part.

One major difficulty for the BBC is that in parts of the world where censorship is rife, news bulletins often cannot avoid quoting official sources; balance and impartiality are sometimes endangered. As News Editor Spaull told us,

There are particular problems in reporting on events in both South Africa and the territories occupied by Israel. You find that not only are you carrying the official Israeli or South African statements, but you end up by presenting them as a BBC story in the form of the Israeli view of what's happening on the West Bank, or the South African view of disturbances. It would be just as important to present the view of the Palestinians or the ANC. Ideally you should have your own eye witness accounts. The danger with South Africa and all the censorship there is that you get tired of repeating such phrases as "I can't tell you what I saw." You end up giving the South African official picture and don't risk boring the listeners by reminding them that this is only a partial, one-sided view of what's happening. It's a constant problem we're up against.

One solution to the problem of describing events in South Africa has been to encourage the English-language African service to build up its own network of correspondents in Southern Africa. There is some concern, however, that if too strong a spotlight were to be focused on such sources of information (e.g., by featuring them more prominently on the global World Service) these stringers would soon suffer the wrath of an unsympathetic regime in Pretoria. This could change, however, if the signs of liberation, heralded by the unbanning of the ANC and the lifting of some media restrictions in January 1990 have a permanent effect on journalists' reporting out of South Africa.

The problems the domestic services of the BBC has had in its relationship to the Thatcher government have also affected the World Service. Decrees and legal decisions restricting the BBC from reporting on court hearings concerning the right to publish Peter Wright's book *Spycatcher* (about the Britsh secret service, MI5) also applied to the World Service. While the BBC was silent, Radio Sweden was transmitting selected excerpts from the text that dealt with joint espionage projects involving Sweden and MI5. In 1988, the British government issued a ban on radio and television interviews with members of various Northern Ireland extremist organizations. Clever legal experts at the BBC soon found a partial route round the restrictions. Interviews with certain individuals from Northern Ireland on the banned list could be transcribed and read aloud in a neutral voice by a studio presenter.

Stability has characterized much of BBC–WS operations over

the past three decades. Even if different British governments
have been tempted to nibble away at the budget (threatening the
existence of particularly the smaller language groups), total
output and format have remained similar, with the same types of
news programmes being broadcast at the same times, sounding
similar as regards style. In 1988, however, BBC World Service
Head John Tusa made a move to keep abreast of the times, as he
saw it. Old brass band themes were replaced by synthesizer
versions. Some announcers were taken off the air and attempts
were made to reach a new generation of listeners by combining,
for instance, science news and popular music in the same
programme. The BBC–WS are also preparing for an expansion of
news for Europe to coincide with the 1992 Single Market,
possibly even introducing a new news channel specifically for
Europe.

More international broadcasters: the Voice of America and related services

The textbook from which we took the flattering quote on the BBC
(p. 126) is less overflowing in its praise of the various international broadcasting services paid for by the US taxpayers:

> The Republican administration that took over in Washington
> in 1981 called for vigorous exploitation of the VOA as a
> propaganda organ. Implementation of this policy caused
> dissension: some staff people felt that new directives tended to
> undermine VOA credibility as a reliable information source
> and as an effective external service. (Head and Sterling, 1987:
> 28)

Ten years earlier, Julian Hale painted an equally confusing
picture. Noting how consecutive administrations had put their
own friends in charge of the VOA after firing their predecessors,
Hale (1975: 35) observed, "The mixture of political appointments
at the top, Congressional wariness and an uncertain chain of
command has led to what one VOA correspondent described to
me hopefully as 'creative tension,' but what can also be described
as plain muddle."

That remnants of the "muddle" still exist is somewhat
surprising; the VOA's current charter is crystal clear and not all
that different from that of the World Service's. Gerald Ford
signed it into law on 12 July 1976, a charter which includes the
following principles:

— the VOA will serve as a consistently reliable and authoritative source of news. VOA news will be accurate, objective and comprehensive
— VOA will represent America, not any single segment of America, and will therefore present a balanced and comprehensive projection of significant American thought and institutions
— VOA will present the policies of the United States clearly and effectively and will also present responsible discussion and opinion on these matters.

Such policies, of course, are difficult to maintain in the BBC fashion when every newly elected President puts a good buddy in charge of the United States Information Agency (USIA) which runs the VOA. Another complicating factor is that the VOA accounts for only about half of the funds the USA spends on international broadcasting. While the VOA (including the Cuban Service, or Radio Marti, as well as RIAS-Berlin broadcasting into East Berlin) had a 1988 budget of about 180 million dollars, other *surrogate* stations with a brief to provide alternative *domestic* services in target areas (Radio Free Europe, Radio Liberty, Radio Free Afghanistan) received 220 million dollars directly from Congress in 1988. Together the total US budget for international radio broadcasting amounted to almost 400 million US dollars, or well over twice as much as the total BBC–WS budget.

Radio Free Europe (RFE) and Radio Liberty (RL), beamed into the Eastern Block from West Germany, often compete with the VOA, sometimes overlapping with broadcasts to the same target areas in the same languages. With the decline of jamming and the inception of *glasnost*, the need for these surrogate stations might well be questioned. Preliminary audience research from January 1989, based on clandestine interviews with a sample of about 500 Soviet citizens, mainly well-educated males in the 35- to 45-year old age group, showed a slight increase in RL listening. Permanent changes in listening patterns, however, take longer to crystallize. The present US policy on the surrogates seems to be to retain them as a sort of "insurance policy," in case the hard-liners take over again in the communist block.

The history of the VOA is characterized by a lack of clarity as to choice of strategy, with actual output varying between the goal of persuasion (selling the ideology and policies of specific administrations, usually as alternatives to communism) and that of providing factual information. The influential *Columbia Journalism Review* has run stories of incidents which suggest that the VOA was used by Oliver North and White House Security Council staff to send coded messages (through the airing of specific records and artists) in the early stages of the Iran–Contra affair. Such stories, of course, hardly add to the organization's perceived credibility, something of which the professional radio people within the VOA are only too aware. The VOA's Head of Audience Research, Kim Elliott (1988: 1), has in fact suggested a radical re-thinking in a paper subtitled, "A New Start for America's Voices."

In it he proposed six fundamental changes to rebuild the VOA's credibility and efficiency:

1 reduce costs and concentrate resources, combine all the existing entities into one organization with a new name (in other words, do away with RL, RFE, Radio Marti, etc. and put them all together)

2 satisfy the "overriding audience desire for credible news" by establishing institutional autonomy for the new organization; block politicians' use of the VOA for their own purposes

3 determine priorities for language services to make the most efficient use of the available budget

4 Use an effective mix of traditional and new technologies to compete in the modern media environment (for example, short waves, medium waves, satellite relays, and DBS when plausible)

5 Privatize some language services to ease the burden on the taxpayer (he specifically suggested the Latin American services)

6 Establish an English-language service for Americans abroad.

Many of these suggestions, if implemented, would produce a VOA much closer in *modus operandi* to the BBC World Service. One possible reason for the lack of discussion or public debate of these issues in the US is the strange condition in which American citizens, in principle, are *not* encouraged to listen to the VOA. In fact, requests for copies or transcripts of VOA programmes by US citizens will not be honoured, though bona fide researchers have recently been given some limited access to the secret world of the VOA/RL and RFE.

International broadcasters attempt television: the VOA and the BBC–WS

Before the advent of satellites, terrestrial transmission of television signals could cover only relatively short distances. Transmission over longer distances required a series of expensive micro-wave links. As satellites began to be used for news gathering and distribution, with CNN building up its worldwide network, the biggest international broadcasters began to wonder whether sound could become sound *and* pictures.

The VOA's Director throughout the entire Ronald Reagan administration was Charles Zwick (later Charles Z. Wick), a lawyer friend from the President's days in Southern California. Wick initiated the USIA's television service, Worldnet. It was an expensive venture, with a 1988 budget of 36 million dollars. Much of transmission time was devoted to linking journalists around the world with spokespeople for the administration in Washington (not always the most exciting television). Viewing figures were not impressive; because virtually the only place that it could be viewed was in American embassies, Worldnet was watched primarily by people waiting in consulates to get their visas. Worldnet's budget for 1989 was put on hold by Congress, and at the time of writing, it lives an erratic existence, occasionally on and occasionally off the air.

Despite the less than spectacular success of Worldnet, the VDA embarked on another TV project in March 1990. This was a TV version of Radio Marti, aimed at Cuba, beamed from Miami to Havana and staffed by exiled Cubans opposed to the Castro regime. The newcomer was not appreciated by the Cubans; within minutes of going on air it was blotted out by jamming transmitters in Havana.

The strategy behind such a VDA TV-operation in times of decreased tension between the nominally Communist and Capitalist worlds is slightly unclear. Presumably, the US administration felt that visual access to US baseball, situation comedies and selected news items might serve to undermine Fidel Castro's apparent resistence to *perestroika*-style winds of change.

Throughout the 1980s, the BBC World Service has also toyed with the idea of a world television service, providing the same range of subjects and countries, with the same degree of reliability, as World Service radio news. Some fifty BBC–WS journalists have done three-month training stints at BBC domestic television news to learn the "new" medium. Initially, the plan was for half-hour packages of news to be satellited around the world. Bush House asked the Foreign Office for eight million pounds to run the project; the funds, though, were not forthcoming. The subject was hotly debated in the British parliament in July of 1987, but despite much lobbying and much support for the idea among various politicians, the British government was adamant. If the BBC wanted to start a world television service, it would have to solve the financing itself.

The idea, though, did not die. Alternative sources of money became the rallying cry. Direct sponsorship was ruled out ("that is perceived as demeaning to editorial integrity," said one BBC staffer), but not advertising. A London firm of merchant bankers, Schroder Wagg, was called in to provide a business plan, one which would involve the taking of commercials. A half-hour segment would contain 24 minutes of news and six minutes of advertising. A BBC press release put it bluntly on 15 November 1988. Extolling the plan's merits, it declared, "For advertisers the key attraction is the exclusive BBC 'brand-label' and all that it stands for."

The BBC–WS television news concept is one of an up-market, up-scale show appealing to a different audience than Murdoch's Sky Channel or Turner's CNN. The BBC's reputation for accuracy would be one of the biggest assets (some might say, up for sale). One enthusiast working with the project had no doubts: "We have the name, BBC. That's the magic word; it's as simple as that!"

Life might not be all that simple for the planned BBC World television news; competition in the realm of television news is fierce. Bearing in mind the medium's dependence on pictures, a news programme which promises to stick to the important stories – whether or not visuals are available – could have a tough time attracting advertisers (and maybe even viewers). Worldnet's "talking heads" have not exactly knocked the world over backwards.

Brave new *glasnost* world: Changes in eastern block domestic and international news

In the late autumn of 1987, the foreign correspondents based in the Swedish capital held their annual party. In keeping with tradition, journalists from one particular nation hosted the gathering; it was now the turn of the correspondents from the Soviet Union. The USSR has nine media men stationed in Stockholm, including three at the APN news agency, two working for TASS, three covering radio and television including a cameraman, and a correspondent for the paper *Isvestia*,

Alexandre Sytchev. After Russian beer and red wine had succeeded in breaking the ice – no vodka in these Gorbachev days – Mr Sytchev announced that he would like to say a few words about the changing conditions Soviet foreign correspondents were experiencing in the wake of *perestroika*. Here follow some significant sections in his address (based on a copy of his manuscript which he kindly provided to us). The picture that unfolds is one of such radical changes that those directly involved have difficulties in dealing with them.

"Try to imagine," he said,

that in your media, not to mention your country, everything is changing. Themes you used to have to cover are not proposed any more. Instead you have to report on events which in the past were always regarded as uninteresting. Your manner of writing and presentation becomes obsolete and does not correspond to modern demands. Can you imagine what would happen in your soul, in your consciousness? I'm sure you will agree with me that changing oneself is a difficult task. . . . In the Soviet Union, not only newspapers, radio and television are changing, the whole country has been involved in this process. As you know, the development is not so easy. What we have to reject today was cultivated for many years and does not correspond to the present. . . I would maintain that Soviet journalists have always tried to be objective. But often we did not always give the whole truth, keeping quiet about certain diasdvantageous facts. So a picture developed whereby everything in the Soviet Union was great, and everything in the Western world was bad. In our stories, we didn't give the opposite point of view. We didn't present Western arguments. The result was that nothing could be understood of the problems or the debate. We divided facts into pleasant ones and unpleasant ones, informing our readers about the former without delay. There were forbidden zones, too. I mean themes which were not recommended for serious analysis. This was most common in domestic, internal issues, but there were areas of oblivion in the international sphere too. We were not allowed, for instance, to discuss the mistakes of our State in foreign policy. Was it a mistake to place our intermediate range missiles, the SS20s, in Europe? Was it a wrong decision to respond to persistent requests from revolutionary Afghanistan to send our troops there? These and many other questions are raised by journalists in the Soviet Union today. A lively and

139

open discussion is underway. . . . Have we gotten rid of all the mistakes and shortcomings? Certainly not. The bureaucratic machine is still powerful. Some State bodies don't tolerate the interference of journalists and try to punish them for their undesirable negative stories. Cases where journalists have been punished by local authorities have been discovered. The phenomenon of taking such cases involving a journalist and a state body to court (to find out who was right or wrong) has become common. Two such cases have involved my own paper, *Isvestia*; we won them both. I think this confirms that we may write without feeling constant fear that someone may dislike it. The only obstacle left, maybe, is ourselves. But we can't maintain our former positions, since newspapers, radio and TV will not accept the obsolete products of our minds any longer. . . . What do we write about today? In the sphere of international affairs we cover problems existing in the West, but we try to look upon them from new angles. We are allowing our readers to discover good aspects of the West, from which we should learn for our best. . . . We have to explain everything both in Soviet life and the international arena truthfully and interestingly. Our task is to teach people to analyse events and think for themselves. Facts and logic are the basis of our work today. . . . If I have not been telling the truth, or following old habits of painting an unreal picture of conditions under which Soviet journalists work today, then you can prove me right or wrong. Read our newspapers and magazines, or listen to Radio Moscow, and you will realise that all I have said is the truth.

It would not be within the scope of a book such as this to speculate on whether the changes described so emotionally here by a Soviet foreign correspondent are of a temporary or permanent nature. Much will depend on whether the Gorbachev era can satisfy the tremendous expectations created by the *perestroika/glasnost* process. The effects so far on the international output of Radio Moscow, however, have been remarkable. From a vehicle dedicated to presenting the gospel according to the party, with long and rather tiring references to speeches by political potentates, Radio Moscow has become a useful source of information about debate and controversy in the USSR.

A letter box programme on Radio Moscow

If European radio listeners were scanning the AM-medium wave band around midnight on 30 December 1987, not far from the Radio Luxembourg pop station frequency, they would have come across one of the many powerful transmitters broadcasting the Radio Moscow "World Service" (a title borrowed from the BBC). The specific programme they would have heard had the intriguing title "Inside Report," and devoted thirty minutes to answering listeners' letters. One of Radio Moscow's English-service organizers, Boris Belitski, was called upon to answer a letter from a listener in Scotland who wanted to know if the *glasnost* principle of "openness" had affected content on Radio Moscow. His answer paralleled the description given by the fervent *Isvestia* correspondent, Alexandre Sytchev. Like all Soviet media, said Mr Belitski, Radio Moscow had moved from an emphasis on presenting glowing achievements to "thoroughly probing our problems." As examples he quoted the inadequate performance of certain industries and, in the cultural sector, the current re-organization of Soviet theatres. "We aim," he continued, "to reflect not only official thinking but public opinion." Public opinion, the listeners heard, is now measured by regular polls in the new Soviet Union. Radio Moscow had also begun to cover natural disasters and industrial accidents, "things which are inevitable in the modern world, but which have been ignored by us in the past." The Chernobyl nuclear accident, he indicated, had indeed been the turning point in this process.

Mr Belitski also addressed the issue of the correct presentation of Soviet history. Radio Moscow, he promised, intended to "fill in certain holes in our history, by allowing historians to expose unwarranted repressive actions against individuals during the rule of Stalin. We are firmly convinced that half truths will not do!"

Any listener concerns that developments in the Soviet Union might mark a departure from socialism were addressed in the answer to a letter from a Mr Share in England. He wanted to know if the growing number of co-operatives, competing with state-run enterprises in the Soviet Union, did not constitute a threat to socialist ideology. Radio Moscow's "observer," Nicolai Gorskov, was called on to explain the facts. Indeed, he admitted, many of these new co-operatives had done well financially, but their profits were not always a reflection of efficiency and service, but more of high prices and a lack of competition. He cited the example of a bakery which could sell cakes at 25 kopecs a piece. The members could each earn a total of 23,500 roubles per annum, an income four times as high as if they worked in a State-run bakery. "The average Muscovite," he added, "finds this hard to accept." But the numbers of co-ops were on the increase, covering a wide range of activities including garages, electrical repairs, and even entertainment. Moscow even had a donkey and pony ride co-op. Even so, the total number was but a "drop in the ocean in this city of nine million."

The two examples above, the Stockholm address and the Radio Moscow programme, indicate radical changes in Soviet media. Any precise evaluation of the significance, however, is hampered by lack of information. Little data are available about the news selection process within *perestroika's* Radio Moscow, data which would allow a more true estimate of its reliability as a source of news about the USSR. The extent of the extraordinary upheaval in traditional Communist media has become even clearer as the winds of *perestroika* have spread across eastern Europe. The case studies from Radio Moscow cited above proved to be a good example of what was to come. Media, both local and external, played an important, though seldom recognized, role in the remarkable events witnessed in East Germany in 1989, culminating with the opening of the Berlin Wall. The East German leadership had long since given up trying to stop their citizens receiving radio and television transmissions from West Germany. The East Germans knew what was going on in the Soviet Union, Hungary, and Poland. Even if the elderly leadership in Berlin decreed that Soviet publications with an excess of *glasnost* should be banned from distribution (the Soviet satirical magazine, *Crocodile*, was blacklisted), they could not stop the newsflow. This, too, was reflected even in the East German radio and television – after all, DDR Radio News could hardly be expected to spread a picture of the world which was totally at odds with what citizens could see and hear from other sources. Long before the Honecker government collapsed, there were signs of a revolt even within the official, controlled DDR media. Youth programmes on DDR Radio, for instance, were regularly playing the Hungarian hallelujah disco hit by Eva, "Clap Hands for Gorbachev."

As we enter 1990, the former propaganda station, Radio Berlin International, has become one of the speediest sources of up-to-date news from an East Germany on the brink of a move towards German re-unification.

142

The trends we noted in Radio Moscow back in late 1987 clearly heralded the start of a development which gathered so much momentum that no one apparently could stop it. Eastern Block media played a vital role in spreading the winds of *perestroika*.

Foreign news in Third World domestic media: examples from the Caribbean, East Africa and Asia

The various actors in the broadcast news arena that operate in those nations generally characterized as "developing" warrant some mention; more specifically the Caribbean, East Africa and Asia offer interesting insights.

A general observation is that the technological developments in the field of satellite distribution have tended to increase the flow of news from richer to poorer countries. As a rule, developing nations within a geographical region have not been able to use satellite facilities to increase inter-regional exchange because of the costs involved. Where television services are available, they normally rely entirely on global services such as CNN, Visnews, and WTN. Frequently the developing nation broadcasters are forced to accept the fact that even news reports about matters of extreme relevance to their own country must be presented through the eyes of a commentator in London or New York, not via one of their own correspondents.

Consider the case of the Caribbean, a group of islands with strong cultural affinity, many with a very low standard of living but engulfed in the media culture of the USA. Even oil-rich Trinidad and Tobago can hardly afford to pay for unique foreign news reports with a relevance to its people and politics. Resting in the footprint of over a dozen satellites pointing at the east coast of the USA, it is much simpler for its broadcasters to take (and occasionally pay for) reports from an American satellite.

The 1987 summer elections in Britain offer a good example of this dependence. The general election campaign was underway in that country, a land with a sizeable population of people of Trinidadian origin. There were more black, ex-Caribbean candidates standing for the British Parliament than in any previous election. The Trinidad press carried numerous reports on the campaign, gleaned both from regular wire services and telephone contacts. TTT (Trinidad and Tobago Television) followed its normal routine of picking up what was available on CNN. The result was a few reports which concentrated solely on the fight between Mrs Thatcher and the Labour Party leader, Neil

8 Satellite dishes in Jamaica apparently are not only for the rich living in luxury mansions. This receiving dish, photographed in a poorer suburb of Kingston, indicates a move down the socio-economic scale

Kinnock, presented in terms of the similarities with the US presidential election. The dilemma is understandable. TTT relies on advertising revenue and sponsorship for its survival. CNN provides relatively inexpensive, guaranteed access to reports on major international stories. CNN's largest market is its subscribers in the USA, for whom a British election battle seen in US presidential campaign terms is a relevant concept. Without a major transfer of resources from richer to poorer nations, there would seem to be no way out of this problem.

The Caribbean nations, themselves, have attempted to pool their local resources and thereby improve regional exchange of news. The CANA news agency is one such example. Exchanging video items between the islands, however, is a cumbersome and expensive operation. A satellite link from Trinidad to Jamaica first requires a trip to a commercial satellite used for USA/European traffic poised far out over the Atlantic. Then the signal must be down- and up-linked to a US domestic satellite and down-linked again in Kingston. It is a wonderful irony that the very technology (satellite), in fact, the very satellites themselves that have made local US television so competitive in the news arena, remain an expensive luxury among local Caribbean broadcasters. Because of the difficulties just described, air freighting of reports remains less expensive. Optic cable links under the sea would conceivably be a practical solution for the islands of the Caribbean, if necessary funds could ever be found.

As things are at present, the spillover from US satellites allows a variety of entrepreneurs to distribute US programmes on the islands at a low cost. A UNESCO (1986: 39) report on television in St Lucia, for instance, presents the case of a local television station, Helen Television:

> It has a 20-foot satellite dish and relays US television programmes 24 hours a day... [Its] programming includes: Cinemax, a movie channel; MTV, a channel devoted exclusively to music; CNN Cable Network News with excellently produced international and US news available at any time; ESPN the sports network which features only sports; Satellite News service, which serves US stations; and finally, the general programming of at least one major US television station, WGN, Chicago. Helen pulls these all direct from satellites which serve the US.

It is easy to understand that with so much available, more or less for free, there is no strong local financial incentive to build up resources for reporting on inter-regional affairs or foreign affairs relevant to the region.

It is also easy to appreciate that the flood of US programming can produce a cultural conflict. Tales are told of how telephone networks on some of the islands broke down when US satellite relays became available. Local viewers in some poor communities assumed that they, too, could phone all those 800 "freephone" or "toll free" numbers for that latest "free" offer to which US television viewers are so accustomed.

The gap in cultural understanding between the USA and concerned persons in the Caribbean is best illustrated by two reports produced in 1986. A USIA report on satellite broadcasting to the Caribbean, "Tracking New Media," concludes that the development is having a "dynamic impact on man's ability to communicate to mass audiences over distance." It goes on to say that the satellite signal has "opened up a new world of communication in both the United States and, by reason of geographical proximity, to our neighbors in the Western Hemisphere." The USIA researchers note that despite a low per capita income, the rise of television set ownership in the region has been dramatic and unparalleled. "Some research suggests that this growth in the Caribbean area is a direct result of regional access to programming from U.S. domestic satellites. No other Third World country has as much access to television programming as does the Caribbean."

A voice from that region offers a somewhat different viewpoint. In a 1986 address entitled, "Influence of Foreign Television on Caribbean People," the president of the Caribbean Publishing and Broadcasting Association, Harold Holt, concluded that a) satellite-delivered television has led to a disproportionate amount of foreign (mainly American) material on Caribbean screens which will eventually subvert local culture and values. And, b) that satellite-fed television is weakening the local and inter-regional broadcasting infrastructure, precluding demand for, and production of local programmes. "In many cases it is not possible to view more than thirty or sixty minutes of Caribbean material in any given day," he said.

> Even then, there are several options on TV dials offering an all-news channel, an all-sports channel, an all-Disney channel, and in some cases a well-prepared mixture of all of these. . . . Our examination of what is taking place quietly in the living rooms of thousands of Caribbean family units, as they sit innocently before their TV sets, frightens us. It is a process of deculturisation which is painless, but also very thorough and long-lasting. . . . In Dominica and St. Lucia, both of which suffer from high illiteracy and unemployment, ordinary folks are happily discussing how President Reagan "looks" or the latest American politics, crime and fashion, without knowing what is going on around the Caribbean community. . . . St Kitts/Nevis, with eleven channels, offers its 45,000 people this heavy diet of up-market pop entertainment which has nothing to do with the harsh realities of the country's socio-economic problems. . . Gil Noble of ABC Television put it aptly when he said that the United States has the capacity through its satellite communications to cultivate a cultural "strike force" capable of penetrating technologically-weak societies. Before we know it, our dependence on foreign programmes will be so strong that external cultural values will displace our national cultural identities.

UNESCO has been running a regional project aimed at redressing these problems through encouraging the establishing of local video production centres. But without adequate funds, and without the membership of the USA in this international

146

cultural organization, little can be done to halt, let alone reverse the present process.

East Africa: the media and strong leaders

Kenya has long been regarded as one of the more stable nations in black Africa, a nation where international conferences can safely be held, where foreign investment is not too risky. Kenya, through its Head of State, has had a series of recent brushes with the BBC–WS. In October of 1988, president Moi publicly stated that "one opposition person who had worked for the BBC was roving around seeking cause to challenge the government. The BBC was supporting subversion". The Head of the BBC–WS, John Tusa, who happened to be in Kenya at the time, regretted the "unwarranted attack. Any recent study of the BBC's coverage of Kenya shows it to be reasonable and balanced." President Moi may have honestly believed that the BBC was supporting a sinister plot in his country. He may have simply been following the time-honoured principle of blaming outside forces as soon as one feels any signs of opposition at home.

It is difficult to tell, because judging the way foreign news is made available in such an environment is difficult. Even gathering domestic news is not an easy task for correspondents based in Nairobi, as we will note in a later chapter. Radio and television there is the monopoly of the Voice of Kenya, a government organization but funded by advertising revenue. Officially the VOK is under the wing of the Ministry of Information. Of late a new ministry, the "Ministry for National Guidance," has taken over a controlling role. The rare occasions when VOK television gathers its own foreign news include those when President Moi goes abroad or when Kenyan runners do great and fast deeds. Otherwise, it chooses from the general Visnews/WTN fare available via a satellite tilted towards the Indian Ocean.

Almost all VOK news bulletins on both radio and television start with an item about the President's activities or occasionally with a report about some senior Minister making a statement about the national interest. This policy can be seen as a constant attempt to ward off pending tribal tension, upping the cause of national unity centred around the person of the President. The situation is not dissimilar in many other Third World countries experiencing growing pains. It is easy to misinterpret in a casual

147

analysis of news in such a country. Consider the following example.

In mid-April 1988, reports were coming in to Nairobi of a massacre of herdsmen in northern Kenya carried out by cattle thieves from the Sudan. On Sunday morning, the major papers (the Sunday *Nation* and *Standard*) carried big headlines about cattle rustlers killing local farmers. The BBC World Service gave the story headline prominence at 9:00 a.m. Kenyan time. The Voice of Kenya 9:00 a.m. bulletin led with a statement from the President warning "wananchi" (citizens) to beware of rumours spread by foreign news organizations.

Why did the VOK ignore the cattle thief story, even when local papers in the capital were carrying full-page spreads? Was it because it was Sunday morning and no-one could make a decision? In Kenya at the time, we put the question to a Voice of Kenya producer. His answer, when considered carefully, was illuminating. He replied,

> We are so official, that if we spread the same story, what might be a rumour would become a fact. We could spread panic and start a major exodus of herdsmen from the northern areas, which would lead to even more chaos. They don't read newspapers or listen to radio transmissions in English. They listen to the VOK in their own languages. We have to be responsible.

An important question raised in this section is to what extent people in a country like Kenya listen to foreign broadcasts. The VOK producer to whom we spoke assumes that his countrymen listen only to domestic programming in their native languages. The dominant regional language of East Africa is Swahili. We have no up-to-date figures for radio listening in Kenya, but an April 1988 study in neighbouring Tanzania suggests that the audience for Swahili transmissions beamed into the region is considerable. The BBC Audience Research Department found that no less than 35 per cent of Tanzanian adults listen at least once a week to external broadcasts in that language. Deutsche Welle was far ahead of the rest, with a reach of 21.4 per cent, followed by the BBC (5.3 per cent) and South Africa (4.4 per cent). The BBC's measurement of listenership to English transmissions from abroad showed more Tanzanian adults listening to the South African Broadcasting Corporation than to the BBC–WS. Shortwave trans-frontier broadcasts, obviously, remain a powerful means of reaching a foreign audience.

An attempt at regional exchange: Asiavision

Countries in Asia are about as far away from the domestic footprints of US satellites as can be. Many do have access to feeds from CNN, CBS and, of course Visnews/WTN via the Intelsat network. Many differences are represented in the region in standards of living, political systems, religions, etc. Even so, several Asian nations have managed to create a mini-copy of the Eurovision news exchange system. Asia is divided into two zones. Zone A includes the official ("State") broadcasters from China, Iran, South Korea, Japan, and Indonesia. Countries in Zone B are Bangladesh, India, Pakistan, Brunei, Malaysia, Sri Lanka, and Indonesia – the latter being the only country in both zones. The operation is run under the auspices of the ABU (the Asian Broadcasting Union). One of the few published studies by Yrjo Lansipuro (1987: 22-27) revealed that in the first nine months of 1985, the exchange handled almost 1,000 items in Zone A and almost 2,000 video reports in Zone B.

The organization also links with the Eurovision exchange network, taking two satellite feeds daily and distributing items to member countries. As one might expect, political items provide a tricky area for many of the co-operating television companies in Asiavision. They are often "prevented from disseminating news about what is going on in the country, while foreign commercial agencies are allowed to cover the same events and feed the pictures to their customers everywhere in the world." When political reports do get fed, they usually consist of news about government potentates, official visits and the like. As might be expected, a large quantity of material fed by the Iranian television company, IRIB, consisted of war footage (no less than 42 per cent).

Lansipuro's study concludes optimistically,

> From being ridiculed for lack of realism, Asiavision has become an object of great attention. . . . Even international newsfilm agencies are now willing to co-operate with it, while on the other hand preparing regional feeds of their own to compete with it. (Lansipuro 1987: 26)

Few other regions with such a heterogeneous mix of nations/ systems have managed to get so far.

7

Meeting the elephant:
broadcast news views the world

This chapter puts a magnifying glass on three weeks of contemporary broadcast journalism, comparing news output in three countries. Three weeks might seem a short time, but in terms of international comparative studies, it is long. The sheer logistical and practical problems of data collection, comparison, and evaluation elevate even twenty-one-day studies to the level of a mammoth task. We have already presented pertinent media trends in our sample countries. What about the events our newscasters had the option to cover or ignore? We start with a summary of our thin slice of history – the three Autumn weeks from the US mid-term elections in November 1986 to Thanksgiving Day – three weeks full of events which not all of us heard anything about on the news. Our summary is based on programme logs from the BBC World Service, which we use as a baseline in our study. The BBC–WS is not always perfect; occasional blemishes do occur in its newscasts. It does, however, provide one of the more reliable summaries of what is going on in the world. This is why we use it as a convenient starting point for a comparative study of news output from different broadcasters. An inter-country or inter-media content comparison tells us what news different broadcasters include. By adding the BBC World Service we can identify some of the news they exclude. So what did the slice of world history look like during those three weeks in November 1986?

These were interesting times. They encompassed the first dramatic period of what became known as Irangate, or the Iran–Contra Affair, including two major speeches to the US by

President Reagan, the first denying any "arms for hostages" deal, and the second admitting that profits from arms sales had been diverted to funding the Contras and their operations in Nicaragua. The Contra part of the Iran–Contra scandal continued in Nicaragua – Eugene Hassenfus, who crashed his plane while on a CIA funded mission to supply the Contras, was tried by a people's tribunal. The plight of the hostages in the Middle East became no better, though two French citizens kidnapped in Lebanon were released. King Hussein of Jordan, meeting the Egyptian President, said that the US arms sales to Iran were an insult to every Arab. The EC debate on sanctions against Syria because of suspected involvement in terrorism continued. So did the Gulf war with attacks on shipping. Another longe-range missile from Iran hit Baghdad. Fighting in Lebanon continued involving Palestinian and Shiite groups as well as the Israelis. The Organization of American States met in Guatemala to discuss Central America's problems. The UN discussed Nicaragua and the Falklands/Malvinas dispute between Britain and Argentina. The UN further condemned the American bombing of Libya earlier that year. France negotiated a peace with Libya over Chad.

There's more. Reports on the growing refugee problem involving the people of Afghanistan were published amid suspicions that parts of a critical UN study had been withheld. Mr Gorbachev, visiting India, announced that the situation in Afghanistan could be resolved and Soviet troops withdrawn. A senior Soviet official announced in Finland that the number of medium-range missiles in Northern Europe was being reduced. A Soviet guided missile carrier visited NATO-member country, Greece.

Still more – the Chilean government arrested more opposition politicians, and Britain supported another World Bank loan to Chile (the US abstained). There was serious rioting in Algeria, possibly linked to Moslem fundamentalist groups. The Pentagon announced it was planning to deploy new missiles along the border between North and South Korea. The Soviet Union later strongly condemned this. A rumour was spread that Kim Il Sung of North Korea was dead.

It was a busy three weeks. There was a court hearing in Australia over the book *Spycatcher* that the Thatcher government did not want to be published. Britain was still waiting for a reply from Israel about the apparent abduction of a nuclear scientist who had revealed Israel's nuclear weapon activities for *The Sunday Times*. In Jerusalem, right-wing Jews held a march and chanted "death to the Arabs."

Yes, still more. The Indian government filed a claim for 3,000,000,000 dollars against Union Carbide for the Bhopal gas leak that reportedly injured or killed 522,000 people. There was a series of serious chemical spills in the Rhine, in both Switzerland and West Germany.

The US breached the SALT 2 agreement. Thirty citizens were injured in a mortar attack on the Northern Ireland/Eire border. Teachers were on strike in the UK. Nurses threatened to strike in Sweden.

There were attempted coups both in Haiti and in the Philippines. Heavy fighting continued in Surinam between government troops and rebels using British and Dutch mercenaries. In Sweden, the Olof Palme murder hunt, in its seventh month had cost five million dollars, involved 71,000 hours of police overtime and was making no progress. A Swedish military explosives depot was blown up; police suspected sabotage.

Barclays Bank pulled out of South Africa. The South African regime hanged six blacks. The Pope visited Australia, where a man with a gun was arrested in the crowd, and the Pontiff suggested that Aborigines ought to be given back their land rights. All in all, a lot of fascinating events.

The above, compressed, mini-history of three simple weeks in the life of the world offers a rough idea of the events and phenomena that news selectors could have pursued. What came out of it? How were different aspects handled?

The first problem in any major study of this kind is how to identify and measure the news that was, in fact, covered in our sample media. Others who have tried similar undertakings have used different means, ranging from the output of official government monitors through academic institutions to the broadcasters themselves.

Sources of data: official big ears and other, smaller ones

Various government sponsored organizations continually monitor the news output of other nations. The BBC's giant radio/television "ear" at Caversham Park constantly records and transcribes domestic and external broadcasts from other parts of the world. Caversham produces a daily summary of world broadcasts

(100,000 words) as well as an edited "news file" detailing main items from broadcasts in over 130 countries. The emphasis, however, is on Eastern Europe, the Far East, the Middle East, Latin America and Africa. This station also does some television monitoring – a parabolic antenna in the grounds receives a variety of signals, including those from Soviet satellites used to relay newscasts from Moscow to different parts of the USSR. Reports from the BBC Monitoring Service are made available not only to government agencies, libraries, and universities, but also to commercial subscribers and other broadcasters. The data, however, are primarily "main thrust," with simple extracts of important items; the sheer volume of material recorded precludes total content analysis.

Sweden, too, puts some effort into monitoring radio transmissions from specific other countries. External service broadcasts in the Swedish language (mainly from eastern block nations) are received and taped in a small attic room at the Political Science Department at Gothenburg University. The PROPAN Project, as it is known, then seeks to identify aspects of and changes in the foreign policy of the transmitting nations that are embedded in the broadcasts those nations beam into Sweden. The theory is that during periods when relations between the Soviet Union and Sweden have been somewhat strained (suspected submarine incursions into Swedish waters, fishing zone controversies, diplomats accused of "engaging in activities not compatible with their status"), analysing radio transmissions can be a useful aid in evaluating information gathered through other, more traditional diplomatic channels.

To take a practical case, when Radio Moscow began broadcasting ironic commentaries about mysterious underwater objects in Scandinavian fjords at the height of Sweden's submarine hunting efforts in the mid-1980s, the Swedes were convinced that there were, in fact, no submarines in their waters that, if found, could prove embarrassing to the Soviets. *Glasnost* seems to have changed this equation. Time will tell if the change is permanent.

The US maintains a number of monitoring operations, some within official diplomatic agencies, some in the military, and some at various universities.

Monitoring, though, is a tricky business, since it relies on translational skill in a variety of languages, and, frequently, reception of signals of varying quality. The rumour that North Korean President Kim Il Sung had been murdered in a coup in

153

November 1986 is said to have originated with a Pentagon radio monitor who misheard a domestic Korean radio broadcast. This misinformation was then passed through confidential channels to South Korean defence officials. Shortly afterwards, the press in Seoul announced that North Korean loudspeakers had been declaring "The Great Leader's" death over the demilitarized zone. In spite of the fact that no recordings of either the original monitored radio programme or the reported loudspeaker messages were available, the mistake became the truth and was carried by most news media as a top story; for some, against better judgement. Even the BBC–WS ran the story of Kim's presumed demise despite advice to the contrary from their own Far Eastern staff. The day after the news was cabled around the world, Kim appeared alive and reasonably well to meet a delegation at Pyongyang Airport.

Satellites can often provide important information for news gatherers and analysts. During the first days of the Chernobyl nuclear accident in April/May of 1986, for example, the tracking station at Stanford University in California picked up newscasts from Soviet polar satellites (orbiting the Poles as opposed to geostationary over the Equator) and noted specific differences between the information that was transmitted from Moscow to far eastern regions of the USSR and that which was sent to the Baltic States. The "official" US ability to glean data about Chernobyl from its own military satellites was limited because the one that would normally have been "aimed" at the Soviet Union was tilted instead toward Libya in the wake of the American air raid on Tripoli.

Accessing content

For someone interested in comparing the news content of broadcasters from different countries, monitoring is only one, and not always the most practical way of proceeding. Television programmes from only a few countries are as yet available on satellite, allowing them to be watched or recorded in one place. Transcripts of broadcasts, when available, can provide additional access to content.

The domestic activities of the American news broadcasters are documented with varying degrees of thoroughness as part of their own institutional memories. The major networks each produce transcripts of their national newscasts as well as logs of their own and their competitors' activities (the "opposition logs").

154

Elaine 5/
55/sub sinks

THE NUCLEAR POWERED
RUSSIAN SUBMARINE
THE WORLD HAS BEEN
WATCHING...
SANK TODAY 1000
MILES OFF THE NORTH
CAROLINA COAST
THE SOVIET SUB
ARMED WITH 16 MISSILES
CABABLE OF HITTING
U.S. TARGETS...SANK
18,000 FEET INTO THE
ATLANTIC OCEAN.
THE SUB HAD BEEN
ADRIFT WITHOUT POWER
SINCE A FIRE AND
EXPLOSION TORE OPEN
ITS HULL THREE DAYS
AGO

28
VTR Full
Count :30

		E	PRESHOW	SS / Coming	Eng/sot VTR/UTR	VO/VTR	26	28	29	1/3 10
STM	1							28	29	
	2		(a.D OPEN)		VTR VTR			25	28	22
	3		OPEN				22	OPEN		
SBM	4		HELLO	SS/10						
SBM	5		BIKE AX	SS Bike Ax	VTR	SOT	29			
SBM TAD 48P	6		Sub Sank	SS Sub sinks	UTR	VO/sot	25			
STM	7		TRAVIS	TIGHT	VTR	SOT	29			
STM	8		SONOMA	TIGHT	VTR	VO	26			
STM	8A		B of A	TIGHT						
48P	9		CARMEL	VTR	VTR	VO	28			
STV	10		RESTAURANTS	SS Restaurants Big TV	ENG VTR/UTR	VO/SOT	25	29		
48P	11		RATHER	VTR	VTR	VO/SOT	28	29		
STM	12		TBE	SS Coming	VTR la anim/tease VTR/UPE	VO SOT / VO VO	26	28	25	22

Bumper #3

7.1 Channel 2, KTVU, record of its programme, 4 October 1986

7.1

These practices are far less common with local television and radio stations whose memory, and thus whose ability to access past stories when researching new ones, is generally limited to a bundle of papers off the teleprompter (rarely offering more than anchorperson lead-ins to visuals) and lists of technical instructions regarding matters such as which studio tape recorder was started at which point in the programme.

The deregulation of the American broadcast system encouraged by the Reagan Administration has specifically reduced require-ments that radio and television stations document content and maintain programme logs. As local radio and television expands throughout Europe the number of broadcasters with short institutional memories will no doubt grow.

Britain's BBC boasts the most sophisticated and all-encom-passing institutional memory. Most network news and current affairs programmes are transcribed and taped. Individual news items, and frequently even raw video material, are numbered, catalogued and stored separately, to facilitate retrieval at a later date. Meanwhile, the BBC's paper archives continue to grow with access enhanced by computers. This has its obvious uses when dealing with obituaries, historical flashbacks and the like. These systems have great internal, and for researchers who can gain access, external value.

The BBC maintains sound archives as well. The introduction of Digital Audio Tape cassettes could significantly reduced space problems. A tiny DAT cassette can hold up to four hours of broadcast-quality material. If these archives are not thoroughly logged and timed, however, they present considerable retrieval problems when searching for specific items.

Swedish law decrees that all nationally broadcast television programmes should be stored for posterity in the National Sound and Vision Archives. Tapes of network news transmissions are therefore retained, but not separate items in specific topic archives. Full transcripts are not produced, but summaries of content (with running times and origin) are prepared daily. One important function of this service is to provide correspondents around the world with instant insight into "what's in the news" at home.

Finally, one important source of television news summaries in the USA is the Television News Index and Abstracts, produced monthly by the Vanderbilt University archives in Nashville, Tennessee. These abstracts have been used in a number of studies and have proved to be quite reliable. James Larson and Andy Hardy demonstrated this in their 1977 study of international affairs coverage on network television news. Larson has made extensive use of the Index and Abstracts in other writing as well.

Al Hester used this same data source a year after Larson and Hardy's work in a study of five years of foreign news on American television news. In 1984, James Weaver, Christopher Porter, and Margaret Evans doubled up on Hester and produced a ten-year analysis of the way in which CBS, NBC, and ABC cover foreign affairs. Their general conclusion, by the way, was the same as Hester's: it makes little difference which of the three networks a viewer watches. He or she will get just as much, or just as little of the same foreign news stories. They, too, relied on the Vanderbilt abstracts, which give a brief summary of each news item, including origin, subject matter, and length, as well as net amounts of total news and advertising time for each news broadcast.

Comparisons and evaluations of international news

In view of national and systematic differences enumerated above, not to mention the logistical problems of acquiring tapes and transcripts from different countries, it's hardly surprising that there have been few international comparative studies of television and radio news output. Most examinations of inter-national news have been national in character, looking at the way a given country's media report that news.

The tendency in these research efforts has been to equate the length of a story with the quality of a story; and studies spanning a long period of time necessarily avoid distortions that might appear in shorter time samples. Much of this thinking was fuelled by the writing of early mass communication theorists like Wilbur Schramm, who saw newsflow in terms of relatively stable patterns interrupted by scattered wars, earthquakes and other natural disasters. Two other frequently quoted researchers, Golding and Elliot (1979), came to similar conclusions in their book, *Making News*, after studying broadcasting organizations and the operations of their newsrooms in Ireland, Nigeria, and Sweden. Very different societies, one might think, but these observers found a surprising number of similarities. The general picture that emerged was one of strongly patterned, repetitive, and predictable work routines, varying only in detail from

157

country to country. "The same institutional areas, dominated by the same events and the same people, dominate the news. . . . [The news] portrays a world which is unchanging and unchangeable," they wrote (Golding and Elliott 1979: 211). These authors are certainly not alone in almost dismissing broadcast news organizations as parts of a heterogeneous establishment aimed at supporting the status quo. But there are dissenters (and the deep rift between the BBC and various British governments over the years is sufficient evidence to discredit such sweeping generalizations).

One opposing view comes from Martin Harrison who conducted a five-year study of the BBC radio current affairs programme "The World At One." He observed that for anyone who listened to five years of that programme, "it would have been a remarkable listener who felt that after that he or she lived in an unchanging or unchangeable world in which all was for the best" (Harrison 1986: 425).

A major problem with long term news content studies based inevitably on summaries and sampling is that flood waves become ripples. The Zeebrugge ferry disaster in 1987 or the Pan Am crash after an explosion over Lockerbie in 1988 become "interruptions" in a predictable news flow, a little spot of D & D (Death and Disaster). A shorter, more detailed examination, on the other hand, with a deeper thematic orientation, might provide greater insight into not only how a tragedy was covered, but also into the particular societal lessons that might have emerged, as well as implications for the future, and, not least, how the media handled the affair.

Another classic text which has been the basis for many a national study of international news coverage dates back to 1965. Johan Galtung, currently Professor of Peace Studies in Honolulu, and his colleague H. G. Ruge, studied news coverage of the Cuba, Congo, and Cyprus crises in the early 60s (Galtung and Ruge 1965; also discussed at length in Tunstall 1971). They argued a number of hypotheses regarding the prerequisites for any particular event appearing in the news media: "negative events" and events concerning "elite nations" are likely to become news items; the further away a country is culturally and/or geographically, the more likely the media of a given land are to carry items which feature elite people and events of those distant places, thus excluding information, and presumably knowledge about ordinary men and women in those places.

As so many activities in the world have become internationalized, Galtung and Ruge's postulates may be less valid today.
Martin Harrison did *not* find that the BBC's "World at One"
concentrated solely on a tiny group of elite nations during his
five-year study. In fact, he concluded that sheer ethnocentricity
was a prime mover in news selection: coverage reflected the
country's own external involvement. Thus, the fall of another
Italian government might not be deemed as newsworthy as the
Galtung hypotheses might lead us to expect, but fifty British
tourists catching salmonella in Rimini would no doubt make the
evening news.

Likewise, the notion of "negative news" is also suspect. There
is, after all, a good and a bad side to most things in life. A
volcano erupting can be good, dramatic news for both tourism
and the television news half-hour. But it can be devastating for
local farmers whose fields and orchards disappear under molten
lava. Hurricane Gilbert, which ravaged Jamaica in the autumn
of 1988, was a catastrophe; the government declared a state of
emergency. In retrospect, Gilbert brought good news. The inflow
of international aid and expertise brought about much needed
improvements. With new poles and wiring, the Jamaican
telephone service has never been so good.

Several American researchers have been interested in how
their own media provide citizens with the information needed to
handle the complexities of modern society and to understand the
significance of global events. A number of the national studies
have concentrated on the three main television networks, others
have looked at the content of particular wire services or
compared different newspapers.

One such ambitious effort was the ten-year analysis "Patterns
in Foreign News Coverage On US Network Television." Its
authors (Weaver, Porter, and Evans 1984) concluded that the
communication explosion has not led to a marked increase in the
number of foreign news stories on American television during
the previous ten years.

Another diligent researcher is Daniel Riffe, currently of the
University of Alabama. In a recent study he and his colleagues
studied the mix of the US network news programmes and
concluded that there was a remarkable similarity in "the view of
the world provided in the (three) networks' news packages (a
rather small world if the networks' heavily domestic orientation
is weighed in – authors' note) and the kind of events that

populate the world" (Riffe 1986: 321). Good stories that provide on-screen action dominate over stories that are important (in terms of information content) but boring in terms of visuals.

Comparative studies

It seems reasonable to assume that the communications explosion must have some effect on the concept of "distance" in news reporting and selection. Has it created citizens, ritually watching the television news, coming to know more about different parts of the world? Or has it merely allowed more people in different countries to partake of the same fare that has always been offered to those owning televisions? Do we hear more, just as much, or even less about parts of the world? Has the traditional flow of news from the industrialized world to the Third World been balanced by an increased return of information in the opposite direction?

Concern over this last issue was reflected in the 1980 MacBride Report from UNESCO, *Many Voices, One World*, calling for a "new world information order" demanding changes in the obvious inequity in the flow of news and information between industrialized and developing nations. The proposals were roundly condemned by some reporters and politicians in the Western world for what they saw as an incompatibility between the principles of a "free" flow of information and press freedom. At the very least, this debate played a role in the departure of the US from UNESCO. Still, others with more of an academic and less of a professional/financial interest in news flow, have pointed out that the same few main streets in the global media village seem to be illuminated, despite all the suburbs that have been built.

Several writers have concerned themselves with the way in which news from the Third World is portrayed in Western media. Much of this discussion stems from debates and studies instigated within the UNESCO family of nations and the "New Information Order" controversy. Riffe and Shaw (1986) studied ten years' worth of Third World coverage in the New York *Times* and the Chicago *Tribune*. They found that the tendency of these two dailies to agree on the selection of stories increased steadily over the decade. Stories of conflicts dominated the output, followed by internal politics and international relations. No less than one tenth of the news about the Third World that appeared in these two major newspapers was about sports. Riffe and Shaw were left with the suspicion that among the "social traits of American news purveyors, a stereotyped bias against the Third World has been nurtured." This tends "to foster images of Third World nations as political systems rife with conflict." Similar findings are noted by G. Cleveland Wilhoit and David Weaver from the Bureau of Media Research, Indiana University (1983) who studied the available foreign news provided by two wire services (AP and UPI) and the operation of the selection process as this material was squeezed through editorial funnels before appearing in print. They noted that most reports from abroad focused on political and military activity and crime, in other words, "official" news from the authorities.

Andrew Semmel drew an even harsher conclusion after his examination of four leading American papers. He wrote,

> The image of the global system presented by the prestige US press is basically Eurocentric, big-power dominant, and Western-oriented. In this news map of the world, only a few countries are important or deemed to be of interest; those societies outside the mainstream of prevailing American world perspectives receive minimal attention or no attention at all. (Semmel 1976: 731)

We can speculate at length about the likelihood of this tendency to increase in the future and what it means about our ability to understand the world around us. With improved communication and the commercial developments that accompany them, it may become simpler for a media organization to purchase reports, films, and the like from international distributors of news than to operate its own news gathering operations in distant places. As this "news borrowing" increases – spurred on by technology's speed and concerns of expense – the burden on domestic gatekeepers to perform the necessary secondary selection (which items to buy, which to ignore) both knowingly and sensibly increases. As Daniel Riffe noted in an address to the Association for Education in Journalism and Mass Communication,

> The potential exists for a readership well informed on international events. Yet the flow of international news is highly selective, and the number of items selected is decreasing because the foreign newshole is shrinking. Simultaneously, a

growing amount of the fare is processed even before it reaches the distant correspondent or wire service reporter. (Riffe 1984: 148)

Fortunately, the expense of keeping an individual correspondent in a foreign country may not be the sole deciding factor in a news organization's decision to maintain a bureau. The 1986 *Presstime* overview, "Covering Foreign News," reported that there were more US correspondents in the Third World than at any previous time in history. Some editors say they "have taken a stand that world realities simply demand more coverage" (Ruth 1986: 29). One senior AP executive was even quoted as saying, "the news mandate is to create additional stories that give meaning to events."

Like most international comparative studies, however, the ones we've identified cover fairly short periods of time (*unlike* the national studies already described). This is due largely to logistical problems involved when attempting to gain access to simultaneously delivered material from different countries.

Moreover, studies which attempt to compare broadcast news output in different countries and societies are prone to other obvious pitfalls. Different media entities organize and report their operations in different ways. Even using local groups of observers to monitor output (of direct transmissions) does not eliminate the probability of coding difficulties arising from semantic and linguistic differences and misunderstandings. Freedom fighters in one country's media can be terrorists or guerrillas in another. Bad news, as we have seen, can be good in another context or frame of reference.

Attempting to compare the world...

A direct follow-up to the UNESCO McBride report was the study: "The World of the News–the News of the World," conducted by the International Association for Mass Communication, based in Leicester, England. Published in 1980, this study aimed to compare international news content in a selection of print and broadcast media in twenty-six countries covering every continent. Two weeks of world news, one "genuine" and one statistically "manufactured," were investigated by teams in thirteen different countries. The evidence collected suggested that there is a sort of "Top 10" of hit news items, with the basic agenda of "hot topics" quite limited and fairly well shared among the examined countries. The same international stories were featured in Iran as in the USA, in the USSR as in Nigeria, even if the "news angle" was not always the same. Eastern Europe, Latin America, Africa and Asia were rarely featured as sources of international news items, except in the news output of their regional neighbours. Western Europe, the Middle East, and to a lesser extent, North America provided international news more generally (though the Middle East's high figures can be explained by the fact that the Camp David accord was being signed during the period of measurement).

When trying to categorize and compare different recurring themes, the UNESCO/IAMCR researchers ran into several methodological hedges. News reports in the subject category "imperialism," for example, gave little indication of the angle, since the study made no attempt to analyse any ideological bias. This is something any international study with participants from East and West happily fights shy of, partly because of the pragmatics of international funding. "Terrorism" is another tricky term in the concept of comparative news analysis since its exact meaning/definition is often in the eyes of the beholder. Terrorism came out on top of the UNESCO groups' thematical analysis of news output, but did Iranian television mean the same thing as did NBC, for example, when it reported on terrorism?

Similar but less serious reservations can be made about another multinational study, the results of which are still in the pipeline to the printers. In the late 70s, ten leading mass communication researchers in five different countries decided to investigate the way in which "social conflict" is presented on television news. Two three-week periods in 1980 and 1984 were analysed simultaneously in the US (the network newscasts), the UK (BBC ITV), West Germany (ARD and ZDF), Israel (IBA TV), and South Africa (the SABC national television news). By concentrating on one subject (social conflict), this study avoided the problem of having to categorize and identify every item that appeared in the television newscasts in the different countries. One predictable difficulty in such a comparative study is the assumption that observers in different countries apply the same norms and values when identifying "conflicts." If "social conflict" is defined as a dispute between two or more parties over some issue, idea, or goal, then an interesting question might be: when does a debate become a conflict? Or consider this case. A football match between Argentina and England might be seen by one observer as an expression of good sportsmanship and brotherly love. Another observer might see it as an extension of the inter-governmental conflict that rages between these two lands over the future of the Falkland Islands (or Malvinas). In spite of these problems, the "social conflict on television news" is an important international study, bearing in mind what the authors of one section (Jay Blumler and Michael Gurevitch) refer to as the "predominantly unquestioned presumptions of cross-national universality" in previous studies of "the content of television news and the social function it serves."

Some of the preliminary results are interesting in part because they confirm generally held impressions and expectations. The study of different actors featuring in television reports of social conflicts showed that newscasts in South Africa more frequently presented conflicts involving the Government and dissidents and the armed forces and dissidents than did those in other countries. Bickering between the official South African white political parties was featured far less than in other countries in the sample. Government to Government conflicts were also highly featured on the SABC television newscasts. This should not be surprising, given the growing international scrutiny of apartheid, but it is undoubtedly valuable new data, adding to our scant knowledge of how one sort of official medium functions in South Africa.

As we shall see later, some of the results of the social conflict study concur with our own investigation. European television news, for instance, seems to devote far more attention than American television to relationships and conflicts concerning employers and employees. Even the more bitter and drawn-out industrial conflicts in the USA rarely cripple the whole nation or even a whole sector. Possibly, then, they are consequently deemed not to be newsworthy on a national level. Apart from the two major projects described above there are a few notable comparative and bi-lateral investigations of broadcast news selection in different countries.

One ambitious international comparison of news is credited to Jack Friedman and colleagues. A short report entitled "The World According to Israel, Jordan, the Soviet Union and the United States" appeared in the now-defunct *Panorama* magazine in March 1981. These observers examined the way these four nations reported the same week's news on television. The period chosen was 10–16 November 1980, the week following the American elections of that year. A surprising number of the stories in those seven days are items that we might recognize well even now, years later. They reported, "It was a week of continuing hostage crisis, of the Iran–Iraq and Afghanistan wars. . . it was also a week of surprises. . . . All day long there were rumours regarding US hostages in Iran." This study looked at the main thrust of the evening television news in these four countries (the CBS Evening News with Walter Cronkite represented the US). The conclusion was that all four newscasts were closely tailored to the needs of the specific market or State: a Soviet news story would further a goal of the State, such as increased production, maintaining social control, or issuing propaganda about some accomplishment. This study, of course, was undertaken in the pre-Gorbachev, pre-Chernobyl "openness" era, when occurrences such as natural disasters and accidents were still shunned by Soviet media. In the US, Friedman noted that entertainment values rated high in the choice of news stories. The American news also tended to accept (and strengthen?) the "polarized world view shared by many Americans, for whom East–West tensions are a given." In Jordan, the television news had a variety of national and regional functions – to sustain the position of the King, to calm the fears of Palestinians, etc. Israeli television news, too, was geared to particular national needs. Friedman wrote,

> The Israeli newscaster reads a brief item on how the Arab summit will probably be delayed because Jordan appears to be on the verge of joining the Camp David talks. This reassures the Israelis, confuses the Jordanians [who can watch Israeli television – authors' note] and infuriates the Syrians.

The study concluded that the Global Village is not "uniformly illuminated. Depending on the hut you live in, you see different patches of light – and fail to see different patches of darkness" (Friedman et al 1981: 65).

The academic–practitioner void: mistrust and suspicion

De-mystification is a vital prerequisite for understanding the media. Watching and recording output is one thing, but the task of analysing and understanding that content is greatly enhanced by familiarity with the production process that lies behind it. This can help one predict developments and notice unexpected deviations.

Scholars produce tools for analysis, but are rarely admitted to the closed world of news production. Even when they are, the on-site, case study mode of working is rarely without its problems (Gans' 1980 *Deciding What's News*, Schlesingers' 1987 *Putting Reality Together*, and Epstein's 1973 *News From Nowhere* are all excellent examples of these efforts and their difficulties).

Practitioners, at work in an environment with deadlines, logistical limitations, and a strong consensus regarding the norms and value systems of their profession, seldom have the time, energy, or ability to sit back and engage in a critical overview. Those in the business rarely have an opportunity to look at their own performance with a breadth that encompasses anything more than the bit of the world represented by their own organizations. Comparisons are limited to shorthand "opposition logs" describing the competitive environment.

This creates a void between the curious academic and the professional producer of news product. With news hardly an exact science, latent conflicts between the two groups are enhanced. People whose work ethic is to "get it right" are naturally suspicious of outside observers who might be checking if it is, indeed, right. This is one reason why there are so few sociological or ethnographic studies of journalists at work. Those in recent years who have been allowed to sit in and observe the working of broadcast news operations have generally been accountants or time-and-motion experts, sent in by the top management to identify areas where costs can be cut.

Bearing this in mind, it must be fair to claim that our study of news content in a number of US, British and Swedish broadcast media is fairly unique. Admittedly it investigated a limited period of time and centred on only three countries, but it did highlight clear differences, similarities, and trends. Here's what we did, how we did it, and what it was that emerged after bouncing the data around in the computer at San Jose State University in San Jose, California.

The US/Great Britain/Sweden Study

Our basic aim was to investigate whether or not television viewers and radio listeners in America, Britain, and Sweden have significantly different opportunities to learn about the world from their native broadcast news. We could not hope to produce a study which was methodologically compatible with a whole series of other such studies, since the latter are themselves widely variable. Studies that have been carried out vary considerably in their use and definition of different parameters, producing a wide range of results. Concepts such as a "news item," or "foreign news," or "domestic news" vary from study to study. While the Glasgow Media Group estimated the foreign news content in the BBC1 television news at 15 per cent, for example, Golding and Elliot arrived at a figure of 37 per cent (Harrison 1986: 412). It was our intention, instead, to compare different news programmes during the one time period, employing one, consistent definitional scheme.

The countries

The USA was seen as an important source nation. Jeremy Tunstall's title, *The Media Are American* (1977), for his book on Anglo-American media is telling in this regard. Trends in European media always seem to borrow from over the Atlantic, even if the stated aims in various policy debates are often related to a desire to *avoid* the American situation.

With the Reagan-spawned deregulation fervour of the 80s, the organization and distribution of broadcast news in America has undergone considerable change. Local broadcasters, as we have seen, provide more and more international news and rely less on the networks. With the resulting upheavals within the traditional Big Three national television network news organizations and the availability of non-stop Cable News Network output provided by most cable systems, what have the consequences been for the consumers of that country's broadcast news? Is there a trend towards more or less news about the world outside their own back yard?

Britain, with its unique role in the history of public service domestic and international broadcasting, was also a natural choice. As was Sweden. This is a small, neutral country with a long history of active involvement in the international diplomatic arena, specifically during the Vietnam war and more recently in the attempts to encourage the Middle East peace process by building bridges between the PLO and the USA. Sweden has also been the biggest individual foreign-aid donor to Nicaragua

167

throughout the Sandinista rule and the long conflict with the US-back Contras. How the world is presented to the Swedes, who re-elect their politicians once every third year, thus becomes an interesting topic for investigation. More than this, however, Sweden remains the last Western European country to have held out against the introduction of commercial broadcasting.

Unlike many other studies, this one was not funded by any external group or organization. Levels of ambition had to be related to our own available resources, which happened to include trained student coders. The three-nation sample itself produced some 2,716 news items during a three-week period, totalling 4,772 minutes of news, or almost eighty hours. A pre-test period of two months preceded the actual study and involved large amounts of data used in designing and testing the methodology. The study was further internationalized by a series of spot-checks in different parts of the world, notably the Caribbean, Japan, and East Africa.

Choosing the sample of news organizations

Americans can flip from one network news programme to another with their remote control switches and have a better than fair chance of coming upon exactly the same story. Larson's (1984) study of network news output shows that selected variables, for example, countries covered and time for foreign news, produce similar levels on all three evening news programmes. The more refined statistical comparison of Daniel Riffe and his colleagues (1986) found a strong consensus regarding both mix and choice of subjects. A combination of common news values and the competitive environment produces very similar output. We chose CBS as our representative of American network television news mainly because it is still considered by most observers to be typical of the network news operations.

CNN, too, is an important news actor. Its half-hour "Headline News" became part of the US sample, as did the Independent News Network (providing a thirty-minute news programme to small, independent commercial stations), because it represents the "new generation" of news options available to viewers.

KTVU-TV, Channel 2 in Oakland, California was chosen to represent the rapidly growing influence of large independent television stations. In fact, like other big indies with hour-long news shows, Channel 2 is distributed to other areas and states in the country by cable operators.

168

Finally, we included National Public Radio and its superb afternoon news magazine, "All Things Considered." NPR is non-commercial, but becoming increasingly dependent on outside philanthropic and corporate sponsorship.

Britain was represented by the BBC's flagship television newscast, "The Nine O'clock News," and its counterpart, "The Six O'clock News" on the BBC Radio Four national speech channel.

Sweden contributed data from two similar news programmes, "Rapport" from television Channel 2, broadcast nightly at 7:30, and the main news half-hour, "Dagens Eko," aired daily on Sweden's national spoken word radio channel, Program 1, at 6:00 p.m.

These nine programmes – five American, two British, and two Swedish – became our basic sample. To widen the scope of data interpretation, we then added the output from the BBC World Service, assuming that this provided a base line of "what was going on in the world." Most studies of news content seek to identify items and subjects that have been included, not excluded by the selection procedure. The World Service, even if not perfectly all-embracing, did provide the best available alternative summary of news stories. As noted in chapter 6, it is a twenty-four-hour news operation employing news agency reports, monitoring, and its own extensive network of correspondents. Including a thirty-minute programme from the World Service ("Newsdesk," broadcast at 04:00 GMT) allowed us to ask some interesting questions particularly about items that were omitted from or were reported in a different way in the rest of our sample.

The timing of the study

The detailed study reported in the next few sections took eight months to plan, execute, and summarize. The data interpretation would not have been possible without another year and a half or so of interviews and discussion with representatives for many of the news organizations whose output we scrutinized. The detailed examination covered a three-week period in November of 1986, chosen to fit between the United States mid-term elections and the American vacation period, Thanksgiving. The period, however, did not turn out to be as "normal" as expected. It coincided with the breaking of the Iran–Contra affair as a major news story. This certainly does not distract from its value – on the contrary, we had a perfect case study in our hands of how foreign news quickly becomes domesticated in the United States while other nations continue to examine international implications.

A number of methods were used for gathering data during the scrutiny period. The four United States television news programmes were taped off-air. The BBC kindly provided full transcripts for the 9:00 o'clock television news, the 6:00 p.m. radio news, and the BBC World Service programme, "Newsdesk." Swedish radio and television provided summaries which our comparisons to the actual broadcasts proved to be quite adequate for our purpose.

The results

The first problem that arises in any news content analysis of this ilk concerns the question of what exactly comprises a *foreign*, as opposed to a *domestic* news story. There are almost as many different definitions and practices as there are studies. The widest definition is that used by a leading investigator of international news coverage, James Larson. For him, any story aired in one country which includes a reference to any other nation is "foreign" or "international," as he prefers to call it. Dennis McQuail, who was responsible for the 1977 Press Commission Report on newspaper content in Britain, used the term "international" to describe any news item in which more than one country is involved, including the "host" country. Thus, with this definition, a foreign news item could end up being geographically located at home in the country of the reporting news organization. Other concepts that have been used for distinguishing foreign from domestic news include "news with a foreign dateline" (Hester 1978) and "International affairs where the United States is involved and foreign affairs where it is not playing an active role" (Almaney 1970). Golding and Elliot (1979) lumped both "foreign news at home" and "home news abroad" in the same international newsbag.

Much of the confusion derives from the fact that there seems to be a "sliding scale" between news that is domestic and news that is foreign. International news reporting tends to reflect the relationships between nations. Even if there is no obvious connection between a train crash in Sweden and one in the US (assuming no American citizens were among the casualties or that the train was not manufactured by an American company), the story might still develop some US "domestic" angle. Does

170

America have the same sort of faulty signalling equipment in use, for example? Is there a limit to the development of high speed trains which the US Department of Transportation might consider?

Obviously, it is quite natural for a foreign news story to glide into domestication. Often journalists will intentionally do this in order to make their stories more understandable and relevant. Herbert Gans, who spent various periods from 1967 up until 1975 observing news production at CBS and NBC network news, concluded in a somewhat disparaging fashion that, "American foreign news is ultimately only a variation on domestic themes."

Broadcasters, as one might expect, have a pragmatic solution to this problem. It consists of distinct organizational divisions, each having access to specialists (commentators) to provide necessary overlap. Foreign news is essentially that which is fed in from outside the country, with reports being selected and sometimes instigated by a home-bound foreign duty editor. This person's activities are triggered either by advance warning (the "diary"), incoming data via news agencies or the morning papers, or by tips from correspondents abroad. Everything in this realm is, by internal definition, foreign news. A home-based specialist correspondent might be called upon to provide a commentary or even advice on the significance of incoming information. An example: a monitored report indicates that a large petroleum refinery in China is on fire. Is this important on a national (Chinese) or even international (price of oil) level? The economics correspondent – the specialist – is called in to advise. Still all in the territory of foreign news. But if a foreign dignitary visits the home country, it becomes the domain of the domestic editor, once again with possible help from the specialists (that is, assuming the organization is big enough to have them). As they might expect, in an organization that has to produce a product several times every day at particular hours, division of work requires pragmatic and clear definitions, with back-up solutions in place for the inevitable system failures.

Foreign news – a five-point scale

To indicate the "foreignness" of an individual news item we employed two 5-point scales, each ranging from 0 to 4. A train accident in India, for example, where there was no obvious connection with the host (reporting) country would be rated 100 per cent foreign (or 4 on our foreign scale). The same story's domestic content would be assigned a zero. Flooding in the mid-West states of the US would be totally domestic (4) in the sample American outlets but totally foreign (again 4 on the foreign scale) in Britain. If suggestions were made in an American news report that these floods were related to the ravaging of the rain forests in the Amazon delta, then a foreign element would have been introduced, estimated at 25 per cent, 50 per cent or 75 per cent of the story's thrust (equivalent to 1, 2, or 3 on our scale). Numerous stories were deemed to be half domestic, half foreign. An example would be a summit meeting between the US and Soviet Presidents in Iceland to discuss arms reductions. Few were coded as 1/4 or 3/4 foreign/domestic, and then only on the basis of consensus amongst the coders. These smaller categories were useful, especially when trying to plot, for instance, the gliding movement from "foreign" to "domestic" in the US radio/television coverage of the Iran–Contra affair.

The news organizations were also evaluated in terms of *numbers of stories* and *duration*. The results showed a remarkable range, from under 10 per cent to almost 50 per cent international coverage (see figure 7.2)

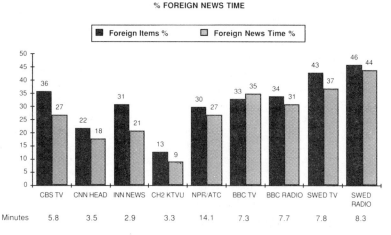

7.2 Percentage of foreign news by time/items in sample of nine programmes excluding weather/commercials/headlines. Values of minutes/day are averaged for actual programmes in twenty-one-day period

When working out relative percentages, the values were weighted according to our foreign–domestic scale.

The comparison above is not perfect for a number of reasons. For one, we were working with programmes of different *net lengths*; that is, the net "news" content, ignoring weather, commercial breaks, and headlines (or "slugs"). Thus an average of 3.3 minutes foreign news a day on Channel 2, in Oakland, was out of a total news content of just over forty minutes per sixty-minute programme. CNN "Headline News" ("Around the world in 30 minutes") produced only 20.8 minutes of news once commercials and programme plugs were removed (of those only 3.5 minutes were foreign news by our definition). Another slight blemish in the data was caused by the fact that more and more news programmes, especially in America, are "pre-empted" at weekends, lifted out of the schedules, usually because of some sporting event. We, and US television viewers, "lost" four days of CBS network news for that reason during the three weeks.

Do these results make sense? Most previous research in this vein has looked at the main US television network news programmes. Our method of extracting foreign content would tend to produce a more stringent result than that used by James Larson, for example (Larson 1984, Larson and Hardy 1977). Indeed Larson, using his definition of "foreign" as any story in which a nation other than the USA is mentioned, charts the increase of foreign reports from 24 per cent of total newstime in 1977 to 38 per cent by the year 1981. He also found that the amount of time devoted to the presenter of the programme decreased from 50 per cent to 30 per cent (reflecting the move from the slower, authoritative, commentating style of Chronkite to the snappier, up-tempo fashion of the Rathers, Brokows, and Jennings mode of anchorship). We would have expected our figures for CBS, for example, to relate closer to those of the Weaver, Porter, and Evans (1984) ten-year study of foreign news as "news reported from outside the USA." Their ten-year average (1972-81) for CBS was 25.9 per cent, not far off our 25 per cent figure. Weaver and his colleagues concluded that his ten-year data did "not support the proposition that the foreign content of the evening news programmes had increased substantially since 1976" (an assumption based on the expected effects of the introduction of news technology such as light-weight video cameras and satellite links).

A number of points can be made from our data:

1 As one departs from the traditional network news and moves towards the new suppliers, satellites, barter dealers, and independents, the content of foreign news in nominal half-hour US television news broadcasts falls rapidly. It must be a very elliptical world that CNN "Headline News" claims to rotate around in thirty minutes.

2 Buying foreign newsfilm from the cheapest supplier, as with Channel 2, Oakland, and providing a daily nominal *one hour* newscast offering local, national, and international news, gives the viewer just about the same number of minutes of foreign news as CNN "Headline News" with its net total news time of 20.8 minutes.

3 With the exception of BBC TV, the proportion of foreign news items is greater than the proportion of time devoted to foreign news. This indicates that foreign news stories are generally shorter than domestic ones. The fact that the gap is greater in the US samples reflects the Stateside habit of running a number of short foreign stories in a sequence, often narrated by the anchorperson. This is not as common in traditional European television news or in radio (including NPR in the States), but could well change in Europe with the introduction of new non-stop satellite news services.

4 As one moves away from the States, first to the UK and then to Sweden, the emphasis on foreign news in both our television and radio samples increases. Swedish Radio's programme "Dagens Eko" holds the record in our study. One possible explanation is that foreign news content is inversely proportional to the size (and presumably, vulnerability) of a country, but this is surely too simple a hypothesis. Working journalists in Sweden tend to attribute that nation's relatively heavy concentration on foreign news to a) Sweden's activity in the international diplomatic arena and b) Sweden's dependence as a trading nation on relations with the outside world.

The ethnocentricity factor – a four-point becomes a two-point scale

We have already referred to Herbert Gans' contention that foreign news tends to become domesticated when pumped through US media news machines. This common notion is frequently expressed in the scholarly and popular American press. Is it valid for the new news suppliers, and how does it compare with Britain and Sweden, considering their involvement in world political and economic affairs?

To answer this we gave each news item an extra code referred to as N, I, B or M. N (national) was for stories which dealt only with one nation. I (international) was the code used for items which referred to stories involving more than one nation, but where the home nation was *not* involved in the reporting (for example, a meeting of Asian nations to discuss trade or security matters, with no reference to the USA, broadcast on Channel 2). B (Bilateral) and M (Multilateral) were used for items which reported stories in terms of the home country's relationship either to *one* (B) or *more* (M) other nations. In this way we could estimate the number of foreign news items which were reported in terms of the home country's interests (the extent of "domestication").

The distinction between N and I, as well as that between B and M, produced little of interest. We therefore turned the four categories into two groups (N+I and B+M). By examining items with *foreign* content to see if they were reported in terms of home interests and involvement or not, tendencies toward journalistic ethnocentricity became clearer. That is, we could gauge a news organization's proclivity for reporting news from outside its home borders in terms of home interest (see fig 7.3).

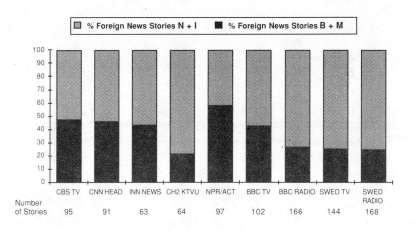

7.3 A comparison of modes of reporting items with a foreign content.
N + I = stories reported in wholly international terms. B + M = stories reported in terms of home nation involvement

The above analysis was based on the judgement of the coders who were looking for references to the home nation in the reporting of foreign news items. The results indicate a general 50/50 rule for CBS, CNN, INN, and NPR. The news independent, Channel 2, seems to be the exception – more on that shortly. Can we compare this to other research findings? Adnan Almaney looked at the same variables in network news during a four-week period in April, 1969 (Almaney 1970). "International Affairs" (with US involvement) accounted for 55 per cent of all foreign news stories on the network news shows; 44 per cent of foreign stories were reported without reference to US interests. Wilhoit and Weaver (1983) applied a similar approach to foreign news stories in the AP and UPI wire services. Based on a sample of 272 news items drawn from periods in 1979 and 1981, they found the same 50/50 rule: 47 per cent were classed as having a "mention of US involvement," exactly the figure we arrived at for CBS network news.

Channel 2 presents an interesting case. Is the 21 per cent figure for foreign news reported with a domestic slant (less than the Swedish ethnocentricity value) an accident or does it represent a trend in the new type of independent presenter of international news? The following quotes from Channel 2's news director, Earl Frounfelter, indicate that specific norms of local newsworthiness, rather than Washington/New York based norms concerning national importance, could be the explanation:

> This is an earthquake area. We are living on a series of faults and are being told monthly that we are eventually going to fall into the sea. Anything concerning earthquakes interests our viewers. When there was the big earthquake in Mexico City, we even did our own deal with Mexican TV getting pictures back over a satellite link. You bust your back trying to get pictures because everyone here is earthquake conscious. The New Zealand earthquake (1987) was much bigger here than in Idaho. We had problems getting pictures of that from CNN. They kept on saying, "pictures are on their way." When they finally came up on the circuit, they weren't even air quality. Three towns were destroyed! I had to change my lead story.

In other words, the international phenomenon of earthquakes is related, not to the USA as a whole, but to the specific interests of the San Francisco Bay area. When Northern California was hit by the big earthquake in October 1989, KTVU found itself in the centre of the disaster area, with part of the double decker highway collapsing only a few miles from the Channel 2 studios.

Consider, too, Mr Frounfelter's comment concerning material from riots in South Korea (a country with which the USA has very close relations and where 40,000 American troops are stationed):

> On the noon show yesterday, I ran some of the anti-government demonstrations in South Korea because we had good pictures. We had pictures of tens of thousands of police firing tear gas into a crowd of nicely-dressed, non-radical suited-up middle-aged men out protesting. That affected my decision to put it on. If I had seen on the wires that 35,000 police had been called into Seoul to scare off demonstrators and a thousand demonstrators showed up and were broken by riot police, and a hundred arrests were made, I'm not sure I would have run it as a copy piece. Since I had good pictures, I put it on. It's television after all, it's not a newspaper. As for the costs, that sort of material comes free in a sense, since we've already paid for it through our contracts with the satellite services.

Had the same story been reported via Korea and Washington (with possible statements from the State Department or the Pentagon) then it would immediately have taken on a US profile. By merely picking up pictures off a satellite, dramatic events abroad can be presented with a short statement identifying time, place, and context. Our measurements suggest that the national producers and distributors of news programmes tend to favour a US involvement angle when reporting foreign/international news. The locals seem to have different priorities, possibly as our Channel 2 producer implies, the availability of striking footage.

Britain and Sweden, on the other hand, showed only-half as much ethnocentricity (excluding BBC television) as the American sample. Figure 7.3 shows that BBC Radio, Swedish radio, and Swedish television imposed a home angle to one-quarter of their foreign news. Few comparable studies are available to which we can relate these results. In Denis McQuail's 1977 study of the British Press, the figures indicate that 798 out of a total of 2,324 news stories were reported in terms of British involvement, a figure of 34 per cent. Martin Harrison's five-year study of the BBC sound radio current affairs programme, "World At One," produced an even higher proportion, namely 49.8 per cent. The discrepancy between these and our figures for BBC Radio News can be easily explained. "The World At One" is a half-hour current affairs programme which follows a ten-minute news bulletin. Its first two or three items are usually related to the main news stories of the hour. The rest of the material can be planned well in advance by a team of researchers, looking, as far as foreign material is concerned, for subjects that will interest listeners. That is the basis for their selection, unless some major event monopolizes the whole transmission. The 6:00 p.m. half-hour newscast which we investigated is far more closely related to the news of the moment, including updates and new stories that the agencies and correspondents have fed during the preceding few hours. Being less governed by forward planning, the "6 O'clock News" may simply have less opportunity to consider home angles, and therefore appears less "ethnocentric." This isn't to say that the British bias is not present. If a ferry goes aground or if there's a minor accident in Sweden, one of the first questions will be: were any Brits involved? Unless it's a very "slow day" in news terms, such considerations often decide the perceived newsworthiness of an individual item. Even so, the percentage of ethnocentric foreign news is half that of the USA.

BBC television produced a 39 per cent rating for stories with a British bias. Our feeling is that this related to the prevalent ideology within television, with a stronger element of explaining and pedagogics. Other contributory factors are the logistics and cost structure of the medium. It is very expensive to send a video crew abroad. But once that decision has been made, there is great pressure to use their reports. During the sample period, BBC TV carried numerous reports from Australia on the legal attempts by the British Government to stop the publishing there of the Peter Wright book on the British Secret Service, *Spycatcher*. There was also extensive coverage of a visit by members of the British Royal Family to the Middle East. Neither of these stories received as much attention on BBC Radio News as they did on television. BBC television had more or less committed itself to covering these stories once the advance decisions to send film crews had been taken.

In summary, the amount of time in US television devoted to news about the world outside decreases as one leaves the traditional network half-hours and moves towards the new independents. The ethnocentricity of the American national suppliers has stayed the same for the last several years (around 50 per cent of foreign stories), but the independent, Channel 2, demonstrated its difference in this respect. British and Swedish news media, while offering almost twice as much foreign news as some of their US counterparts, showed only half as much ethnocentricity.

Here we have a striking example of the schizophrenia that characterizes contemporary media development. Decentralization and localization, made possible by technological, financial, and political/legal developments, are associated with a degree of internationalization. Channel 2 in Oakland may give us less foreign news in terms of the percentage of its available news time, but in a sense, its international output may be less home-biased than the output of the most respected of the traditional networks.

Countries involved in the news

Our aim here was to investigate the existence of geographical "black holes" in news reporting. Despite large variations in attention paid to foreign news and home involvement in interpretation, was any country in our sample of three any better or worse than another in covering the entire world?

For each news item, the countries that were featured were coded acording to a combined list of regions and specific nations. Aware that foreign news is often reported in terms of a domestic perspective – as demonstrated in the previous section – our geographical coding covered all items, not only those that were purely foreign.

The common practice in earlier studies of including an extra code for "international stories" (related to activities at the UN or UNESCO, for example) made no sense for any of our programmes except the BBC World Service. In 1986, with the activities of such international bodies being almost ignored by the Reagan administration (the US withheld its UN dues and left UNESCO during those years), reporting on such matters all but dried up in most Western media.

One example of this phenomenon was provided when the World Bank decided to give a controversial loan to Chile, despite the misgivings of many of its members concerned about General Pinochet's record of human rights abuses. The meeting at which the decision was made was held in Washington on 20 November

1986. It did get a short, ten-second mention on the CBS "Evening News," confirming that the loan had been approved, but that "the USA abstained from voting because of Chile's human rights record". The emphasis was on the USA and Chile, with little or no weight given to the international debate within the world bank.

The BBC World Service, with its more global view, gave this fuller and more enlightening report:

Loans given by the World Bank are supposed to be approved or rejected according to purely economic criteria, but Chile's request for two hundred and fifty million dollars was quite obviously assessed on political factors as well as particularly the Chilean government's records of abuses of human rights and freedoms. It's understood, for instance, that Italy, Denmark, Sweden and Norway voted against the loan for these reasons only. On the other hand, Britain voted in favour of it because the economic performance of the government had been a good one. Reduced unemployment, lower inflation and agricultural and industrial growth. The United States was evidently caught between two stools and abstained. Yet in July, the Assistant Secretary for Inter-American affairs, Mr. Elliot Abrahams, said that in his view the United States should vote against the loan. Explaining the apparent changes in policy, a spokesman for the State Department said later that while the United States recognised the merits of the Chilean government's adherence to the free enterprise system, it also recognised the absence of a correspondingly free political environment. It could therefore neither reject nor approve the loan.

The US abstention, coupled with Britain's approval, was an important factor in this controversial loan being made. The short CBS comment hardly made that clear. The story was ignored on the other US television programmes we monitored. NPR's "Morning Edition" listeners, however, did receive a three-and-a-half minute report on the issue, noting the disappointment of US human rights groups over the Administration's intention not to take a stand against the loan. BBC domestic news did not carry the Chile loan story, despite the British role in pushing it through (Iran–Contra variants dominated the US content on BBC national radio news).

The apparent lack of US media interest in the activities of the world's international bodies during this period would seem to support Gans' contention that "journalists often follow American foreign policy in selecting foreign news because it supplies a quick and easy importance consideration... this solution also discourages State department criticism." (Gans 1980: 149) In other words, it lessens the risk of being accused of un-American leanings. If the President indicates the feeling that the UN and UNESCO are a waste of time, then the media follow suit, not necessarily through collusion but via exclusion.

Coding the countries – patches spotlighted or empty

Since different countries are often referred to in the same news item, especially if that item concerns conflicts between nations, we allowed two coding possibilities per story when necessary. One example would be a report on American companies debating whether to pull out of South Africa.

Our categories included a mix of regions (Africa, the Middle East, Latin America, South America, Western Europe, Eastern Europe, and Asia) as well as several specific nations. The latter included the study countries, of course, as well as the USSR, Japan, and China. Coding was related as far as possible to the contents of an item rather than the origin (dateline). Datelines can be misleading. When the Chernobyl accident occurred in 1986, reporting for the first twenty-four hours came out of Sweden. The Swedes had noticed an increase in radioactivity, and after excluding the possibility of one of their own nukes being the culprit, they identified the probable location within the Soviet Union. Experts sitting in at home can often produce an item which concerns a totally different nation. One has to be wary of such when analysing broadcast news.

Here are some of the results of our small temporal peek at the geography of broadcast news.

By coding all items (both domestic and foreign) we could produce a comparison of coverage of the traditional news source areas (North America and Western Europe). The results showed remarkably small differences, with the World Service the lone exception. Not even our Swedish sample differed, despite that country's strong foreign policy involvement in far-away places (Nicaragua, Angola, the Middle East, etc.) and strong foreign news priority in her broadcast media. The USA and Western Europe accounted for about 75 per cent of all countries covered in the news. For CNN "Headline News," this tendency was even more marked, whereas CBS "Network News" had slightly wider coverage in terms of countries covered. This, of course, could be a result of the move towards shorter, snappier items about far away places in the American network newscasts.

The British results in Figure 7.5 (BBC TV, 77 per cent and BBC Radio, 73 per cent) can be compared to Dennis McQuail's similar measurement, admittedly ten years previously. He concluded that 60 per cent of foreign news items in leading British dailies focused on Europe and the USA. Larson also noted that during the period from 1972 to 1981, the USA was the most mentioned country on CBS (no surprise), featured in 60 per cent of all stories. Our figure of 67 per cent is not so very different.

The consistency in the amount of coverage in British and American media devoted to Western Europe and the United States that is evidenced in these different studies and ours, together covering a span of fifteen years, is paralleled in Sweden. Two studies conducted in that country (Hammerberg 1981 and Giljam and Hedberg 1981) presented data on the amount of coverage of these geographic areas in Swedish radio and television in different years. As can be seen in the following table, there is remarkable consistency over time and between their findings and ours.

Year	1972		1979/80	1986	
Source	Hammerberg		Giljam/Hedberg	Wallis/Baran	
Programme	SWED Radio	Swed TV	SWED TV	SWED Radio	SWED TV
% Foreign Stories North America	6	1 3	1 3	1 0	1 4
% Foreign Stories Europe (excluding Sweden)	2 9	2 4	2 8	3 2	3 3

7.4 Stability over time – Swedish broadcast news' coverage of northern America and western Europe

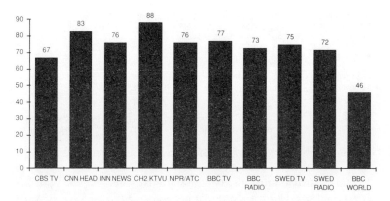

% ITEMS REFERRING TO
USA & WESTERN EUROPE

7.5 Western Europe and the USA dominating the geographical spread, on similar levels. Percentage focus for different stations (maximum of two countries coded per item, total *N* countries 3,374)

The BBC World Service's coverage, introduced here for the first time in statistical terms, had a far wider geographical reach: over 50 per cent of its stories dealt with countries *outside* the USA and Western Europe. The British content originated mainly from the regular eight-minute "news about Britain" section which is a standard segment of the 4:00 a.m. GMT "Newsdesk" programme.

Black holes in foreign news coverage

With our sample of domestic newscasters returning an average of 76 per cent of all stories referring to Western Europe and the USA, it would seem natural that other areas of the world end up being blank spaces in the news, despite the improved means for communications with every corner of the globe. Our look at various regions and nations showed this to be the case. The giant continent of Africa is essentially reduced to a few stories from South Africa. Vitally important current and potential trading nations rarely make the news (e.g., Japan and specifically for the USA, Canada). The USSR and China feature low on the list, except at times of super power summits and, since *glasnost* in the Soviet Union, when disasters and political upheavals occur.

183

	CBS TV	CNN HEAD	INN NEWS	CH2 KTVU	NPR ATC	BBC TV	BBC RADIO	SWED TV	SWED RADIO	BBC WORLD
Middle East %	12.4	5.2	5.7	2.5	10.7	8.3	7.2	12.2	9.3	13.1
Central America %	4.3	2.7	2.6	0.9	2.5	0.3	0.2	1.2	0	1.8
South America %	0.4	0.3	0	0	0.7	1.4	0.6	1.2	0.7	4.9
Eastern Europe (excl) USSR %	0	0.3	0	0	0	0	0.8	0.6	1.2	2.1
STATIONS	CBS TV	CNN HEAD	INN NEWS	CH2 KTVU	NPR ATC	BBC TV	BBC RADIO	SWED TV	SWED RADIO	BBC WORLD

7.6 Regular and less-regular areas of news geography

Eastern Europe hardly existed during November 1986, and little from South or Central America is deemed to be newsworthy. The Middle East, on the other hand, does crop up regularly; this has been true for nearly twenty years, and will continue to be, fuelled by a variety of factors ranging from Israel and the Palestinians to religious fundamentalism and oil (see fig. 7.6).

The "holes" in news coverage are darker in some countries than others. News consumers find out more about events in South America, Eastern Europe, Africa, and the Soviet Union if their source is British or Swedish broadcast news. The increment, however, is not always very staggering, but it's there. Let us consider some of these details and add a few reactions from people in the business.

South and Central America

Few foreign news editors would deny that coverage of South and Central America is less than satisfactory. It's a part of the world where military dictators have come and gone (though some have stayed on), where nations have staggering foreign debts (but one of them, Brazil, is becoming a major supplier of arms to Third World nations), where armed confrontation has been a constant feature of the 80s (Falklands/Malvinas, Grenada, Nicaragua, Panama, and so on), a part of the world which supplies drugs to the USA and Western Europe. No one could claim such areas were not of interest, that they do not warrant the general attention of those wanting to know about the world.

For Channel 2, the US independent in our sample in which 1

per cent of the stories were related to Central America during the three heaviest weeks of the Iran–Contra débâcle, the reason for the scarcity of coverage was pecuniary. "I would love to do more on Nicaragua, but there's not much video coming out," said producer Frounfelter,

> This is television. Otherwise I could run three copy stories a night telling people what's going on in Nicaragua. I would love to send a reporter to Costa Rica and let people know what's happening, that the oldest democracy down there, which has no army, is getting sucked into this. A story hits the wires that the Administration is asking for 300 million dollars for El Salvador and that 100 million will be for earthquake relief. Anyone who knows anything knows that that's not the truth, but you can't go on air and say it. We don't have any stringers – we can't send people down there. When people wearing American uniforms start dying maybe, but until then . . .

This news producer could clearly see that more reporting from Central America could also benefit his station locally – large groups of Central Americans live in the San Francisco area and are presumably interested in events back "home." Money, though, was the stumbling block.

With local television news in the States competing heavily against the networks for advertising revenues, many stations are beginning to send local reporters abroad. Martin Bell, the BBC's longstanding Washington correspondent, said,

> The affiliates are taking on the role of the network news. The airtime for local stations is growing, their revenues are growing and so is their appetite for at least a cosmetic show of reporting the world. If you're in Central America, you'll often find reporters from a Seattle station or one of the other big city stations, and not only doing things with a local connection, American advisers from the home town or something like that. There they are, out there competing with the networks.

Bell agrees that different countries treat foreign news in very different ways as regards geographical coverage. "The Germans take Central America very seriously," he said, "they have resident correspondents who can speak the language. You come across the Swedes and the Canadians as well. We (the BBC) should be able to do a lot better. We tend to concentrate on certain stories, like the US elections."

When unexpected events occur and are deemed important, the news business' response, according to Bell, is predictably gregarious:

> Journalists here tend to be like starlings on a telephone wire. One flies off and the others follow. Large parts of the world get neglected until something dramatic happens. Then they either buy in pictures (and voice them in New York) or send a top reporter.

Costs and logistics are clearly factors that colour home-base judgement about covering different parts of the world, as this quote from Richard Ayre of the new BBC News Directorate demonstrates. "South America is about as far away from a BBC Television enclave as you can get," he said.

> It is inevitable that there will be whole periods when there is no BBC Television coverage of South America at all. It is equally possible that once there is a big enough story, like Pinochet and the Chilean elections, we will send reporter John Simpson and a crew, which will cost scores of thousands of pounds, while they are there they will be expected to blatter off half a dozen stories to keep up the dose of South America.

Africa

Stations	CBS TV	CNN HEAD	INN NEWS	CH2 KTVU	NPR/ ATC	BBC TV	BBC RADIO	SWED TV	SWED RADIO	BBC WORLD
% stories Africa	2.7	0.8	0	0.6	0.7	1.7	6.4	3.1	4.9	7.0
No of African stories	7	3	0	3	9	5	32	10	18	20
No of South African stories	5	3	0	3	7	5	22	8	14	10

7.7 Coverage of Africa as compared to coverage of South Africa, based on reference to countries in foreign news stories

Coverage of the continent of Africa is also an interesting feature. Our figure of 2.7 per cent of CBS stories referring to Africa is exactly the same as that found by James Larson in his 1972-81 study, thus indicating, once again, an element of stability in news agenda. Africa, however, when it is in the news would seem to be *South* Africa. During our study period a peace was negotiated in Chad (involving France and the Libyans), there was political uncertainty about the leadership of the guerillas in southern Sudan, and the Catholic Bishops in Kenya voiced their fears for democracy as the one-party state got stronger. Little of this reached Americans via radio and television. Europe, on the other hand, got a more embracing picture of the continent.

There has been a considerable degree of internal debate within the BBC about reporting on South Africa and the possible neglect of other important geographical areas. The dilemma would seem to be without a solution, as these comments to a 1988 BBC seminar on South Africa from BBC correspondent, Michael Buerk, clearly show. He said,

> Why do we concentrate so much on South Africa when the biggest human problems on earth are actually sandwiched between the Sahara and the Limpopo? An area where living standards, life expectancy and food supplies are all falling, and the highest birth rates in the world are rising. Where there are a dozen, apparently unstoppable wars, where independent reporting is discouraged, suppressed, censored or banned; where economies are in a state of collapse, and cities falling apart? Yet we concentrate on South Africa. Why? One answer is that South Africa is quite clearly the most important country in Africa, because of its mineral wealth, its economic infrastructure and its military strength. This combination allows it to dominate and destabilize half the continent. More important, it is a moral story. South Africa is the only country in the world where racism is institutionalised, enshrined in law. It is an issue on which there are no negatives, unlike all other world causes.

The debate will certainly continue. For the BBC World Service as a whole, the bias towards South Africa is not as great as our figures indicate. As we've seen, the BBC also has a specific African Service, served by a large net of local stringers who provide regular reports on other African nations.

The big and super powers

Coverage of the Soviet Union, bearing in mind the news opportunities which are becoming available and the resources required, will no doubt become a major headache for the US networks. That is, unless they choose to merely buy from the BBC (via Visnews/Eurovision/Intervision) or other European

SUPER POWERS

STATIONS	CBS TV	CNN HEAD	INN NEWS	CH2 KTVU	NPR ATC	BBC TV	BBC RADIO	SWED TV	SWED RADIO	BBC WORLD
USA %	57.1	76.9	66.1	85.4	68.0	8.6	6.6	7.0	4.6	13.8
USSR %	2.7	0.5	0.5	1.8	1.4	0.7	3.4	3.7	3.3	7.0
China %	0	0.5	0.5	0.2	0.3	0	0.2	1.2	0	1.8

7.8 Coverage of three super powers, as indicated by reference to countries in foreign news items

TRADERS

STATIONS	CBS TV	CNN HEAD	INN NEWS	CH2 KTVU	NPR ATC	BBC TV	BBC RADIO	SWED TV	SWED RADIO	BBC WORLD
Japan %	0	2.0	1.5	1.1	0	0.3	0.6	0.3	0.2	0.3
Canada %	0.8	0	0	0.4	0.7	0	0	0.3	0	1.5

7.9 Coverage of nations which are important traders with the USA, based on a count of references to these two countries

broadcasters. China, too, is an even larger challenge for television news bearing in mind the anti-*glasnost* trends that have emerged since May of 1989. In radio, the BBC has a Chinese correspondent, attached to the World Service but servicing even domestic radio and television. Swedish Radio has an Asian correspondent, based in Hong Kong, whose beat stretches from Australia, through China and India, and includes Japan, Malaysia, Indonesia, and the Philippines – quite a few miles of land and sea!

The trading nations

With balance of payment problems threatening the economy of the world, it's strange that general news is not more oriented towards other parts of the world on which nations are dependent for trade. Canada is not only the US' northern neighbour sharing a 5,000 mile common border, but it is also one of its biggest trading partners. The US exports twice as much to Canada as it does to Japan. Canada supplies 21 per cent of California's natural gas. Military security in the North is a joint effort. Our findings are a repeat of Chris Scheer and Sam Eiler's (1972) conclusions in their research comparing the news output of CBS and the Canadian national service, the CBC. They observed no news about Canada in the States, but plenty the other way round. Big stories that made the television news in Canada but not in the States in their 1972 study included Dow Chemical's refusal to compensate fishermen put out of work by mercury pollution; a Canadian vote to extend its territorial waters and widen its offshore jurisdiction to prevent pollution; and attacks on US investment in Canada made at the Canadian political conventions. What did make the news over the border on CBS was a short twenty-five second item about the kidnapping of a British diplomat by extremists.

Japan, too, seems to be generally ignored by the media unless there's a natural disaster, the Emperor dies (which doesn't happen very often), or the price of meat exceeds some gigantic figure. The important trade stories apparently are too tricky to handle, and are definitely not deemed attractive in the competitive environment of US radio and television.

Do the Japanese ignore the West? Do we find the same phenomenon as in the case of Canada *vis-à-vis* the USA? A mini-study reported to us by Thomas von Heine (1988: personal communication) indicates this not to be the case. He compared a scattered eleven-day sample of television newscasts from the semi-State-run NHK and its commercial counterpart, NTV. The amount of NTV's foreign coverage was twice as high as that of NHK, but both concentrated on the USA as soon as important developments concerning US–Japanese trade occurred. Von Heine concluded that the amount of foreign news reporting was directly proportional to a country's economic significance to Japan. Despite this, reporting from other parts of the world was not absent. Correspondents' reports, though, were not always very enlightening. "In a four minute report from Cairo, 70 per cent was devoted to talking about sand storms and the view from the reporter's window," he wrote (Von Heine 1988: personal communication).

China, too, with the world's largest population, receives only the slightest coverage in our sample and was also more or less absent from von Heine's study as well.

With the rapid expansion of financial and business reports in most European broadcast media, this situation could change. China as a potential market may still become more newsworthy despite the political clampdown and the ensuing freezing of international relations after the events of May/June 1989. Business experts who understand broadcasting may be able to make the mysteries of Japanese and Chinese trade informative, interesting, and even entertaining.

Summary of our news geography findings

The amounts of foreign news, both in terms of numbers of stories and time devoted, vary considerably among our sample. The further one departs from the traditional broadcasters into the new suppliers, the more those totals diminish. The Europeans give more than the Americans. By comparison, the differences are smaller in terms of regional coverage. Almost 70 per cent of all coverage we sampled is devoted to Western Europe and the USA. The main exception is the BBC World Service where over 50 per cent of the items covered concerned nations outside these areas.

Europeans can expect to learn more about the USSR, South America, Eastern Europe, and Africa than Americans who rely on broadcast news for their window on the world. Africa in the news, however, is generally restricted to the southern tip and the activities of the Pretoria regime. Important trading nations live a quiet life in broadcast news, as does the world's most populous country, China. Illumination is indeed very patchy on the global media village.

Activities and themes in the news

Our examination of the areas of activity that are reported in the news was also confronted by the same problems of choice and definition of categories that we faced in our earlier analyses. The few other studies available show little consensus on these methodological matters. They often attribute different significances to the same words. "Topic," "Activity", or "Theme" all appear, referring sometimes to general classes of subject matter (e.g., International Conflicts), and sometimes to more specific ongoing or current phenomena (e.g., Fighting in Lebanon or AIDS). We use the term *activity* to denote general classes of subject matter included in the news, and the term *theme* to refer to more specific subjects that played a prominent role during our actual period of investigation.

Many systems of categorization also try to distinguish between items containing conflict and non-conflict. The distinction here, however, is thin, sometimes to the point of invisibility. Any comparison between *non-violent* conflict and *violent* conflict, for example, is very much in the eyes of the beholder. Wilhoit and Weaver (1983), comparing foreign news in UPI and AP, had a

190

category for stories in which "no conflict was discernible." One example of such a story they quoted is *"The Times* and its associated London Publications have been sold to News International headed by Australian press magnate Rupert Murdoch." Particularly to a European, this would seem to be a somewhat naive academic classification given Labour's unfriendliness toward Mr Murdoch and the year-long tumult that followed the takeover.

Because of these difficulties in defining exclusive categories of news activities, comparisons between different surveys should be treated with caution. We will restrict our own observations to internal comparisons in our own sample.

Our catalogue of activities numbered nineteen classes, the last being "others not covered by the first eighteen." The pedigree can be traced to Herbert Gans' division of activities in the news (Gans 1980: 16) that he devised for his analysis of domestic news in US television and magazines. On the home front, the Columbia University researcher makes the sweeping statement that "year in, year out, about 15 per cent of domestic news is given over to disagreements and conflicts within and between parts of the government and the public officials who personify them." Here's a piece of statistical curio; our analysis of all news items classed as totally domestic (with no foreign element) showed Gans' observation to be still valid for the traditional broadcasters in our sample survey. The figures for stories relating to government conflict and disagreement were: CBS 16.7 per cent, BBC TV 16.2 per cent, and Swedish TV 13.0 per cent. The only significant differences in the television field were local television (Channel 2) and Cable News Network, with the latter devoting only 6.5 per cent of its stories to this particular activity. Even if the world is a dynamic place, some things change very little in the make-up of the traditional "flagship" newscasts. The style might evolve, but some elements of content remain the same. Let's return to coverage of politics abroad.

Gans divides the large political chunk of news reporting into a piece covering "government conflicts and disagreements" (reporting and commenting on government affairs) and the more formal information on "government decisions, proposals and ceremonies." We retained this division, being interested partly in the process of "news borrowing," in other words, for our foreign survey, finding out to what extent news is collected and presented by the news organization, and to what extent it consists of repeating official statements, proposals, and decisions.

Studying such phenomena in a wider context, at least one US researcher, Daniel Riffe (1984) addressed the problem of the dependence of news gatherers on official news agencies, statements by other news organizations, and the like, thus decreasing their ability to check sources independently. As costs for foreign correspondents rise and as cost cutting hits the broadcast media (with the exception of the BBC), the amount of second-hand news can be expected to rise.

The distinction between relatively independent looks at the activities of a government and the repeating of official statements/ proposals produced some interesting differences in our sample. Figure 7.10 shows the percentages of activities for the two categories in all stories with any foreign content at all. As in the previous news geography analysis, a maximum of two activities per news item was allowed, following the journalistic tradition of giving "both sides of the story." We found that the number of news stories devoted to reporting the doings of specific foreign governments varied considerably within our sample. The BBC World Service figures do reflect their habit of regularly quoting official statements by other governments or government media. The relatively large per cent for borrowed news on CBS also surprised us. In part this reflects the tendency to say "Tass stated today that..." rather than "CBS Moscow correspondent has learned ..."

Our coding system is also relevant here. If CBS reported on parliamentary conflict in Iran, coupled with a statement from the US Secretary of State, then the result would be a contribution to *both* percentages in Figures 7.10 and 7.11 below.

Oddly enough, BBC TV and our US independent returned the highest percentages for reporting on political events abroad, coupled with the lowest for reporting official statements (either from the home or a foreign government) about such events.

BBC Television news, at the time of our analysis, was in conflict with the British Government and the Conservative Party over coverage of the US bombing of Tripoli in April 1986. It is quite possible that a desire to validate and demonstrate their independence as a reporting and commentating organization produced a smaller propensity to distribute "official" versions.

Meeting the elephant

GOVERNMENT CONFLICTS/ACTIVITIES %

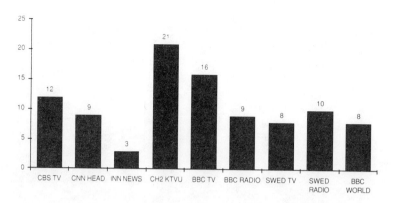

7.10 Percentage of news items covering government conflicts/activities of parliament, elections, etc. (foreign news only)

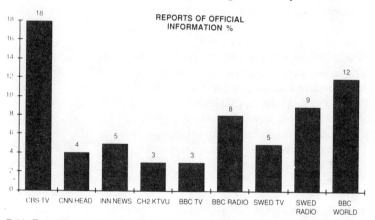

REPORTS OF OFFICIAL INFORMATION %

7.11 Percentage of news items covering official statements, proposals, etc. (foreign news only)

International disputes, negotiations, military moves and violence

While reporting on political events in different countries accounted for about 20 per cent of all activities in the news, another group added an extra 45 per cent or so. International disputes and negotiations returned an average of 18 per cent in terms of activities covered in broadcast news with a foreign

193

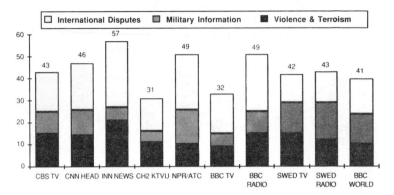

7.12 Combined percentage of distribution of three activities in foreign news items (international disputes and negotiations, military activities, violence and terrorism), coding allows a maximum of two activities per news item

element. Violent crimes, group terrorism, and state terrorism accounted for yet another 12 per cent. BBC Television and the US independent returned similar figures.

INN, supplying small US television stations with news on a barter basis, returned the highest figure for reporting on international disputes or negotiations, but, as we saw in our previous figure, the *lowest* figure for reporting on political conflict and disagreement in different foreign countries. (See Figs 7.10 and 7.12 above).

What may appear to be statistical quirks in the graph above actually represent differences in the nature of our various news organizations. INN relies, more than any other sample member, on Visnews' international feed for its foreign coverage. Moreover, it disseminates its programme to any number of disparate areas of the US. In the absence of any regional or demographic identity and dependent on the resources of others, the choice of easily understood items, good v. bad, us v. them, material seems logical. These types of stories also tend to be more visually dramatic as well, rendering depth of understanding and familiarity unnecess-ary. The BBC, conversely, believes that its audiences want more in-depth analysis and has the resources to match that mandate. Channel 2, as we've already seen, tends to be regionally ethnocentric, making foreign conflict and military action with no San Francisco Bay Area angle unworthy of coverage.

Reporting on *international crimes, scandals, and court proceedings* was a low priority on the CBS "Evening News" but four times higher on BBC TV. An important contribution was the British Government's dealings with the Australian courts on the MI5 *Spycatcher* book during these times and possibly, as we've already seen, the fact that BBC TV had committed itself to sending a film team to Australia at this time. Neither Swedish radio nor television showed any great interest in international crimes and scandals, nor for that matter did Channel 2 in California. For Channel 2, INN, and CNN the percentage figures for foreign scandals and crimes ranged from 7 to 11 per cent. The equivalent figures for their coverage of this category in domestic stories ranged from 12 to 17 per cent.

Disasters and Accidents are *not* major sources of foreign news. Conventional wisdom says otherwise, but both our data and that of Wilhoit and Weaver (1983) say it just isn't so. Coding in this category returned percentages of news items in the 4 to 11 per cent range. The highest figure came from Channel 2, 11.2 per cent, with INN not far behind at 9.4 per cent of all activities reported on in foreign news stories.

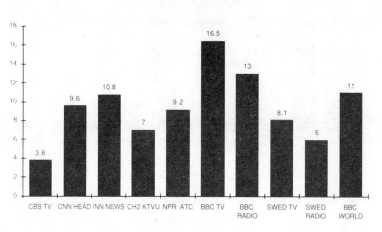

7.13 Distribution of activities, crime, scandals, and investigations in foreign news items, based on a coding allowing maximum two activities per item (foreign news only)

DISASTERS,
ACCIDENTS %

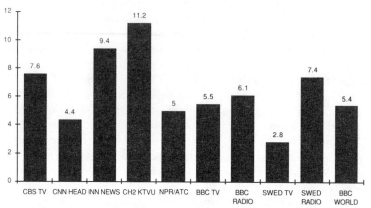

7.14 Percentage distribution of activities, disasters, and accidents, in foreign news items, based on a coding allowing a maximum of two activities per item

VIPS, ROYALS
ODD THINGS %

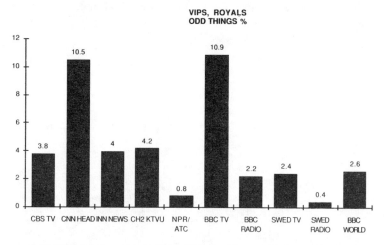

7.15 Distribution of activities, VIPs, royalty, and other oddities, in foreign news, based on a coding allowing a maximum of two activities per item

Figure 7.15 reflects the combination of two different activities in our classification scheme, both of which concern lighter items. The chart reflects reporting on the activities of various VIPs (film stars, monarchs in their purely ceremonial roles, tennis players off the courts) as well as coverage of unusual activities, oddball records, lottery winners, treasure trove finders and the like. BBC TV came out on top, partly due to extensive coverage of Prince Charles and the Princess of Wales' visit to various States in the Gulf. Not far behind the BBC came CNN "Headline News," with regular oddities, many of them reported out of London: new clothes fashions for poodles, how to buy a genuine English telephone box at an auction and freight it back to the States, or an aristocrat's title. An international "tiddlywinks" competition was covered, and Ted Turner, CNN's owner, was given airtime to support the principle of colouring old black and white movies (one of the more expensive projects within "his" film company, MGM).

The activities of the British Royal family, and indeed other European monarchs, are said to be attractive news stories by US news producers. It's not exactly clear where the BBC stands on this issue. News editor Jenny Abramsky admits, "There was a tendency at one stage to cover the Princess of Wales (Diana) wherever she went. It was absolutely ridiculous, false news judgement, hype." Coverage of the British Royals may have been encouraged during our study period by editorial memos reminding the newsroom that the Royals "make good copy." In the spring of 1988, with the Birt revolution within the BBC, the British press, at least as represented by the *Daily Telegraph* (26 April 1987), was referring to BBC television news as being "propelled out of its populist mould of the past two years, and being forced to become more analytical."

Half a year later, the editor of the new combined BBC TV News and Current Affairs, Tony Hall, was quoted in the *Independent* (7 September 1988) as reflecting with "pride on the BBC's decision to carry news of the birth of the Duchess of York's baby as the last item on the 9 p.m. news; its rival, ITN, led on it." The dilemma of the Royals and their newsworthiness can hardly have been removed by internal organizational manœuvres, or by ignoring the competitive environment. As one of our own sources within BBC news put it, "If you, by giving a minute to the Royals, can up your listeners by 2 million, who would say No out of principle? You cannot ignore the listeners." Another comment from inside Auntie was, "ITN must be gloating now. All these long, boring stories on the 9 p.m. news are just losing us viewers." The "mission to explain" requires much determination, but also general conviction and the ability to make the "explain" bit interesting, important, and gripping!

Jenny Abramsky on the Beeb's radio management side, commenting on our study, said we would find coverage of the Royals much more limited now. However, she does recognize the news value of Prince Charles since he has emerged as an undaunted maker of statements about the environment, social evils, inner-city decay, and other subjects which some critical politicians think an heir to the throne should not touch with a bargepole. Said she, "Charles is an interesting story. We have virtually decided that whenever Charles makes a speech, we ought to be at it. It could become a news story."

Before any Stateside reader begins to feel too superior to those "silly Brits," we are bound to report that in this all-important category, "VIP and unusual activities," our US sample media contributed an average of nine minutes per station devoted exclusively to animal stories: moose falls in love with a cow and the like.

Former news director Ed Joyce's summary of life at CBS mentions other animal tales, one concerning singing sheep. His explanation involves the influence of Welshman Howard Stringer

> offering amusing slices of English life.... In addition to a succession of stories about Princess Di, the Evening News took its viewers to the English countryside for stories about growing giant cabbages... or a village contest for quartets of singing sheep.... Imagine you are correspondent Phil Jones and you got a turndown on the Evening News on your story about the congressional hearing on the import tariff... and after a minute and forty seconds, the broadcast is devoted to a quartet of British sheep bleating their little hearts out. (Joyce 1988: 178)

Stringer, in an interesting irony, took over for Joyce when the latter was fired in 1975 and later moved to head the CBS Entertainment Division in 1988. None the less, Ed Joyce's assumption that the inclusion of animal stories in the news is a phoney English (Welsh?) quirk is not borne out by our study. The category was more or less entirely absent from our European sample. The nearest anyone got was a thirty-four-second report on BBC Radio that European environmental ministers had adopted new measures to regulate the use of live animals in experiments, the aim being to stop cruelty and ban the use of endangered species.

Coverage of notable events in the financial/industrial, medical/technological, and social/human spheres

Are there differences in selection criteria for foreign and domestic news stories within given categories of activities? In other words, are there some activities that tend to appear more in foreign than in domestic news or vice versa? We tested this in three "notable events" categories of activities, namely events in the 1) economics/business/industrial sphere, 2) in the medical/technological sphere, and 3) in the social/human sphere (social conditions/welfare, starvation, hardship). These ranked far higher in domestic than in foreign news selection. In other words, a lot on wages, prices, medical cures, poverty at home, but relatively little on such matters from overseas. Television and radio, it seems, are not good at informing us of the macro problems of international trade, currencies, and starvation, but are much more enthusiastic about these issues when they are on their own doorstep (see fig 7.16 below).

% ECONOMIC MED/TECH SOCIAL IN DOMESTIC & FOREIGN NEWS ITEMS

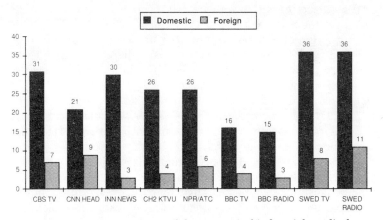

7.16 Comparing the coverage of the economical/industrial, medical, technical, and social/human spheres in domestic news items and items with a foreign news content, maximum of two activity codes per item

The results show a remarkable similarity, not between types of broadcast media or news suppliers, but within our sample countries. Swedish Radio and Television stick to the same proportions, as do BBC Radio and Television and to a certain extent the whole of the US sample.

That technical/economic/social news from abroad finds little receptivity in domestic newscasts back home is an accepted *modus vivendi* for many foreign correspondents. Medical innovations only become international news items when they've been legitimized through presentation at some international gathering of the medical elite, even though they have invariably been made official earlier in their country of origin. Sometimes the lack of ripples is surprising. Two recollections from Sweden should suffice to illustrate the point.

The first concerns run-away cars. Hundreds of incidents of vehicles suddenly accelerating for no apparent reason, killing and injuring people, had been reported throughout the US. Several cases were in the courts. In the summer of 1988, the official road safety lab in Linkoping, Sweden, published a report with a possible explanation of the phenomenon. Scientists there had observed that the sudden acceleration usually occurred in vehicles with automatic transmission and a cruise-control mechanism. Their analysis showed that a cold solder in the cruise-control circuits could lead to an engine going to full throttle at a certain critical speed.

The subject of run-away cars had been hotly debated in the USA, yet the Swedish report hardly caused a ripple in US media. NPR was the only major organization to pick it up and, in fact, received considerable listener response. Apart from that there was very little reaction even in the UK where the first cases of the phenomenon had been reported. Why? Maybe the thought that some small lab in a far away place like Sweden could crack the riddle was not compatible with news expectancies.

Event two concerns a business story with a certain relevance for millions of consumers around the world who buy well-known brands of toothpaste. It also originates from Sweden. In 1987, Colgate and Palmolive each launched a new advanced "anti-plaque" formula toothpaste. They then sued each other in the Swedish consumer court (an official court of justice that monitors marketing practices), with each manufacturer claiming that the other company's plaque-removing qualities were bogus. A six-week period of hearings and deliberations followed. The toothpaste giants called in experts from all over the world. Local business experts saw this as a test case which could have international ramifications. Judgment was finally passed in December 1988. The court found that neither manufacturer could substantiate its claims. They were given half a year in which to remove the unacceptable slogans from their tubes (conveniently long enough to sell off product already on the shelves). Surely this is a story having relevance in those parts of the world where brand-name toothpaste is bought by the majority, with brand loyalty often based on hopes regarding its dental value. For some reason, it just didn't hit the airwaves. That toothpaste is one of the most important products advertised on commercial television is not the only possible reason. One public service news broadcaster turned it down with the comment, "maybe if it had been a slow day." Swedish Radio carried it as a lead story.

Although Swedish radio and television follow our total sample's proclivity for presenting a greater number of economic/medical/technical stories in their domestic rather than their foreign news, as Figure 7.16 demonstrates, they lead the league in these latter categories. Fully 36 per cent of all the activities reported in their domestic coverage referred to economic, medical, and technical matters. Twenty-four per cent of all the news items' categories, in fact, were in the realm of economic, labour, and industrial issues.

The apparent lack of interest in international stories in the economic/technical/social spheres demonstrated by our sample media is balanced, as we have noted, by a concentration on politics/international disputes/military activity/violence and terrorism. During our study period, CBS, CNN "Headline News," INN and BBC TV included more activities in the "VIP, Royals, Oddities" categories in their foreign news coverage than they did in the economic/medical-technical/social-human fields. Our radio sample, particularly NPR, Swedish Radio News, and the BBC World Service, however, returned an entirely opposite picture of news priorities in these relative fields.

Themes in broadcast news

It's worth the reminder to say that every news content analysis is a child of its time. A breakdown of activities reported is obviously related in some way to what is going on in the world; that is, unless all reporting is static or rigidly predefined by immutable rules. Our activity analysis above does indeed point towards certain trends and preferences in foreign news reporting. Just like news geography, some areas are left untouched, others make up the bulk of the output. But not only do the times influence *which* activities are covered, they affect *how much* attention is given to them. A post-analysis of themes that dominated the news, therefore, seemed appropriate.

Our thematic investigation involved coding each news item according to a list of categories agreed on *after* the end of the study period; based, in other words, on our combined views regarding recurring themes.

Different views of the Iran–Contra affair

We've already illustrated how the Iran–Contra story came to dominate the US network newscasts. The débâcle became an obsession with them, as CBS, NBC, and ABC involved themselves in a game of cat-and-mouse with the White House. It was a game that a great showman like Ronald Reagan could hardly lose. He took them on, at first denying what everyone knew was the case (that an attempt had been made to trade arms for hostages). Reagan ended our three-week period by openly admitting that funds had been siphoned off from Iran deals to feed the Contras with guns, despite a congressional ban. Reagan blamed subordinates who were fired. With the journalists waiting for more blood, Reagan then went silent for three months, until the publishing of the Tower Commission report in March 1987. It was brilliant news management from the White House's perspective. There was overkill in the news media, which probably led to large sectors of the American body politic becoming bored with the whole affair. With the broadcast media concentrating on White House secrets, Oliver North shredders and the like, the foreign aspects of the story received less and less prominence. During our survey period, there was considerable consternation among Middle East nations usually friendly to the USA. The Gulf war and the fighting in Lebanon continued. The American hostages were not freed. And in Nicaragua, the trial of Eugene Hassenfus, the CIA-supported pilot who had crashed in the jungle, continued to reveal interesting links in the Iran–Contra chain. Most of this never made it to the US evening news.

We examined the proportion of total newstime devoted to Iran–Contra. Our particular interest, however, was in comparing

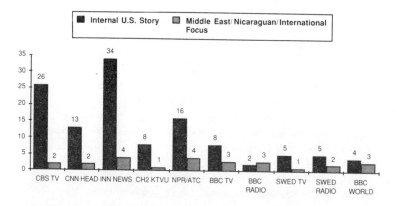

% TIME IRAN-CONTRA AS INTERNAL U.S. STORY VS
% TIME AS MIDDLE EAST OR NICARAGUAN STORY

7.17 Percentage of time devoted to treating Iran–Contra as an internal US story, as opposed to a story concerning the Middle East and/or Central America

the percentage of net newstime given to reports that treated it as an internal US story as opposed to news that covered its relevant Middle East and Nicaraguan aspects (Figure 7.17).

The possibility of yet another US president being toppled over Iran, or even yet another being involved in illegalities, clearly inspired fervour among all our sample stations. This was most markedly so in the States, but even to a certain extent in Europe, including the BBC World Service. BBC Radio, and somewhat surprisingly, INN, devoted the biggest percentage of their time to the foreign affairs side of the coin. INN's 4 per cent international slant on Iran–Contra was dwarfed, however, by the 34 per cent of its *total* newstime devoted to it as a purely domestic story. CBS, too, presented a similar disparity between the two angles.

Accidents and crimes

We also ran a breakdown of disaster, violence, and crime, to see how selection worked in different areas for different news programmes. In all news, both domestic *and* foreign, CNN, Channel 2, BBC Radio, and TV as well as Swedish Radio returned the same sort of percentages of newstime for the category "violent crime." Violent crime was on the rise in Britain, with 1800 rapes (up 29 per cent) and 10,000 cases of the use of firearms (up 16 per cent), all according to a Home Office report quoted by the BBC TV news presenter on Thursday 20 November 1986. Swedish Radio was still involved in the as-yet-unsolved Olof Palme murder. Over the Atlantic, Oakland, where Channel 2 is situated, was approaching a new annual record for murders, over 200. The independent was the champion of our violent crime reporting league, but only by a slim margin over the other, more traditional members of our sample. CBS, interestingly and most likely because it wishes to differentiate itself from independent stations, presented virtually no news on violent crime.

With Wall Street not quite sure of what to make of the Ivan Boesky insider-trading scandal, white-collar crime still had a clear presence in the news. CNN "Headline News" devoted as much time to the machinations of the rich as it did to the problems of hostages, terrorism and anti-terrorism sanctions (which were very much in the news at the time). White-collar crime received far less prominence in our European sample. Swedish television was the lone European exception, most likely because it was involved in covering economic issues, particularly at the time of our study, tax manipulation.

% NEWS TIME OF VIOLENT CRIMES
& WHITE COLLAR CRIMES

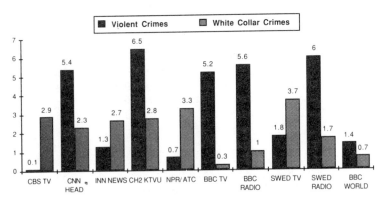

7.18 Relative amounts of time devoted to violent and white-collar crimes per programme in our total sample of news items

Disasters were divided into two categories for comparison, the natural type, that is, volcanoes and earthquakes, and the man-made, environmentally dangerous type. Volcanoes became active in Japan and on Hawaii. Taiwan experienced an earthquake. The chemical spills in Germany and Switzerland left the Rhine a dead river, and there was an oil spill in the San Francisco Bay.

Man-made disasters were clearly deemed more newsworthy on Swedish Radio and Television than anywhere else in the sample, with the partial exception of the US NPR. The Swedish figures were not the result of an excess of small, local pollution scandals. Possibly we identified in our study signs of the emergence of an ecological concern in Sweden which was to lead, two years later, to the Swedish environmental party becoming the first new party to be elected to parliament in almost sixty years. NPR's interest in pollution was balanced by a smaller degree of attention to natural disasters; volcanoes aren't as dramatic on radio after all.

The BBC World Service clearly did not regard volcanoes and chemical spill as being worthy of more than shorter mentions in news telegrams.

That Channel 2 in California and CNN in Atlanta have the highest bars in Figure 7.19 tallies well with their news ethic of "spot reporting," with Channel 2 closely monitoring the local police emergency services in order to be first on the scene of an

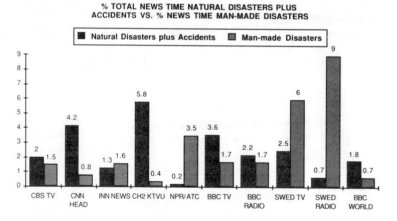

7.19 Percentage of newstime devoted to a) natural disasters/accidents, and b) to man-made disasters (pollution/environmental problems), based on coding of all relevant news items per programme

accident and CNN aiming for similar goals on an international plane. Pollution is a difficult matter for such operators since neither bad air nor poisoned water provide very dramatic television pictures (unless there are an awful lot of dead fish in the latter).

Other popular broadcast news themes

"Medicines and cures" was another of our thematic categories. To what extent was knowledge about solving the pains of the human body something which was regularly featured in newscasts? Our US sample averaged 5 per cent of its total newstime in this area. INN came out on top with 9.4 per cent (INN's regular "Health Beat" segments are partly financed by drug manufacturers). BBC TV and domestic radio news averaged just over 1 per cent and Swedish Radio/TV 3 per cent of their newstime.

AIDS was another theme. Here the BBC returned the highest country average, just over 3 per cent of BBC radio and television's total newstime was dedicated to coverage of the disease. All the US news programmes had less on AIDS than the BBC, with the exception of the independent in Oakland, just across the Bay from San Francisco (5.2 per cent).

Each country's media had certain subjects that appeared frequently in the news. Irangate for the US national news programmes; disasters, AIDS, and crime for local television in northern California; the environment in Sweden; wage disputes in Britain and Sweden (these latter, as we've seen, were virtually non-existent in US national radio and television news).

Also, the BBC made sure that the Royals and the MI5 book scandal were not forgotten. The "9 O'clock News" had fourteen items totalling forty minutes (about 9 per cent of its total time) on the *Spycatcher* trial in Australia and the British government's attempts to make sure that a book already published in the USA was not officially available in the Commonwealth. The other favourite of the BBC was British monarchy and all that it does or is asked to do. BBC TV had nineteen stories in three weeks in this category, totalling thirty minutes (almost 7 per cent of its time). For BBC "Radio News at 6", the totals were eighteen stories lasting twenty-one minutes, or 4 per cent of news transmission time. In a business where thirty seconds is regarded as a long time, thirty minutes is an eternity.

Our thematic post-analysis demonstrated the universal tendency in the broadcast media for certain subjects to dominate, excluding many others. Irangate in the USA, Royals or MI5 books in Britain, the unsolved murder of a Prime Minister in Sweden were our examples.

This may be an inevitable feature of a medium that presents news in short, time-bound programmes. What of other news? What of other information that allows viewers and listeners to form a better, deeper understanding of the elephant? Significant stories can be and often are "still born" in the shadow of those dominating events. A prime example in our study was Gorbachev's first announcement of the probable Soviet withdrawal from Afghanistan. Contragate shouted it down in the USA.

But, if one function of foreign news reporting is to alert both decision makers and the body politic to significant signals of events ahead, then selection practices should not be constrained by the momentum of the present. Are there alternatives to this inevitability?

We've met the players. We've seen them at work in a three-week period. Next, we'll look at how these organizations and the people who work in them come to perform as they do and examine their potential for giving us news of the world as technology, economies, and politics change.

8

Which news and why?
Understanding the forces that
shape the news

Three military conflicts from the 1980s, the Falklands conflict in 1982, the invasion of Grenada in 1983 and the American bombing of Tripoli in 1986 offer dramatic evidence of how foreign news reporting has changed in the wake of the political, economic, and technological developments of that decade.

In the Falklands conflict between Britain and Argentina, the UK government literally took selected members of the media to the scene; board, lodging, and sea-sickness pills, c/o Her Majesty's Navy. Reporting back was heavily controlled. The media in the UK found it easier to get material distributed by satellite out of Argentina, but that presented problems of usage and reliability. It was, after all, the enemy's version. What's more, any mention back home on the BBC of opposition to the Falklands venture was decried as treason by certain political groups.

The task of balancing demands from the Government and the military with the professional journalists' standards of impartiality and reliability was almost impossible. Mrs Thatcher and her advisers were involved in a gamble that could have gone wrong. The Argentine move into the Falklands/Malvinas Islands was primarily intended to boost the morale of the ruling military junta and direct its citizens' attention away from other aspects of domestic importance in Argentina. The balancing act, particularly in relation to the Thatcher government, created significant instability within the BBC, the effects of which are still evident (Milne 1988).

Then, in 1983, came the Reagan decision to invade the tiny

Caribbean island of Grenada, a decision publicly based on the fear that Grenada would become another Cuba, bringing the "evil of communism" closer to America's shores. Much to the infuriation of the US media, they were kept out of the action during the first few hours of the invasion. In fact, enterprising journalists who attempted to reach the tiny island by private boat were turned away by armed American naval warships. Former CBS Head of News, Ed Joyce, quotes statements from officers at the Pentagon that they had, "learned a lesson from the British in the Falklands" (Joyce 1988: 285). This comparison, though, is hardly correct. The British Government took reporters across half the world to the Falklands and then exercised "news management." The Pentagon, on the other hand, simply denied media access to the Grenada exercise until it suited them.

British television reports of the Grenada episode were confusing, despite what one would have expected to be an advantage from a former colonial presence in the Caribbean. After all, here was the USA invading a member of the British Commonwealth. Hetherington (1985: 101-09) chronicled the confusion that ensued: the doubts about what Cubans were doing on the island, the facts that took so long to emerge about the number of US casualties resulting from marines shooting each other by mistake, and the unintentional bombing of a mental hospital. He found that the BBC had followed official US information sources far more faithfully than did the rival ITN.

The lessons in manipulating one another that the media and governments learned from Grenada and the Falklands were ultimately applied in our final military skirmish, the bombing of Tripoli. This event best illustrates both the possibilities and difficulties of reporting on international military activities and the political aftermaths.

The attack occurred in the early morning of Tuesday 15 April 1986. It was in reprisal for the bombing deaths of US servicemen in a West German discothèque, an event Reagan blamed on Gadaffi-supported terrorists.

The British Government allowed the use of US bases in the UK for launching the attack. Its official position was that the attack was "a necessary and defensive action against a military dictator who was using the resources of his state to carry out acts of barbarous terrorism against innocent people in foreign countries" (Conservative Party Document 1986: 1).

According to a series of newspaper articles printed in the

American press, the main aim of the action was to murder the
Libyan leader, Gadaffi (Hersh 1987). Gadaffi survived but
members of his family were injured and his adopted daughter
was killed.

In the course of the raid, the French Embassy in Tripoli was
mistakenly bombed, as was a residential area, resulting in
numerous civilian casualties. These errors were at first denied by
Caspar Weinberger, the US Secretary of Defense, but were soon
proved to be fact thanks to television pictures received by the BBC
and the US networks from satellite transmissions emanating
from Libyan ground stations. The incident became the basis of a
claim by the British Conservative Party that the BBC "took a
number of editorial decisions the effect of which was to enlist the
sympathy of the audience for the Libyans and to antagonize
them against the Americans" (Conservative Party Document
1986: 4), a claim which the BBC rejected.

Coverage of the Libyan bombing is enlightening because it
demonstrates the impact of the technological, organizational and
political factors on foreign news reporting.

Access to functioning technology, everything from ordinary
telephone lines to satellite links, provided the means for
journalists to feed material out of Libya. The White House no
doubt had overlooked their potential; Casper Weinberger would
otherwise not have made his early categorical statements on the
success of the raid and his denial of civilian casualties.

Kate Adie, the BBC reporter in Lybia during the attack,
recalled,

> Telephones in to the hotel worked. Telephones out were a
> problem. It had been like that for four years ever since an
> attempted coup. There were four lines into our hotel which
> worked for the next five days (after the raid). One was the NBC
> line, one was the BBC line, one was used by ABC and there
> was one left for all the other journalists. The BBC held their
> line open. Once it was up it was held open for two and a half
> days. A large organization can do things like that.

She also detailed how access to the scene and the technical
facilities were dependent on the approval of and help from the
Libyans. "We had to get out of the hotel, which was a problem,"
she said.

> We knew bombs had dropped nearby, half a mile away. We

210

9 Kate Adie reporting for BBC Television from Tripoli. A still taken from a video tape in a bombed building at 4:00 a.m., just a few hours after the US bombing of the Libyan capital

knew the area but were physically prevented by armed people. It was very chaotic in the dark. Then at 4 a.m., to our great surprise, the Libyans turned up with transport. We asked ourselves, "are we going to see what we want to see?" There's no doubt we saw what we should have seen. We were allowed to go to the area of greatest devastation (which we knew about because we had seen it from the hotel balcony). It was a residential area which has the embassies. We saw part of the French Embassy flattened. I've been in it. I knew it.

The Libyans assisted the filming of civilian casualties, restricted access to military areas, and then facilitated transmission out of the country. "We weren't allowed to go to the barracks," she continued. "We went to the hospitals; there were no restrictions on who we could talk to. We brought the material back to the hotel, edited it and by mid-morning had got the local television station to open up. That was unusual. Usually, there's no one there until midday." By shortly after 10:00 in the morning, Libyan time, a ground station was feeding BBC material back to London.

211

Kate Adie again.

They are part of the Eurovision satellite network. They can also send by ground links. They have all the facilities, excellent equipment just like any European station has. They are incompetent at using it at times, but it's rarely been subjected to censorship. We got out everything we wanted that first morning, with endless caveats about what might have happened and what we might not have seen. We were careful not to speculate. I knew Gadaffi was alive an hour-and-a-half after the raid, both from a contact and from the fact that the army would have been on the streets if he had been dead. They weren't, there was general calm. The technology functioned as well as it might have done anywhere in the West. We got everything across. The technology pushed it out, and it caught a lot of people by surprise.

The journalists thus found themselves in the position where they knew more, apparently, than the US administration and had their own eyewitness observations and sound and visual documentation to prove it.

Caspar Weinberger in his first press conference said, shortly after the air raid, that there had been no civilian casualties and that the only damage to the US forces had been the loss of part of a wing of a plane. He lied, because there was no doubt from our very first reports reaching London via telephone, literally while the raid was on, that civilian areas had been hit. The American network people told us that there was jubilation in the US where it was regarded as a brilliant military strike, without any civilian losses. We had just seen corpses. It was the biggest credibility gap you can imagine

was reporter Adie's postscript on the event.

Major news *organizations* have not only the money to pay for telephone lines open days on end, but they also have personnel resources that allow them to have staff in place. The fact that BBC radio and television both had correspondents in Libya was the result of a suspicion that some sort of action was afoot, action which would be newsworthy. All three US television networks made the same judgement.

There had been a lot of activity over US air bases in Britain during the day before the raid, but this was dismissed as "routine exercise" by the British Ministry of Defence and this information never reached Kate Adie in Tripoli. The BBC Arabic Service (World Service), however, did receive a tip regarding the time of the raid and the intended targets twenty-four hours beforehand from a stringer in Washington. He claimed to have gleaned the information from sources in the Pentagon. The World Service did not deem this information to be sufficiently reliable to warrant transmission. "If we had done so, they [the Americans] probably would have had to change the time and the targets anyway," explained senior news editor David Spaull.

Politics influenced not only media coverage, but the timing of the attack as well. Domestic publicity took priority over military considerations. The scheduling of the bombing was chosen to coincide with the American networks' evening news shows so that President Reagan's account would have maximum domestic political impact. The BBC's Adie noted,

> Shortly before 2 a.m. in the morning we got a call from the BBC in London saying they had received a tip-off from the networks in Washington that something big was afoot – President Reagan had apparently asked for time on television. Then the raid started at exactly 2 a.m. Later it turned out that this was not what the Pentagon had wanted; they wanted a raid at 4 a.m. local time, when people are most drowsy, when the streets are empty, the time in the middle of a military shift. Why did it happen at 2 a.m.? Because that was prime time newstime in New York and Washington, 19:00 hours. It was the politicians' desire to use the media dictating the Pentagon. It was specifically timed, rather cynically, not to use maximum military advantage, which *is* cynical because any military person will want to minimize casualties or dangers to themselves. If you try to maximize the PR, at danger to your own men, that is a cynical use of it.

The USIA, in particular its director, Charles Z. Wick, was also involved on the political and propaganda front. As soon as the bombs started dropping over Tripoli, an editorial was read on the Voice of America that included the following exhortation:

> Colonel Gadaffi is your head of state. So long as Libyans accept his orders, then they must also accept the consequences. Colonel Gadaffi is your tragic burden. If you permit Colonel Gadaffi to continue with the present conflict, then you must share some collective responsibility for his actions. (Alexandre 1987)

Colonel Gadaffi survived the attack. The US "proof" that the Libyan leader was directly responsible for an attack on the American servicemen in Berlin has never been made public; the West German police have laid the blame on the Syrians. But Charles Z. Wick was not satisfied with the treatment received from British media, particularly the BBC. Its footage coming out of Libya had made the White House publicity exercise look rather silly. A senior BBC news editor in London told us that Wick personally complained about a commentary by the BBC's man in Washington, Martin Bell, on US reactions to the bombing and its legality in international law. When asked why the BBC should be concerned about the opinions of the USIA Director, the editor ominously replied, "Charles Wick is a close friend of Ronald Reagan." One source also claimed that, prior to the bombing, Mr Wick had asked for and received a positive assessment from high-ranking members of Britain's ruling Conservative Party on the British media's likely reaction to an attack on Libya originating from British soil.

Like Wick, the Conservative Party was not satisfied with the BBC's performance. In October it published its report accusing the BBC of bias, naming eight different BBC reporters but strangely enough, avoiding any direct mention of either Kate Adie or Martin Bell, a point emphasized by the then BBC Director General, Alasdair Milne (1988: 191). Presumably these two reporters enjoy such status in Britain that the attack was aimed at the institution of the BBC rather than at particular individuals.

The Conservative Party report, "Media Monitoring: The US Raid on Libya," consisted of a textual analysis comparing individual BBC headlines and pieces of comment with those of the rival ITN "News at Ten." The Conservatives explained that their study was the result of "a growing wave of correspondence and telephone calls complaining about various aspects of the BBC." They did not specify how many complaints had been received, when they were received, or their nature. The fact that ITN tried, as the Conservative Party saw it, to mitigate chagrin over the fact of civilian casualties by reporting that they were caused by "bombs meant for terrorists" was praised by the report. "Only in the last breath did the BBC make any reference to *Libyan Terrorists*" (1986: 6).

The BBC responded with a line by line rebuttal which was returned to the Conservative Party and the leader of its anti-

BBC campaign, former minister Norman Tebbit. The bickering persisted for a while. Tebbit countered with a new analysis of the BBC defence from an unidentified "independent, non-political source." Ultimately, the squabble died when an academic study conducted by Nottingham University demonstrated that there was, to quote Kate Adie, "not an iota of truth in the suggestion that we had been some sort of Libyan agents." The BBC did, however, admit to some minor error of judgement in news copy written in the newsroom in London; but no factual errors could be found in any of the reports from correspondents abroad.

Reporter Kate Adie, though, did not avoid having her personal reputation questioned in public. The *Daily Express* newspaper, with Conservative Party sympathies, accused her of providing coverage sympathetic to Colonel Gadaffi, claiming that, as a result, she had been granted facilities not available to other broadcasters. She took legal action against Express Newspapers and, in an out of court settlement, was vindicated, winning substantial damages (The *Guardian* 1988).

Was the attack on the BBC an example of close co-operation between the Reagan and Thatcher regimes? Kate doubts it.

> I think it began to coincide with the Americans' feelings once it got going, but this is part of something which has been observed by everyone. There has been a sustained campaign, not only from certain political quarters, but also from commercial quarters, from people with commercial interests which they wish to expand. These are people who own stakes in newspapers, who own parts of huge conglomerates, entre- preneurs, who wish for a slice of the television audience in the UK and find it very difficult to get it. The BBC is the big animal they would like to slice up.

Kate Adie's description provides a good illustration of the complex, conflicting web of pressures on both broadcasting organizations as a whole and individuals within them (conflicting with their professional standards of factual reporting). Those supporting the Reagan administration's position on the Libya bombing might indeed claim that she and her colleagues were manipulated by Gadaffi. The decision to allow all foreign news teams satellite facilities in Tripoli may well have been based on a desire to create positive publicity for Libya by showing civilian casualties to the world. But how different is this from the US administration's manipulation of the network news?

For the traditional broadcasting organizations, both public service BBC and the American commercial networks, the changing mode of political pressure as well as the emergence of new groups trying to exercise control has created considerable upheaval. With deregulation entrenched in the USA and the philosophy of protected Public Service broadcasting being challenged in Europe, a mixture of pressure, mistrust, and jealousy among the political power centres is shaking the roots of these institutions.

Borrowing models from organizational theory

How would traditional mass communication theory explain these convoluted events and their possible outcomes? Functional approaches (Siebert, Peterson and Schramm 1956, for example) would focus on the media's performance. Effects perspectives would offer insight into how the culture might respond (Meyrowitz 1985) or how individuals would come to understand the workings of important public institutions (Berger and Luckman 1967; Gerbner *et al.* 1982). But what both would no doubt miss is the fact that news media are organizations. They are bureaucracies. Many are institutions with all the structures that years of survival produce. Their aim may not necessarily be to simply maximize audiences (or profits); organizational researchers have long held that even straightforward manufacturing companies are not merely driven by profit-maximization goals (Dean 1951). In all organizations, a process of "institutionalization" occurs over time, with *survival* a value in itself for management and other members (Selznick 1957). Above all, organizations are not isolated entities; they are always dependent on an environment where other organizations and groups compete for resources, place demands, and offer rewards.

In the 1930s, such observations led to the emergence of Chester Barnard's *equilibrium theory* (Barnard 1938). He saw the survival of a company as dependent on the continued contributions from different groups of "participants" on which the organization depended for its survival (customers, owners, suppliers, etc.). Later, the sociologist Philip Selznick's interest in the institutionalization processes led to a focus on how managements perceive the conditions necessary for survival, i.e., which *strategies* they adopt (Selznick 1957). Strategies can change, but only at a rate compatible with internal institutional factors.

Institutionalization produces strength, loyalty, and predictability, but also sluggishness in certain situations where change is required. In a firmly established institution, change requires a strong measure of consensus about the *need* for change. Otherwise, attempts to move the organization in another direction will be painful or unsuccessful.

Barnard's participation model, like all models, is an over-simplification. The different groups associated with an organiz-ation, making contributions and placing demands, are not always totally free to come and go. Staff cannot walk out of the door the moment something doesn't satisfy them. Nor can an organization engage in random firing as soon as a management decides on a change of direction. This theoretical approach, however, is useful, particularly if we regard the organization as seeking to attain equilibrium through balancing demands and rewards of different participant groups.

A broadcasters' overall goal, in other words, is not merely to maximize audiences, even if this is an important factor. Our interviews with staff at both CBS, the BBC, and a small local television station in California showed this to be the case. The organization is involved in a constant process of balancing the demands of owners, power centres, professional principles of journalism held by the staff, etc. Strategies are altered as management perceive and react to changes in such balances.

A Swedish researcher, Lars Engvall, used a similar approach when studying how newspapers adapt to changing environments. He studied how publication/editorial policy changed when a newspaper's initial goal of political advocacy evolved as it was becoming a general company (Engvall 1986). He followed strategy changes aimed at providing rewards which would attract and/or retain more readers, noting varying policies on the inclusion of lighter/heavier material, as well as the newspapers' handling of two different types of customers (readers and advertisers).

This is not so different from the organizational dynamics of the news media we have described in previous chapters. Management can oscillate between strategies of *entertaining* and *informing*, depending on how they perceive the demands of the consumer of news programmes (the hunt for consumer loyalty is related both to short-term success and long-term survival). In large broadcast news organizations, periods of what we might term trivialization have often been followed by an emphasis on a more "serious" or

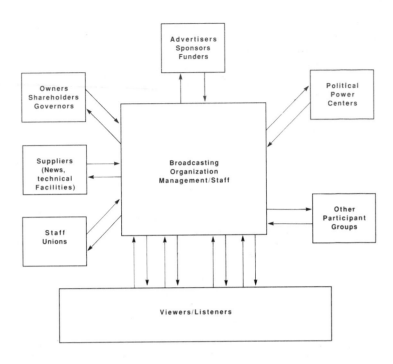

8.1 A broadcasting organization and some participants. A system of demand–rewards relationships seeking equilibrium

"pedagogical" approach. Both CBS Network News and BBC Television News have demonstrated the phenomena of changing policies, not necessarily in terms of a permanent drift, but rather as attempts to adjust the balance of participants' demands and rewards as the environment changes. This drift in strategies and emphases over time helps explain changes in principles of news selection.

Technological, economical, and political factors at work in and on the organization

We can now knit together the complex web of factors that determine the international news gathering, selection and presentation process. From there we can predict opportunities and problems that are likely to develop. We start with

Which news and why?

Table 8.1 *Significant technological developments and some o₋ effects on foreign news gathering, processing, and presentation*

Decade	Changing roles and methods in foreign news gathering
50/60s	Few foreign correspondents but with fixed bases abroad. Use radio correspondents/wire services for news material. Television reports mainly film in the cinema Newsreel tradition. Film freighted to homebase by air. Film cameras and fairly large crews required. Even radio reporters still sometimes have sound engineers who accompany them.
70/80s	Video technology replaces film. Satellite ground stations in 30 per cent of nations by 1972 up to 76 per cent by 1981. Airfreight replaced by satellite links. Telephone lines improved quality, facilitating radio reports from virtually anywhere. Increased opportunities for censorship (pulling the satellite "plug"). Deregulation cuts satellite link costs in the USA and allows for SNG.
	Foreign-based correspondents replaced to a certain extent by travelling "firemen" or "super star reporters" using possibility of speedy air travel.
	Development of digital techniques for editing and graphic designs. Small, low-cost amateur video equipment comes on the market, allowing news gathering when large crews not possible.
	CNN network provides real time coverage of large events; available in most newsrooms. Requires monitoring and editing resources for best use.
90s	Digital development continues. Radio reporters can transmit tape recorder quality reports using broad-band, standard telecommunication links (over the phone not via expensive, unique music quality lines)
	Oligopoly of big agencies will use two or three person crews to cover much of the world. Lone reporters with high-quality small video cameras provide more unique film. More "tourist" journalism with pictures taken by travellers/businessmen/diplomats, etc. Portable ground stations facilitate links via satellite from anywhere. Monitoring of television programmes from other countries also facilitated as more use satellites for domestic distribution. More local monitoring and taping of unique local output as part of news borrowing exercises.
	Expansion and fragmentation of audiences increases demand on specialist news programmes, with specialist material. Demands on speed of editing increase even further.

technology, by charting how foreign news gathering has followed technological developments over time, as well as making some predictions as to likely developments during the next decade.

Technology can both *assist* and *impair* news gathering. A "technological drive" exists, forcing the use of the latest equipment or methods. Much news technology is concerned with speeding up the process of news gathering and selection. Instant access can range from CNN covering a press conference live to local area computer networks (LANs) providing immediate summaries of hot stories and speedy access to the organization's institutional memory. This puts a new sort of pressure on news selection decisions (everybody wants to be first with a news flash) and affects the production process.

After news terminals were introduced to the NPR newsroom in Washington, for example, one of the editors said that journalists tended to concentrate more on spot news and to be less analytical and less willing to move to other, non-terminal-delivered stories as a result. The "newness" of the technology increased its salience. With a high level of competition (everybody watching everybody else), the concentration on *speed* can also lead to journalistic errors. A rumour becomes a fact and starts off a chain reaction.

The rumour that North Korean leader Kim Il Sung had died, which was initiated by a US agency monitoring North Korean radio, virtually became fact and was carried by all in a "follow the leader" fashion in November 1986. With CNN-type non-stop news stations aiming for speed and enjoying a presence in all newsrooms thanks to modern satellite technology, accuracy enters a risky duel with urgency. If one usually reliable source makes an error, false statements can get picked up and spiral. Deadlines and the increased quantity and frequency of news bulletins can enhance the dangers. When things were slower, when it took two days to get reels of film back to the home base, broadcast journalists had more time and opportunity to compare different sources, including the printed press. A foreign correspondent can still get a call which goes like this: "Daniel, there's an interesting piece in this morning's *Guardian*, should we do something on it?" But this happens noticeably less often than in the not too distant past. On the whole, the technology of instant news access seems to be replacing the report-initiating status of the serious press for the broadcast media.

Which news and why?

The false second Chernobyl

On 3 February 1988, at one minute past 3:00 p.m., the Swedish News Agency, TT, sent out a flash that there had been another nuclear power station disaster in the Soviet Union. The story, which had apparently originated in financial circles in London, had come to the attention of the BBC earlier the same morning. They ignored it. The TT flash, however, was picked up by Reuters (with which TT co-operates closely) and soon after, by CNN. According to a Swedish study by the official Board for Psychological Defence, 42 per cent of the Swedes had heard of the false accident with thirty minutes. An hour later, Swedish national radio news was still referring to details of "the Soviet nuclear accident." In the USA, the "rumours swept the market and pushed up the dollar" according to the Reuter's wire.

Some local radio stations in Sweden, however, had what the Swedes idiomatically refer to as "ice in their stomachs." Radio Uppland, in the same region as the Swedish Forsmark nuclear power station, took the precaution of phoning the engineers at Forsmark. It was there that measurements had first indicated the Chernobyl accident in 1986. This time, Forsmark had noticed nothing unusual in its sensitive measuring devices, and Radio Uppland refrained from carrying the accident telegram from TT.

Later, it was suggested that the rumour originated from someone getting access to a series of coded test telexes which the International Atomic Energy Agency (the IAEA) in Vienna had sent to member countries as part of a test of international preparedness for accidents. The IAEA, however, though agreeing that such telexes had been distributed, denied that they included the words "nuclear" or "accident."

The Arafat–American Jews meeting in Sweden

Yassar Arafat came to Stockholm in December 1988 to meet up with a small group of prominent American Jews and discuss the Palestinian situation. The meeting was unique in many ways; US Jewish organizations had previously dismissed the PLO as a terrorist organization and refused to have any dealings with Arafat. The meeting had been organized by the Swedish Government; few knew at the time that it was acting as a go-between for the US. The actual aim was an attempt to get the

PLO leader to be more specific about his stance on terrorism and Israel's right to exist.

The actual wording of what was said at the final press conference was of crucial political importance. There were some interesting aspects of the technologies used for covering it.

Many radio and press journalists are now issued cellular radio telephones. A representative from one of the major wire services who was at the conference used such a device. When Arafat said something he deemed to be of interest, he would jot it down, move into a corner and ring it into his office (presumably missing what was said while he was phoning). This was the only way he could be expected to work; for him the technology and the situation demanded it. Afterwards there was much discussion on semantics regarding what Arafat had actually said. Different wire services had differing accounts. Different quotes were already circulating in bulletins before those who had recorded the whole conference on tape, the BBC for example, had a chance to select the most relevant statements (those in which Arafat was most specific).

Opportunities, logistics and that precious commodity, time

John Mahony, BBC Foreign News Editor, discussed another difficulty inherent in new technologies, the problems of using them once you have them. "Television is totally logistics dominated," he said.

Logistics often get in the way of the story. Arrangements for satellite transmissions are very onerous and complicated. That's the big problem in using the technology. When a correspondent has to spend the bulk of the time making arrangements, and is not on the story, then you have a very uncomfortable situation and so does he. Sometimes, we send along a back-up person who just deals with logistics. Even your own portable ground stations which are getting smaller are not always easy to use. Governments are getting more sensitive. We took our ground-to-satellite station to Gibraltar for the IRA inquest (three suspected IRA terrorists were shot there by British security officers in 1988). Even there it took quite a bit of negotiating to get frequencies we could use. ITN had similar problems in the Sudan, when they were there for the flooding; they had a hell of a fight with the authorities to set it up.

Even if satellite news gathering has been developed into a fine art by companies like Conus in the USA, internationally it is far from easy to use, even with your own 800 kilos of ground station equipment and 50 boxes. High-cost technology means high operational costs as well. Mahony estimated the cost of maintaining a film team with a portable satellite up-link for two weeks in the Sudan to be about £35,000.

Technology and relationships with participant groups

In 1974, Herbert Gans, writing primarily about domestic news in the USA, observed that the news media can be viewed as a communication channel which various interest groups and subcultures of American society attempt to fill with news that positively presents their viewpoints and those of their opponents negatively. Whoever gains the most access to this channel secures the best chance to influence the audience (Gans 1974: 39).

In 1989, technology has proved Gans' observations true in the realm of international news reporting. Modern communications technology opens up new ways for participant (i.e., interested) groups to:
1 check quickly what the journalists produce
2 increase their demands on the news organization or its individual members by offering facilities or threatening sanctions, and
3 at times unilaterally affect news output.

Consider this example related by a BBC World Service reporter who was following the Contra–Sandinista peace talks in Managua, Nicaragua, in March 1988. After a press conference he observed the reporters from the Washington *Post* and the News York *Times* tapping away at their portable computers and then feeding copy via modems over phone lines to the USA. They then retired to the bar for some drinks. An hour or so later, Sandinista officials approached them with telefax copies of their articles, taken from latest editions in New York and faxed back to Managua, and started discussing their contents with them.

Portable computers, phone lines, and fax machines allowed the quick checking of these reporters' work, and that instant evaluation would not have been possible had the authorities not been satisfied with their output. Apparently the Sandinistas were satisfied enough not to unilaterally affect the news; that is, pull the plug on these newsmen. The same was not true, however, for CNN and the American television networks in May 1989. They were in China to cover the historic meeting between Gorbachev and Chinese Communist leaders. That presence soon became an embarrassment to the Chinese government as the massive student demonstrations became the focal point of American coverage. Originally invited to show the world Sino–Soviet friendship, the modern electronic broadcasters had the plug pulled (all satellite up-links were denied them) just as martial law was declared.

Economic and political factors influencing news selection

Unless something exceptionally unusual happens, news bulletins on radio and television are on at fixed times. They are the end station of a news-flow process. Their durations are fairly stable; a thirty-minute programme has to be filled with thirty minutes of "news."

All foreign correspondents have heard the phrase, "a slow day," signifying that stories which would not normally raise an eyebrow might get on the air. Sometimes the opposite is true.

With a steady flow of material feeding regular broadcast outlets, decisions on "deadlines" comprise one of the most sensitive points in the selection and production process. Ideally,

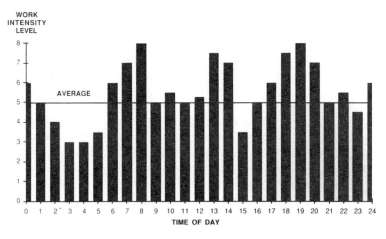

8.2 A steady flow of news through the production process includes periods of high intensity preparing for bulletins

final decisions on the make-up of a newscast should be made as late as the technology and editorial work allows. This provides the flexibility to be "first with the news." But an urge to be first can lead to less than perfect decisions as far as fact checking is concerned. Because the deadline decisions have to be made, the organization becomes somewhat vulnerable to influences from outside.

A common trick of "news management," for example, is to feed a good story or tip to a news organization as near the deadline decision time as possible. Swedish radio faced this problem in covering the issue of possible illegal arms deliveries from the Bofors company to countries banned for Swedish military exports. The story had been something of an ongoing saga throughout the 1980s, but came to a head in 1987 when Swedish Radio disclosed that money had been paid by Bofors to numbered accounts in Swiss banks in connection with a billion-dollar deal for field-guns to India. A grass-roots peace organization in Sweden that had spent most of the decade trying to expose more about sales of Swedish arms to forbidden places, then took upon itself the task of feeding Swedish Radio with more news (much of it gleaned from moles within Bofors and the Civil Service). Their enthusiasm and clever use of publicity led to a minor conflict with some of the journalists at Swedish Radio, but not because they were opposed to the disclosures: they simply resented being manipulated.

Two senior radio news reporters claimed that the Swedish peace organization in question had "cleverly utilized every opportunity in a situation which placed the organization in the center of things." Press conferences were held and new "disclosures" were released shortly before main newscasts on radio and television. This made it impossible for the broadcasters to thoroughly or even sufficiently check the peace organization's claims (Remdahl and Mosander 1987: 16). The reporters also claimed that internal competition between different news programmes had led to representatives from the peace organization receiving financial rewards for exclusive news items. They never maintained that the information was incorrect, merely that the situation, exploiting a weakness in the production process, was not acceptable.

Big stories interrupting the steady flow of news

The steady-flow model (with certain ups and downs) can, of course, be interrupted by a sudden event which is deemed particularly newsworthy. The death of a Prime Minister at the hands of an assassin, for example, would totally disrupt the picture above.

Over a longer period of time, the bigger news events do produce peaks of intensity in the news gathering and presentation process. The organizational problem here is that a new peak (a new important story) can take over before another one has been completed. This creates a somewhat schizophrenic situation. To move from an on-going story to a new, fast-breaking one is like reading a detective story with the last page ripped out. But journalists cannot ignore the next major event.

Organizational changes within news organizations can also affect news flow priorities. BBC television is starting up specialist units, the majority of which are concerned primarily with domestic issues. This could impinge on the relative importance of foreign news in the flow. John Mahony expressed this concern,

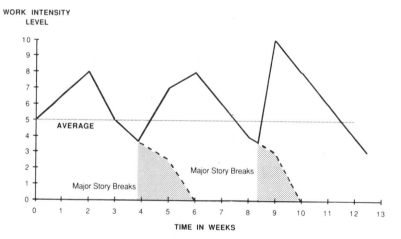

8.3 Unpredictable major events lead to peaks of intensity. Sometimes newpeaks "take over" before details referring to the previous peak have been processed. The shaded area requires resource reserves for the sake of continuity and clarity

My worry is getting my second foreign line story on; it will always lose out to a good home story. That's a worry with the trend towards specialization. If we've got all these home specialists pitching good stories, there will be less time for my good and worthwhile story from abroad.

Foreign News Editor Mahony's primary concern may be the exclusion of foreign news items, but embedded in his lament is a second problem of flow, the sheer amount of foreign news. Our study of the relative importance of foreign news (as opposed to domestic) in chapter 7 showed that foreign news items, as a rule, were shorter than domestic ones. On television, they are often bundled together in a few short bursts, with pictures to suit. An up-tempo collage of foreign news visuals adds to the slickness of a television bulletin. It adds drama, a sense of urgency, and gives the impression that a professional job has been done. It gives the "around the world in 30 seconds" feeling. Style tends to dominate; the substance becomes almost irrelevant. In such an environment, the serious broadcasters, wishing to provide analysis, endeavouring to give the viewer time to digest the significance of the items, have a tough task ahead.

We were in Kuwait in February of 1988 and watched, of course, the local evening television news. Much of the foreign content (and there was a substantial amount) was clearly semi-edited material from the major agencies. One item concerned a major pile-up on an icy, foggy Dutch motorway. The filmed story ran for almost two-and-a-half minutes (an eternity in television news). But a minute into the drama we began to study the material in a different fashion. It wasn't just another multiple accident. There were all the different aspects: the human suffering, the cost, the inefficiency, the dangers involved in such modes of transport under such weather conditions. It was an interesting and unusual media experience, one which would have been impossible in a high-tempo, slick "headline news" type of broadcast. Such a use of video material in TV News becomes less likely as the debate on blood and violence (fictional and real) in the small screen progresses. New BBC producers' guidelines, for instance, stress that TV News should not linger too long on pictures which are likely to cause distress to the viewers.

A model for news flow

The selection of news items and the choice of mode of presentation is carried out by members of organizations, that is, human beings. They have personal feelings about what is important in the same way as their organizations have norms and traditions governing their relative priorities. Outside the organization there are also groups and interested parties holding their own values and looking to apply them.

The resulting output is in part a result of interaction between different personal beliefs, collective norms and external pressures. The stronger the news organization is in terms of such factors as audience support, financial independence, and institutional cohesion, the less the selection process will be affected by complaints or pressures from interested outside participant groups.

The folowing diagram illustrates the types of influences and decisions which characterize a news organization's handling of the information it receives about the changeable world it seeks to describe.

Budget considerations (1) fix an overall frame of reference for the operation of the news organization. The actual structure (2) the organization develops (number and type of staff, number of foreign correspondents and their location, co-operation with other news gathering agencies, etc.), is based on a combination of factors. These include past experience, the traditions and expertise which the organization has developed (3) as well as input from the competitive environment (4), what the opposition does or is thought to be thinking of doing. The organization which is created (2) then gets on with the business of choice of subjects to be covered (5), thus triggering further news gathering and a choice of how each subject or item shall be covered and presented.

All the way along, the process is guided by those formal and informal rules which society as a whole applies (the legal framework, libel and other laws, respect for and expectations of the press and media). The competitive environment (4) also plays a particular role; some events become "must-carry" stories, simply because everyone else is giving them exposure.

The actual choice of items and the choice of treatment (5) are obviously related to what is actually happening in the world, but it is also tied to priorities set in the news organization. One BBC

228

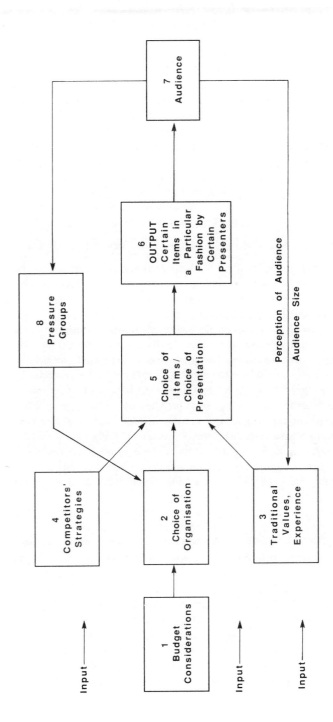

8.4 Newsflow in terms of decision-making and strategy

seminar agreed that "stories are sometimes overplayed, but it was also pointed out that the newsroom does not set priorities. Human Rights was an issue under the Carter presidency because of President Carter, not because of the Newsroom" (Buerk *et al.* 1988).

The audience also plays a role in the process (7), partly directly through measurements of audience size but also indirectly, via the organization's perception of audience expectations and interests. Pressure groups (8) emerge which can affect not only the choice of items and their presentation (5, 6), but, if they are powerful enough, even the choice of organization (2).

Collective and individual norms of the news broadcasters

Whether the organization and its members' perceptions of that audience are correct or not is immaterial. The fact is, they contribute to the general norms and values of the staff. Perceptions of the audience may make only a small contribution to those norms. Other norms, developed within the organization, reflecting the collective and individual values of the newspeople, certainly contribute more. The newsroom, for instance, collectively develops rules for what to cover. "People with headphones on don't make good television," one local television news producer in the States said, explaining why he was not enthusiastic about covering debates in the UN, even when they concerned the USA. Group norms also affect the news gathering process abroad. The tougher the task, the more likely foreign journalists are to co-operate, pooling information and sometimes dividing up different story lines, though the latter is more common among printed-press journalists on competing papers.

Radio and television reporters working in Moscow, for instance, have traditionally lived a very cloistered life, establishing security through internal co-operation. This reality tends to produce a streamlining of output. The same can be said for Eastern block journalists working in the West. They tend to stay within their own groups, relating closely to their embassies. Once again, *perestroika* can slowly change this equation.

That difficulties in gathering foreign news lead to increased journalistic co-operation among correspondents stationed together is obvious from this Kenyan example. Most of the foreign media representatives in Kenya have their offices in the same corridor of the same building in central Nairobi. BBC stringer Lindsey Hilsum observed that,

Other journalists passing through are sometimes surprised at how much we do collaborate with each other. I think it's vital, simply because it's so difficult to get any information out of anybody. Getting anything out of Government is really getting blood from stone. If you do get anything, you will obviously want to get in first, but then you will want to share it. So much of it is luck rather than skill. If you've been lucky, you tend to share because it works the other way as well. Obviously you check out the information as far as possible, but it's the same here as anywhere else; you know who the good journalists are. You know who not to trust as well. The local papers, for instance, are the seed of many stories, but you never take them as truth.

Collective norms not only affect selection, they impact modes of processing and presenting news as well. The news gatherers and processors develop standards for describing different phenomena which sometimes can act as a bias against understanding in the audience. The journalists' shorthand habit of labelling actors in the news and their choice of vocabulary become important elements of their presentations, as this example from the BBC South Africa seminar shows:

> It was also felt that there were problems over vocabulary, the meaning of *nationalist* or *Conservative*, particularly in specific cases. . . . In the Crossroads squatter's camp, those opposed to the UDF-supported vigilantes might more accurately be described as "elderly and middle-aged gangsters, running protection rackets while fed and protected by the South African security forces." There was no consensus over labelling except to say that it was useful but frequently misleading, especially in terms of blacks. (Buerk *et al.* 1988)

Collective norms and actions of journalists can even lead to situations where they create uniform expectations when presenting forthcoming events, and, in some cases, make sure that those expectations are satisfied (irrespective of actual courses of events). The media, in other words, can mould reality. We propose that the tendency to do this is greater with foreign than with domestic news events, since a) immediate response to inaccuracies is less common – foreign authorities trying to redress inaccuracies are less likely to have an impact than domestic authorities – and b) collecting correct information is often harder in a foreign country than at home. The visit of some

231

English football fans to the Swedish capital in September 1989 presents a good example.

Football "Riots" in Stockholm 1989

"WAR IN STOCKHOLM" was the headline in some of the British tabloids the day after England and Sweden drew in a World Cup qualifying match on Wednesday, 6 September 1989. Even radio, television and the serious press gave an impression of a devastated city, although there was not a single picture to show actual damage or even personal injuries. The impression the general public must have got, both in Britain and Sweden, as well as the rest of Europe, was that English football hooligans were at it again, causing trouble, ruining the game, and Britain's reputation. Comparing the reporting with the facts as they emerged in retrospect raises some interesting points.

In response to previous problems involving English fans at European matches, the English Football Association had refused to sell any tickets to British fans for this away game, saying that all tickets had been sold in Sweden. This manœuvre was intended to deter fans, in particular those classified loosely as "football hooligans," from going to Stockholm. Some diehards did make the trip to Scandinavia. A few hundred bought tickets to the match which were freely available through ticket agencies in the Swedish capital.

The game was on a Wednesday evening. Reports started filling the European news media on Monday 4 September, with accounts of several hundred fans rampaging on a ferry bound for Gothenburg on Sweden's west coast. The ferry had to return to its English port, Harwich, where a large police reception committee was waiting. *Facts*: there was some rowdy behaviour on the boat, though many passengers noticed little more than the return to port. In one serious incident a passenger fell overboard and drowned. Manslaughter or murder was suspected; this was why the ferry turned back to England. At the end of the week, only 50 football fans arrived in Gothenburg to take the ferry back to the UK. Assuming that most outward passengers would have bought cheap return tickets, then reports of several hundred fans on board rioting would seem to be a clear exaggeration.

By Tuesday, radio and TV media in Britain were reporting that fans had been arrested in Stockholm for fighting and would appear in court to face charges. On Wednesday, the day of the match, journalists in Stockholm were quoting the number of English fans as high as 2,000. A bus had been overturned – some said it had been set on fire. The soccer hooligans had charged into a large downtown department store and looted its contents. There was media consensus that there had been no trouble inside the ground, even though those English fans who had not managed to get tickets had been allowed in by Swedish officials. After the match, which ended in an uneventful draw, a uniform media reported that fullscale warfare had ensued in central Stockholm involving the police, and English and Swedish soccer fans. Damage to property was said to be considerable. Several hundred Brits had been arrested. Official British government reaction was swift. Mrs Thatcher expressed concern, demanding that hooligans should be resolutely dealt with. The Sports Minister asked the English FA to cancel a match against Holland planned for later that year (which they did). And when the Swedes released all the fans without bringing any charges, concern was expressed in London that Sweden had given a mass amnesty to hooligans who deserved to be punished. A week later, the British Home Secretary announced the creation of a new special police force for dealing with football hooliganism, citing, according to a report in the *Independent* (12 September 1989) "Last week's events in Stockholm" as reinforcing " the need for a unit such as this".

Facts:

— A small group of fans who congregated near Stockholm's central station did behave in a fairly offensive, and particularly noisy fashion. Their deviance included drinking lots of beer (though complaining about the price) and testing out the reaction of the average Stockholmer to swear words and annoying gestures (Nazi signs and the like). Many Swedes on their way home from work probably were frightened by this unusual sight. But no bus was turned over. No windows were broken.

— The manager of the big store which was said to have been looted said afterwards that he had experienced no trouble whatsover. A group of English youths had passed by, but had not tried to enter the store. Possibly one or two pedestrians might have been "bumped into."

— Of the total of 283 persons who were temporarily detained by the police, 181 were Swedes, most of whom admitted they had gone along to see some action. There were no regular arrests on the day of the match. The police – almost 500 of them in riot gear – applied the controversial Swedish "temporary detention law." This allows an officer to detain a person in custody for a few hours without filing charges if there are reasonable grounds for believing that the suspect would otherwise disturb the peace. English fans interviewed on Swedish TV after their release from police cells gave the impression of being sheepish, embarrassed adolescents rather than thuggish hooligans. Many complained that they had been provoked by jeers from Swedish counterparts.

— The day after the night before left *no* traces of a war in Stockholm. The City Works and Roads Department confirmed that there had been no mess to clear up. Their biggest problem had been to help close off certain streets because the police expected trouble.

— A British diplomat who had been liaising with the police summed it up: "the media came here looking for a story; they made sure they got one." The same diplomat estimated that the total number of fans who travelled to Sweden was well under 500, possibly as low as 300. Journalists quoting estimates in the thousands must have either been in the world of fantasy, or had failed to note that some 11,000 British citizens live in Sweden, mostly in Stockholm – many went to the match. The Swedish Minister for Home Affairs told Swedish radio that he had discussed the events of the week with his British colleague who wanted assurances that no amnesty had been granted to troublemakers. The British Government, he said, did not seem to be aware of the use by the police of preventive detention, allowed under Swedish Law.

Why was the reporting from Stockholm so out of proportion to what really happened? Several facts could have been checked; a phone call to the big store confirmed that they had not been looted. The local bus company confirmed that they had not lost a bus. The Works department's number is in the phone book. It's good to have at least a rough understanding of the law when reporting on police actions in a foreign country. Few of the visiting journalists seemed to be aware that Swedish police can apprehend a person even if a crime has not been committed, i.e. merely on the suspicion that a misdemeanour is intended or likely to occur. The police used this to defuse the situation, a fact the British embassy in Stockholm made clear to anyone who asked.

Was the reason that much of the reporting was done by sports reporters whose real job was to talk about football, but who have become hooligan specialists? If so, why didn't the checks and balances function back home? One slightly mitigating circumstance should be mentioned. Reporters in Stockholm and desk staff back in London were somewhat misled (or rather, allowed their expectations to be confirmed) by statements from Swedish police spokespersons, who *also* seemed to be caught up in the euphoria of the media-high. The police gladly confirmed the seriousness of the situation, even though they were not capable of quantifying exactly the extent of any damage to persons or property (there wasn't any). Swedish police interviewed by journalists also seemed to be unaware of the need to distinguish between the words "detain" and "arrest." Despite this, it is amazing that checks, balances, and standard practices of inquisitive journalism did not lead to correct reporting.

The sequence of events outlined here is not unique in media history. In fact it's almost a carbon copy of the observations of those who studied phenomena such as media coverage of riots in the 60s between the so-called "Mods" and "Rockers" in Britain. Stanley Cohen wrote in his book *Folk Devils and Moral Panics* (1972: 162):

> If one is in a group of twenty, being stared at by hundreds of adults and being pointed at by two or three cameras, the temptation to do something – even if only to shout an obscenity, make a rude gesture or throw a stone – is very great and is made greater by the knowledge that one actions will be recorded for others to see.

There were plenty of examples of this in Stockholm. Other parallels can be drawn. Cohen describes how the British media exaggerated out of all proportion the devastation of the seaside resort of Brighton after Mods and Rockers moved in during the Whitsun holiday in 1964. Actual damage was later estimated to £400, and costs for police overtime to £2,000. In Stockholm, damage caused by the fans was negligible – the police action cost £50,000 (or $90,000). Stanley Cohen shows how the media, in such situations of deviant behaviour, tend to amplify that deviance by a) creating expectations and b) exaggerating reports of deviance. Control systems (e.g. police presence and actions) also unintentionally, but inevitably contribute to this amplification effect. Even though the actual numbers of deviants, or to be more precise, ringleaders, might be very small, the parameters of the system involve the majority. The whole thing becomes a vicious circle. To paraphrase Cohen's flow process (Cohen 1972: 143): initial deviance leads to an inventory stage (what are the characteristics of the deviance?), followed by sensitization. The public identifies the stereotype hooligan. The latter two phases feed back on each other to produce an *over-estimation* of the deviance, often with the help of the media. This produces an escalation in the control culture (societal control via police actions, administrative regulations, etc.) which in turn can serve to amplify the deviance. The media's role here, as a catalyst – via exaggerated reports and rumour spreading – was patently obvious in Stockholm during that first week of September 1989. Surprisingly, even the "quality" media (electronic and print), both Swedish and British, were caught up in this process when reporting on English soccer fans in Sweden. The rumour that a big store had been blasted by the fans apparently originated in the afternoon radio magazine programme, After 3 (see our earlier chapter on Swedish Radio). It became fact and was even printed as such in Sweden's largest morning daily the next day. Swedish foreign correspondents stationed in Britain managed to introduce a new term into the Swedish language, "Hooliganer" (= "hooligans") to describe English soccer fans. Swedish youths also learned what the media expected of them and did their best to comply.

In conclusion to this contemporary media story we can but note that history repeats itself. In 1972, Stanley Cohen rounded off his book on the Mods and Rockers riots with the telling prediction that the ways in which moral panics are produced and disseminated by the media do not date. Stockholm was another example of what can happen when the starlings on the wire all fly off, blindly following any directions they can get from a rumoured leader. In Stockholm, group dynamics in the foreign correspondent collective (albeit with a few sports reporters included) overruled demands of responsibility and restraint.

The regular BBC reporter in Stockholm (Roger Wallis) was out of town for the first two days of this drama. He took over reporting in the early hours of the morning after the match. A last report out of Stockholm read as follows:

Official figures are now available for the number of people detained by Stockholm police in their bid to thwart disturbances among football supporters in the City centre. Of the 283 taken into temporary custody, only 102 were British. All were held for a few hours and then released. No charges have been brought. The police say that most of the minor scuffles between English and Swedish supporters were provoked by Swedish youths trying to pick a fight. There is no evidence to confirm earlier reports of English soccer fans looting in stores and vandalising property. The general impression one gets in Stockholm is that the so-called riot was more a figment of the imagination than real. Nervousness, an enormous police presence of at least one officer per visiting English fan and expectations of trouble explain the many detentions. Rowdy English fans drinking copious amounts of strong beer certainly frightened the people of Stockholm. There was no riot or vandalism.

This was the final report filed to the BBC from Stockholm, on Friday 8 September. Over the weekend, the British government finalized plans for a special intelligence unit within the police to deal with football hooligans. Events in Stockholm, as we have noted, were quoted as a reason for the urgency of this move.

From collective to individual norms affecting news selection

Individuals in institutions not only are aware of the organization's commonly held norms, but they also have personal feelings about a whole range of worldly issues. Hetherington (1985: 21) observed, "Journalists may often be unaware of the way their own social or personal backgrounds affect their judgements or their phrasing." Indeed, a hermetic sealing off from personal emotions and commitments would be an inhuman demand on reporters; it is an impossibility. Where issues are contentious, personal feelings are likely to impinge on the selection/presentation process to a greater degree.

Apartheid, specifically, or racism in general is an obvious such area. Hanging and/or the death penalty is another. A third, the Palestinian issue, offers us an illuminating story concerning a reporter who was filing for a US news programme on statements made by Yassir Arafat about the PLO's position on terrorism. An editor's strong emotional tie to the State of Israel clashed with his report. Our reporter had referred to Arafat's refusal to condemn the Palestinian uprising in the occupied territories (Ghaza/West Bank) in his report from the Stockholm meeting between the PLO leader and a group of American Jews. The item had been recorded. A few minutes later, the US newsroom phoned back and one of the intake editors asked for a re-read with a few changes in the script. One request was for the replacement of the words "Arafat refused to condemn the Palestinian uprising in the occupied territories" with "Arafat refused to condemn acts of violence against Israeli officials in the occupied territories." When the correspondent remonstrated, complaining that this was not what Arafat had actually said, he heard, "I know, but I have a senior colleague who feels very strongly about this and it would help get them off my back!"

Out in the field, of course, foreign correspondents have to have strong faith in what they are doing. Life can be difficult. Tales of danger, harassment, and loneliness abound. Foreign reporters rely heavily on moral support not only from the collective at home (Hammerberg 1981) but they are forced to draw strength from their own commitment to their craft. People like Kate Adie, sitting in a Tripoli hotel, waiting for American bombs to fall about her can't let fear intervene. They need an almost insatiable curiosity.

Lindsey Hilsum, the BBC stringer in Nairobi, went to the University one morning in 1988 when Kenyan students were protesting. "I heard there were demonstrations at the University and the students were throwing stones," she recounted,

so I went up there, arriving before the rest of the journalists because I got a lift. I went round the back and found some students to interview. While I was showing them my ID card to prove who I was, the police arrived. The students ran off and I ran to the side and hid behind a wall (not wishing to be amongst students being chased by the police; I could have got shot). Basically I was just trying to get out of the way of the police running after the students. I crouched down but the police spotted me and four or five of them came up and started beating me with heavy clubs. I just started shouting, "I'm a journalist, you can't do this to me, I work for the BBC," which was rather a pathetic thing to say when there's five enormous men bashing you with clubs. Eventually they stopped, arrested me and took me in for three hours of questioning.

10 Lindsey Hilsum, BBC reporter who was beaten up by Kenyan police during student demonstations. "It's just like falling off a horse. You just get back on again," was her reason for returning to Kenya after the incident

The injuries Lindsey sustained led to complaints from the BBC, the British High Commissioner and various journalist organizations. A Kenyan "enquiry" led nowhere. The President of that country later implied that there was something fishy about journalists knowing about the students' riots and that it was their own fault for being there (three other foreign journalists were also arrested). After the event, Lindsey Hilsum left Kenya for a while, but then returned. Her reasoning, "It's like falling off a horse. You just get on again."

Balancing demands and rewards

Technological, economic, and political factors affect news selection as we've seen. Now we need to return to the issue of how this relates to the organization's survival strategy when confronted by different demands from different participant groups. Strong audience support (high ratings/large income) offers insulation from outside pressure groups hoping to affect selection. It can also lead to a sense of "over security," producing an air of paternalism, verging, at times on *arrogance.* This is when rumours don't get properly checked and fiction finds it easy to become fact.

So emboldened, journalists are sometimes tempted to bend the rule of faithfully reporting reality (even as they see it) in the hunt for a "good story." Here's a BBC anecdote, related by Ann Sloman from her days with a television documentary unit.

> I remember a reporter who went out to do a story about private old people's homes in Eastbourne. He got down there and wanted to cover a funeral where nobody came. He got down too late. In fact there had been relations, one or two, there. After they had gone, he bribed the undertakers to dig up the coffin and stage it. I remember him coming back and telling this story. Everyone else was roaring with laughter. I thought it was so wicked. But that was an atmosphere that prevailed, an atmosphere of arrogance.

The opposite situation no doubt can develop, where editors shun sensitive stories, where outside pressure groups increase their influence, where the institution fears for its survival, and where a state of deference characterizes news selection. Most news organizations exist between these two extremes, but where they sit on the continuum varies with time, according to perceived (feared) and actual (available sanctions) participant demands.

Models such as this lead inevitably to semantic problems. Paternalism might be seen by some as arrogance, deference as subservience. Even the term "watchdog" is not without problems. BBC Head of Editorial development Richard Ayre said, "I don't like the term 'watchdog.' It suggests consumerism. I prefer 'reportage.' We are merely there to observe what others do. We don't have a mission to improve the world. It's up to others to set standards."

In a situation where a news organization has experienced strong pressure from political groups, categorical statements like this become understandable. A second BBC editor put it more pointedly, "This place isn't in the mood for taking any chances at the moment."

Politicians, as we have noted in countless previous examples, assume an interesting role in this scenario of demands and rewards. They have responsibilities, ambitions to be re-elected, opportunities to use the broadcast media for their own messages,

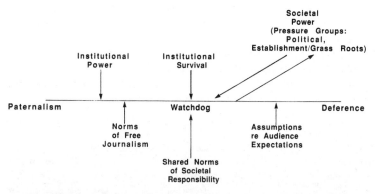

8.5 The pressure model. A strong institution provides a shield against various pressure groups. In practice there are movements along the scale, reflected in news selection/presentation resulting from competing participant demands as well as the technological and competitive environment

and specific and often powerful sanctions that can be applied.

Michael Grade, Head of the UK's fourth television network, Channel 4, for example, suggests that the current fragmentation and deregulation fervour in Britain can be related to government's mistrust of strong, national broadcast media. In a 1989 interview on Swedish television he admitted, "Part of it is technology-led. With all the satellites and other inventions, change has to be managed, after all there are still limited frequency spectra." But, according to the Channel 4 boss, deregulation/fragmentation also provides benefits to any government, not just Mrs Thatcher's.

It provides a wider range of views and filters through which the government's policies are questioned and put under the microscope... the more it (that scrutiny) is fragmented, the less powerful they think it will be. They also have a false perception of the media. All we do in fact is communicate. But they are politicians, concerned with getting re-elected. Somehow the unelected electronic media seem to be in their way most of the time. They rather despise us and would do anything to neutralise our power. One way to do that is to have a lot more broadcasting channels. Most politicians would be much happier if TV was a medium of entertainment and didn't do news and current affairs.

In terms of the pressure model, Grade might have argued that the politicians' enthusiasm for fragmentation of the media is designed to move it toward the right pole of the model; that is, toward deference.

Campaigns against the electronic media, symbolized overtly by verbal attacks from the likes of the Helmes and the Irvines in the USA or Mr Tebbit and other ardent BBC monitors in the UK, all have their effect. Sometimes, one is surprised by the magnitude of the disturbances they create. The former British Conservative party Chairman, Norman Tebbit (active in the Libya story chronicled earlier in this chapter), launched a new attack on the BBC in February 1990, for using the word 'conservative' to describe, among others, those in the Kremlin opposed to *perestroika*. His inference was that this was a plot to miscredit those with a conservative political label in general. In a Tebbit talk to students at Oxford University (reported generally in the British press, e.g., the *Independent*, 22 February 1990), BBC journalists were referred to in terms of "insufferable, smug, sanctimonious, naive, guilt-ridden, wet, pink orthodoxy of that sunset home of the third-rate minds of that third-rate decade, the 1960s." Even if criticism of the BBC's use of the word 'conservative' can easily be dismissed by simply referring the critic to any good dictionary, such attacks do indeed function as disturbances. They reflect the desire of different power groups to both tame and utilize the power of the news media, tending to produce a move along the scale of our pressure model, unless the news organization in general, and management in particular, feel they have enough institutional strength to stand firm.

The pressure model embodies a number of assumptions. The right–left scale is *spatial*, and not related to the right/left of traditional political analysis; both right-wing conservatism and left-wing totalitarianism can seek the subservience of the media. Our pressure model proposes that the greater the power of various external groups (political, business, grass-roots/popular movements), the more to the right on the scale news media organizations will find themselves; unless, of course, there is significant external pressure for the development or maintenance of high standards of journalistic independence; unless, of course, what those groups mean by journalistic independence is coverage deferential to their own views. Thus, two arrows on the model's right extremity.

Power centres can manipulate or exert pressure on the news

242

organization by applying sanctions (governments can review franchises, pass laws limiting journalists' freedom, etc.), overt pressure (letter campaigns), or through more covert news management. The latter tactic is becoming more common. News management can be positive (supplying news, but in a form satisfactory to the giver) or negative (restricting access to information except under the giver's terms). As we observed in a previous chapter, the official civil servant spokesman who gave little, but reasonably accurate information is being replaced by the PR Officer with tons of information, all couched in terms intended for maximum selfish benefit.

A number of internal factors also affect the organization's position on the scale at various times. Norms of free journalism will exert pressure to move it toward the left on the scale, towards greater independence. Assumptions about audience expectations, as a rule, can be expected to push to the right (not wishing to offend or shock listeners and viewers). Norms of social responsibility – seeing itself as the responsible monitor of society – will support a more central position.

The concept of broadcast news organizations constantly changing their positions on the spatial left–right scale of our pressure model is a useful aid to understanding developments, particularly during periods of turmoil and realignment. Other parallel spatial scales can be linked to our model. When an organization is more to the left (strong and independent) then it will tend to build up permanent resources (both staff and equipment). When not so sure of itself and its future, i.e. when moving to the right in a period of realignment, the organization will tend to rely more on freelancers and short-term contracts. Rather than building up its own technical production resources, it will tend to purchase services from outside suppliers, thus increasing its flexibility and (as the management perceive it) its means of withstanding pressures from outside in the future. Such developments have been clearly noticeable in the BBC, the US networks, and Swedish radio and television over the past few years.

The static, two-dimensional nature of the printed picture of our model might seem to imply a worst case scenario, where media, even those with strong libertarian ideologies, move inexorably through a phase of social responsibility toward an organizational positioning that leaves them vulnerable to influence by strong, authoritarian power centres. But technology also offers a more optimistic view of the media's development. The schizophrenic combination of internationalization (a few large international news suppliers closely interlinked) and localization (a multitude of smaller and/or independent broadcasters employing low cost technology or small elements of high technology) could produce just the opposite movement.

News might develop like the popular music industry has. A few large companies now provide the resources and technology for the international flow of recorded music. But they cannot monopolize it all. A plethora of small and/or independent producers is constantly active, occasionally using services provided by the giants, taking the risks in the market-place, and giving exposure to new and different content, content that the Bigs could not and would not touch (Wallis and Malm 1984).

In our epilogue we will touch on further parallels between broadcast news and the music media, including some of the varied conclusions such a comparison necessarily produces. One prediction can be made here, however; it will be the medium-sized, public service broadcasters and the larger independents with resources to invest in international news gathering that can be expected to produce the most unusual and adventurous forays into foreign news reporting. They will have the greatest need to develop unique, specific competences. The Bigs will be too involved in maintaining their status quo *vis-à-vis* competitors and other participant groups. On a lower level of magnitude, there will always be small, shoe-string budget operators interested primarily in minimizing costs and therefore buying their foreign news material from the cheapest sources.

Epilogue

What will we know?
What should we know?
Comparing broadcast news to developments in other media sectors

The issue is relatively simple to articulate, "What will individuals, organizations, and societies do with the new news communication technologies?" The answer, though, is less clear. The electronic news business is in a confusing state of flux, even turmoil. Established broadcasters seek new strategies or tighten old ones. Public service broadcasters lose the advantages of protected status. The BBC adopts a survival policy of moving up-market; more in-depth, specialist analysis is deemed the recipe for staving off the increasingly threatening competition. Other broadcasters on both sides of the Atlantic move down-market, increasing their dependence on up-tempo presentations and light-weight items. New entrepreneurs, backed by enormous financial resources, hover at the tabloid end of the news. Gigantic investments flood into the perceived El Dorado of European deregulated broadcasting. In America, the Big Three commercial networks falter and public broadcasting is all but commercial.

Where will all this lead? Even if the media do not entirely dictate the message, as some technological determinists would have us believe, we do agree that radio and television have inherent, limiting parameters that affect the efficiency of the communication process of which they are part. They are dramatic, emotional media, like film and phonogram. A monotonous voice or a talking head reading information that listeners and viewers care little about will not lead to a situation of functioning communication. Unlike the printed press, viewers and listeners can't go back to the previous page. Radio and television are *immediate*, emotional media. The emotional prerequisite for successful communication in the broadcast media means that news, ideally, should be both informative and dramatic if it is to grip. If news consumers have high motivation to find out about an event, the emotional involvement is naturally established.

Plane crashes and apartment house fires are visually dramatic, creating their own emotional lock. But even for the most complex story, radio and television have the ability to create the emotional involvement necessary for communication to succeed. When they squander that power, watching and listening become little more than social or personal rituals, mere parts of a person's audio-visual environment, warranting no more attention than trees lining a forest road. If the audience gets bored, it will tune out or tune in to another alternative.

This leads us to two conclusions. First, these media place certain limits on the way in which news can be successfully presented, in terms of maintaining and informing an audience. Second, the all-too-common strategy of dichotomizing between informing *or* entertaining the audience is doomed to fail. A combination is a prerequisite for success. This explains why the habit of oscillating between these extremes, so common in the strategies we have described in earlier chapters, never seems to lead to any degree of permanence. The result is an output which tends to be *either* boring and incomprehensible *or* frivolous and superficial. The result is rarely newscasts which are consistently gripping, informative, and stimulating.

The observation that the nature of the broadcast media limits how they can be used leads us on to an interesting parallel. Broadcast news is characterized by structures and developments bearing a remarkable similarity to other sectors of the entertainment industry. They exist in areas as diverse as organizational and financial structure, production practices, and distribution. One can speak of a broadcast "news industry" much the same way as one refers to the "music industry." The past two decades have seen the rapid international integration in the structure of the so-called "cultural industries" (radio, television, film, music, etc), and this is just one instance where the news and recorded music industries match.

In the music industry, companies producing and marketing recorded music have experienced a radical process of horizontal and vertical integration, on local, national, and international levels. Hardware companies have bought software producers.

Larger companies have swallowed smaller ones, producing a small group of gigantic firms, controlling a large percentage of sales of recorded music around the world. In a second round of integration, these companies have themselves become minor players in gigantic corporations with a variety of activities. CBS Records has been bought by SONY of Japan; RCA by the West German publishing complex Berthelsman, and operating as BMG. These trends can be seen in the broadcast news indutry. NBC becomes a part of General Electric; ABC a part of Capital Cities. The Visnews/WTN duopoly is carved up between major news actors NBC, ABC, Reuters, the BBC.

Even larger combines are moving into traditional music industry territory, providing rewards and placing demands. Coca Cola, Pepsi, and Nestlé's sign exclusive contracts with artists like Michael Jackson and Madonna. Sponsorship is on the increase in the music business and although Pepsi hasn't yet made Dan Rather an offer he can't refuse, commercial sponsorship in exchange for the status of associating with Public Broadcasting is a reality in America, on its way in Europe, and mandated as an important form of financing in Britain.

The comparison between the music and news industries becomes even more obvious in other areas:

Table 9.1 *Similar developments and trends in the music and broadcast news industries*

Aspect of Comparison	Music Industry	News Industry
Control of international distribution	Oligopoly of transnationals	Oligopoly of transnationals as deregulation opens markets and cuts satellite costs
	Many small companies (National and Local)	Many small companies (National and Local)
Forms of distribution of products	Radio/TV Satellite (MTV) Cable Cassettes	Radio/TV Satellite Cable (Cassettes)
Non-stop programme channels	Music Video Channels	CNN, SkyNews, etc.

Table 9.1 *cont'd*

Aspect of Comparison	Music Industry	News Industry
Division of responsibilities regarding "raw material" for production	Big operators own big international stars/sources of talent. Smaller take risks/sell new discoveries to the Big ones	Big news/film agencies cover major international stories. Smaller produce unique items and sell to major distributors/users
Dependency on advertising/sponsorship income	Increasing as less income from actual phonogram sales, and more from sponsors. Advertisers' influence over music in media increasing, as music becomes vehicle for selling products/life style	Increasing as a) public funds dwindle b) news required to make large profits.
Universal products	TOP 10 similar in many parts of the world	TOP 10 news items Some of them universal
	Same small no. of items available to growing international audience in more countries	Same small no. of items available to growing international audience in more countries
Production norms	Norms govern "sound" and video clichés	Strong norms govern audio/visual style
Life-span of products	Limited. Sharp rise for hits. Slower fall	Limited. Sharp rise big items. Quick fall when new story takes over
Institutional Memory	Old material stored and re-released (eg often after a star's death)	Major operators store old material and re-use in new packages (eg obituaries)
Selection of products based on:	Assumptions regarding expectations/interests of audience	ditto
	Norms/experience from previous	ditto

Table 9.1 *cont'd*

Aspect of Comparison	Music Industry	News Industry
	selection Gatekeepers' own preferences.	ditto
Predictability/ inevitability through planning/marketing	Commitments through forward planning Big stars hits can be predicted (via marketing efforts)	Much can be predicted. Commitment of resources makes specific output more predictable
The Star system a) Presentation	deejays/veejays chosen for looks/ charisma rather than subject knowledge	news "jockeys" ditto
b) Product Stars	Megastars main concern of biggest operators	Certain international actors recur
e.g.	Julio Inglesias Madonna Pavarotti	George Bush Yasser Arafat Mrs Thatcher
Time-span from unpredicted event to product	Unexpected "hits" require a matter of weeks to be established. Global benefits (Band Aid) can create stars overnight	Unexpected events can be news in hours or even minutes
International/ National/Local relationship	Internationalization/ Localization occurring simultaneously. Pressure on national music industries. Local music stations thrive with international music (cheap access)	Internationalization puts pressure on traditional *national* operators. Local news stations get cheap access to international news
Management recruitment trends	Top management with music expertise replaced by lawyers, accountants, or marketing experts	ditto

The similarities are remarkable. The only major difference concerns the time-span within which "hits" or "major stories" can be created. But even this could change as machines that allow digital sampling, advanced sequencers, and sophisticated synthesizers become commonplace in the music business, turning the phonogram into a veritable "news item." Produce it quickly, borrow quotes freely, and chuck it away – much the same way local TV news functions.

These parallels are not mere academic curios. The risk is that news organizations, those who control and work in them, will be swept along in this drift. The changes in both the music and news industries that have evolved over the last two decades may have been inevitable. But surely news is different from music. The prime aim of the latter industry is not to inform us about those things that will allow us to perform our duties as citizens (even if some individual artists comprise occasional exceptions); it is not to give us the data we need to live effectively and efficiently in a changing and complex world. The aim of the global music industry is primarily to make money while entertaining. If individuals who consume news, organizations that gather and disseminate news, and societies that depend on news ignore this, the results can, shall we say, be somewhat interesting.

Whittle Communications, an American company that specializes in reaching highly-targeted audiences (and 50 per cent owned by Time, Inc.), began trial transmissions of its Channel One in six US high schools in March 1989. Called a product of the "MTV school of journalism" by the *Columbia Journalism Review*, it is, according to Whittle, "a network quality news program" beamed daily by satellite from Los Angeles to captive high school audiences. All a school has to do to earn the right to receive the programme and the "gift" of $50,000 worth of electronic gear necessary for that reception, is to agree to show the complete newscast to the entire student body every day. Hoping to reach 7,000,000 young people in 8,000 schools every day by 1990, Channel One has

> the look and feel of a music video, heavy on the bass, with "anchors" who look like vee-jays. "Up Front" was the news – an airline strike, trouble in the Middle East, arms control talks in Vienna – presented at pinball pace. More care had been lavished on the snazzy graphics than on the newswriting. . . .

The shows were peppered with ten-second factoids in various guises. (Tate 1989: 52)

The ten-minute news programme is down-linked accompanied by two full minutes of commercials presented in thirty-second bursts.

Is Channel One the logical and inevitable product of developments in the technology, politics and economics of news? Does anybody care other than some old-line, print-oriented journalists and a few liberal academics? Does the audience care? Does it want news, especially foreign news? Ed Planter, NBC Bureau Chief in London, has one answer.

Do they care two hoots about the elections in Pakistan, the Palestinian National Congress meeting in Algeria or turmoil in Albania? Ninety eight per cent probably couldn't care less. That doesn't mean we shouldn't do these stories, since we have an editorial duty to inform. If we were driven by the public's taste, we'd be putting out the sun every night. You have to take a chance that someone out there is going to be interested.

A Harris Poll has a different view:

the survey indicated that media personnel underestimate the public's interest in international news, for while 41 per cent of the (US) public surveyed expressed great interest in foreign news, only 5 per cent of the sample of media practitioners believed media consumers to be concerned with this news category. (Kaplan 1979: 239)

Is NBC's respected Ed Planter correct or is the Harris poll? If our pressure model is accurate, this is the crucial question; the audience is, after all, the most powerful of the participant groups.

On the other hand, if our pressure model is correct, the news organizations have responsibilities and traditions that virtually compel them to offer what people should have as well as what they want. In this way, Planter is most definitely right. The issue, in other words, is not only a matter of what these media have traditionally given us, and whether they can go on doing it. It is also a question of *what* do we want to know, and what *should* we be told.

This book has concentrated on what the broadcasters tell us. It would be irresponsible to conclude without a few comments on the audience's desires and needs, as we see them.

At the beginning of the evaluation stage of this project we did dabble gently in the area of audience preferences and expectations. A small group of US citizens, representing a wide range of occupations, ages, and education was given a list of all the major foreign stories the BBC World Service featured during our three-week study period. They were asked to categorize the events into two classes; those which they would have been interested to hear about, and those events which they would have expected the US broadcast media to cover (the actual wording was: those about which they would have been surprised if US Radio and Television News had *not* covered). The results of this mini-survey seemed to produce little. All the sample, without exception, expressed a strong interest in knowing more about items ranging from a ceasefire in Chad to refugee problems in Afghanistan. The second category scored slightly less, indicating that our respondents' expectations of Broadcast News' ability to present the world were less than their perceptions of their own interest in knowing more about the world.

In retrospect, we recalled a study by Vernon Sparkes and James Winter, published in the *Gazette* back in 1980 (1980: 149–70). They found a similar trend in a larger sample they asked to comment on the selection of foreign news in the media. These two researchers went one step further with a follow-up interview which suggested that people do indeed want foreign news, but not always the sort the broadcast media traditionally give. News of elections, a coup, or a train crash were the things respondents thought they probably would hear about, and ought to hear about, on the news. Reminding us that "what people say they do and what they actually want are not always the same" (1980: 167), Sparkes and Winter found that what people really seemed to want to know was how ordinary folks live in other countries, how other nations and peoples solve similar problems to the ones one battles with at home.

This tallies with another set of observations we made during a series of lecture tours around various US universities in 1987. We regularly visited classes of students studying Mass Communications and Journalism and asked them *if* and *why* one needs foreign news coverage on radio and television. One or two bright sparks did admittedly give the speedy response that international news was good as a filler if it was "a slow day" in America. A slower and more consistent answer gave two solid reasons which

252

we would like to share with you. One was that broadcast news could and should provide the means for an impartial appraisal of your country's foreign policy. The other was that international news on radio and television could conceivably help us to find out more about how others live and think in the world around us. In other words, we can tentatively conclude that people do wish to be informed about the elephant, but not always via the choice of information media traditions say we should be given.

If this is what people *want* to know, then what are the things people *should* be told? Why is it important that people everywhere know about human rights abuses in Haiti, about torture in Chile; about entrenched racism in North America and in Europe, about apartheid in South Africa? By remaining ignorant of the world we have created we remain ignorant of ourselves. What kind of leaders will we then elect? What kinds of solutions will we then favour? What will we add to the weight of world opinion against hate and suffering?

That's what foreign news, essentially, should be all about.

Postscript:
A Challenge to European Traditions of Broadcasting

Throughout the seventy years or so of broadcasting history, much innovation in the media business has occurred in the USA. Up to the the mid-1980s, the traditional European response to North American media developments had been one of critical caution rather than open admiration. The very founding of the BBC in the early days of radio marked a conscious attempt to avoid what were seen as the cultural problems of free-market commercialism. The BBC model was borrowed by numerous other broadcasters the world over. That was back in the 1920s.

Again in the 1950s, the British model of regulated commercial television was introduced as an alternative to the model that had developed in the USA. It forced commercial television companies to retain a high degree of public service responsibility, whilst providing them, via regulation, with a high degree of financial protection in the form of monopoly franchises.

Now, as we enter the 1990s, Europe finds itself facing a similar dilemma. New technologies and deregulation have typified developments in the US electronic media throughout the 1980s. But the tradition of critically appraising such developments – a tradition so firmly entrenched in the European broadcasting debate for most of this century – seems to have waned.

History repeats itself. Hopefully, European media policy-makers, and indeed concerned citizens in the USA who look to Europe for inspiration, will sit up, take note, and react; before it is too late.

254

Appendix

Results of study 10 November – 21 November 1986. Nine news programmes, six on Television and three on Radio.

Station	Days logged	Items total	Total time seconds	% Foreign (items)	% Foreign (net newstime)
CBS news	16	214	20805	36	27
CNN Head	20	347	24989	22	18
INN news	17	164	17496	31	21
Ch2 KTVU	20	429	48616	13	9
NPR ATC	20	262	65939	30	27
BBC TV	21	259	26373	33	35
BBC Radio	20	423	31459	34	31
Swed TV	21	292	26883	43	37
Swed Radio	21	326	23765	46	44
BBC World Service	21	367	25200	–	–
Total Items/Time		3083	311525 (= 86½ hours net newstime)		

255

News Geography. Percentage distribution of countries/regions reported on. Coding allows but does not require a maximum of two countries per news item.

Station Area	CBS news	CNN head	INN news	CH2 KTVU	NPR ATC	BBC TV	BBC radio	SWED TV	SWED radio	BBC World S
USA	57	77	66	85	68	9	7	7	5	14
W. Europe	10	4	8	2	6	6	7	12	9	9
UK	0.4	2	2	0.2	1	62	59	1	2	24
Sweden/Scan	0	0	1	0	0	0	0	54	56	0.3
TOTAL	68	83	77	88	75	77	73	74	72	47
USSR	3	0.5	0.5	2	1	1	3	4	3	7
CHINA	0	0.5	0.5	0.2	0.3	0	0.2	0	0.5	0.6
JAPAN	0	2	1.5	1	0	0.3	0.6	0.3	0.2	0.3
Asia (rest)	8	3	10.6	4	5	3	7	6	6	9
Australasia	1	1	2	1	0	7	2	1	2	2
S. America	0.4	0.3	0	0	0.7	1.4	0.6	1.2	0.7	4.9
C. America	4.3	2.7	2.6	0.9	2.5	0.3	0.2	1.2	0	1.8
E. Europe	0	0.3	0	0	0	0	0.8	0.6	1.6	2.1
Africa	2.7	0.8	0	0.6	0.7	1.7	6.4	3.1	4.9	7.0
Middle East	12	5	5.7	3	11	8	7	12	9	13
Station	CBS	CNN	INN	CH2	NPR	BBCTV	BBCR	SWTV	SWRA	BBCWS

Distribution of activities covered in stories with foreign content
(Foreign = 1, 2, 3, or 4).

Stations Activities	CBS news	CNN head	INN news	CH2 KTVU	NPR ATC	BBC TV	BBC radio	SWED TV	SWED radio	BBC WorldS
Politics internal										
1 disputes etc.	12	9	3	21	13	16	9	8	10	8
2 gov. decisions etc.	14	4	5	3	9	3	8	5	9	12
TOTALS	26	13	8	24	22	19	17	13	19	20
International disputes/										
negotiations	18	22	26	9	23	14	24	15	16	17
Military	10	13	8	9	16	10	12	15	16	14
Violence/Terrorism	14	11	23	13	10	8	13	13	11	10
TOTALS	42	46	57	31	49	32	49	43	43	41
Crimes/scandals/courts	4	10	11	7	9	16	13	8	6	11
Non-violent protests/ strikes/opinions	7	4	5	3	6	2	3	7	6	7
Disasters/accidents	8	4	9	12	5	5	6	3	7	5
Notable Events										
1 industry/economics	5	4	3	0	3	2	2	4	6	7
2 medical/technical	1	1	0	3	1	0	0.5	3	1	0.3
3 social/welfare	1	4	0	1	2	1	0.5	1	4	3
4 Culture/Arts	1	2	0	1	2	1	1	1	0.4	1
VIPs/Royals	4	3	3	4	0	9	2	1	0.4	3
Odd/lucky activities	0	7	1	0	1	2	0.4	2	0	0
	CBS news	CNN head	INN news	Ch2 KTVU	NPR ATC	BBC TV	BBC radio	SWED TV	SWED radio	BBC WorldS

Themes in the news – a "post-analysis" of recurring topics
% time devoted to 26 categories

Station Theme	CBS news	CNN head	INN news	Ch2 KTVU	NPR ATC	BBC TV	BBC radio	SWED TV	SWED radio	BBC World S
Iran/Contra										
1 USA internal focus	25.9	12.7	34.2	7.9	16.4	8.0	1.7	4.6	5.0	4.5
2 international focus	1.9	1.8	4.0	1.1	3.7	2.9	3.3	1.0	2.3	3.4
Philippines	3.7	2.5	0.9	1.5	3.4	0.8	1.1	1.9	1.8	1.4
Kim Il Sung (dead?)	1.5	0.6	0.5	0.2	1.1	0	1.1	0.8	0.6	0.8
Lebanon fighting	0.8	0	0	0	0.5	0.5	0.9	0.8	2.3	1.8
Iran/Iraq war	0.1	0.6	1.6	0	0.4	1.4	1.2	0.2	0.3	1.6
terrorism hostages	5.6	2.3	2.2	0.1	2.7	4.7	2.5	1.9	1.3	2.6
OAS meeting	0	0.1	0	0	0.5	0	0	0	0	1.0
UN etc.	0	0	1.2	0	0	0.7	0.3	1.2	0.5	3.3
International arms negotiations	2.4	0	0.1	0.3	1.3	0.4	3.0	0	1.2	2.3
Afghanistan/refugees etc.	0	0	0	0	0	0.1	0	0.4	0.2	1.5
S Africa	1.4	0.6	0	0.3	2.2	2.6	5.0	1.4	3.4	2.6

	CBS news	CNN head	INN news	CH2 KTVU	NPR ATC	BBCTV TV	BBC radio	SWED TV	SWED radio	BBC WorldS
Disasters										
1 natural	2.0	3.7	1.1	2.1	0.2	0.3	0.2	1.1	0.2	1.1
2 accidents	0	0.5	0.2	3.7	0	3.3	2.2	1.4	0.5	0.7
3 man-made	1.5	0.8	1.6	0.4	3.5	1.7	1.7	6.0	9.0	0.7
Crime										
1 white-collar	2.9	2.3	2.7	2.8	3.3	0.3	1.0	3.7	1.7	0.8
2 violent	0.1	5.9	1.3	6.6	0.7	5.2	5.6	1.8	6.0	1.4
Wage disputes	0	0.1	0	1.2	0.5	5.4	6.0	3.9	5.1	0.3
Jobs (+ or -)	6.0	1.8	0.9	0.1	1.1	2.0	2.7	1.6	1.6	0.3
Medical cures	5.2	5.2	9.4	0.2	4.0	2.6	0.1	5.9	0.4	0.0
AIDS	1.3	2.0	1.3	5.2	0.2	3.1	3.5	1.9	1.0	1.7
Animal tales	1.2	1.9	0.4	1.5	1.9	0	0.2	0	0	0
STATION	CBS news	CNN head	INN news	CH2 KTVU	NPR ATC	BBCTV TV	BBC radio	SWED TV	SWED radio	BBC WorldS
Total time(m)	346	416	292	810	1099	440	525	448	396	420
Total items(n)	214	347	164	429	262	259	423	292	326	367

References

Adams, V. (1986) *The Media and the Falklands Campaign*, London: Macmillan.

Alexandre, L. (1987) "Inciting the Libyans," *The Nation*, 20 June.

Almaney, A. (1970) "International and foreign affairs on network television news," *Journal of Broadcasting* 14, 4: 499–509.

Altheide, D. (1976) *Creating Reality*, Beverley Hills, CA: Sage.

Ariel (1990) London: BBC Staff Publications, 30 January. Summary of Phillips Report.

Baran, S. J. (1980) *The Viewers' Television Book*, Cleveland: Penrith.

Barnard, C. (1938) *The Functions of the Executive*, Cambridge, MA: Harvard University Press.

Berger. P. L. and Luckman, T. (1967) *The Social Construction of Reality*, New York: Anchor Books.

Boyer, P. J. (1988) *Who Killed CBS?*, New York: Random House.

BBC World Service (1988) *Bush House Newsroom Guide*, London: Edward M. Brown.

British Government (1988) *Broadcasting in the 90s: Competition, Choice, and Quality*, London: Her Majesty's Stationery Office, November 1988.

Buerk, M. *et al.* (1988) *BBC, Apartheid, and South Africa*, London: Report from BBC World Service Seminar.

"CBS chief denies he's a penny-pinching tyrant," (1987) San Jose *Mercury-News*, 26 March.

Cohen, S. (1972) *Folk, Devils and Moral Panics: The Creation of the Mods and Rockers*, Oxford: Martin Robertson.

Cohen, S. and Young, J. (1973) *The Manufacture of News*, London: Constable.

Conservative Party Central Office (1986) *Media Monitoring: The US Raid on Libya*, London: Conservative Party Report.

Deakin, J. (1984) *Straight Stuff: The Reporters, the White House and the Truth*, New York: Morrow.

Dean, J. (1951) *Managerial Economics*, Englewood Cliffs, NJ: Prentice-Hall.

References

De Fleur, M. and Ball-Rokeach, S. (1975) *Theories of Mass Communication*, New York: McKay.

Drummond, W. (1986) "Is time running out for network news?" *Columbia Journalism Review*, 25, 1: 50–52.

Dunkley, C. (1988) "The Nine O'clock News goes serious," *Financial Times*, 16 November.

Elgemyr, G. (1987) *Dagens Eko 50 År* ("50 years of Dagens Eko"), Stockholm: Sveriges Radio Førlag.

Elliott, K. (1988) "International broadcasting on a budget: A new start for America's voices," Voice of America working paper, Washington.

— (1988) "The future of shortwave in international broadcasting: problems, opportunities, and proposals." Voice of America internal report, Washington.

Elstein, D. (1986) "An end to protection." In C. MacCabe and O. Stewart (eds.), *The BBC and Public Service Broadcasting*, Manchester: Manchester University Press.

Englund, K. (1986) *BBC External Services*, Stockholm: Swedish Foreign Office Report.

Engvall, L. (1986) "Newspaper adaptation to a changing social environment," *European Journal of Communications* 1, 327–41.

Epstein, E.J. (1973) *News From Nowhere*, New York: Random House.

"Fewer radio listeners are hearing the news," (1986) New York *Times*, 28 December.

Fortner, R. S. and Durham, D. A. (1988) "The future of shortwave for international broadcasting," Voice of America briefing paper, Washington.

Friedman, J. *et al.* (1981) "The world according to Israel, Jordan, the Soviet Union, and the United States," *Panorama* 2, 3: 62–5.

Fulbright, J. W. (1975) "Fulbright on the press," *Columbia Journalism Review* 14, 4: 39–45.

Galtung, J. and Ruge, M. H. (1965) "The structure of foreign news," *Journal of Peace Research* 1, 1: 64–91.

Gans, H. (1974) *Popular Culture and High Culture*, New York: Basic Books.

— (1980) *Deciding What's News*, London: Constable.

Gates, G.P. (1978) *Airtime: The Inside Story of CBS News*, New York: Harper & Row.

Gerbner, G. *et al.* (1982) "Charting the mainstream: Television's contribution to political orientation," *Journal of Communication* 32, 2: 100–27.

Giljam, M. and Hedberg, P. (1981) *"Rapport's bild av omvärlden"* ('Rapport's' picture of the world), Department of Political Science, Gothenburg University, Sweden.

Golding, P. and Elliot, P. (1979) *Making the News*, New York: Longman.

Goldstein, T. (1986) *The News at Any Cost*, New York: Simon & Schuster.

Granada TV (1988) "The Taming of the Beeb," *World in Action*, 29 February.

Hadenius, S. and Weibull, L. (1985) *Massmedier*, Stockholm: Bonniers.

Hale, J. (1975) *Radio Power*, London: Paul Elek.

Hall, S. (1970) "A world at one with itself," *New Society*, 18 June: 1056–1058.

Hammerberg, T. (1981) *Massmedier Och Var Bild Av Omvärlden*, Stockholm: Prisma.

Harrison, M. (1986) "A window on the world? Foreign coverage by a British radio current affairs program," *Critical Studies in Mass Communication* 3, 4: 409–428.

Hartley, J. (1982) *Understanding News*, London: Methuen.

Head, S. and Sterling, C. (1987) *Broadcasting in America: A Survey of Electronic Media*, Boston: Houghton Mifflin.

Hersh, S. M. (1987) "Gadhafi's survival of attack was seen as 'an accident,'" San Jose *Mercury News*, 23 February.

Hester, A. (1978) "Five years of foreign news on US television evening newscasts," *Gazette* 24, 1: 88–95.

Hetherington, A. (1985) *News, Newspapers, and Television*, London: Macmillan.

Holt, H. (1986) "Influence of foreign television on Caribbean people." Paper delivered to the Caribbean Publishing and Broadcasting Association, Port of Spain, Trinidad.

Hulteng, J. L. (1979) *The News Media and What Makes Them Tick*, Englewood Cliffs, NJ: Prentice Hall.

Hvitfelt, H. (1989) "Nyheter och verkligheten" ("News and reality") Department of Journalism, Gothenburg University, Report 1989:1.

Irvine, R. (1988) "Give up on Public Broadcasting," *Wall Street Journal*, 28 March.

Jay, P. (1984) *The Crisis for Western Political Economy and Other Essays*, Totowa, NJ: Barnes & Noble Books.

Joyce, E. (1988) *Prime Times, Bad Times*, New York: Doubleday.

Kaplan, K. L. (1979) "The plight of foreign news in the US mass media," *Gazette* 25, 4: 233–243.

"Kate Adie wins damages," (1988) *The Guardian*, 14 June.

Killian, J. R. (1967) *Public Television, A Program for Action*, New York: Bantam Books.

Knight, G. (1982) "News and ideology," *Canadian Journal of Communication* 8, 4: 15–41.

Lansipuro, Y. (1987) "Asiavision," *Intermedia*, January: 22–27.

Larson, J. (1984) *Television's Window on the World*, Norwood, NJ: Ablex.

— and Hardy, A. (1977) "International affairs coverage on network television news: a study of news flow," *Gazette* 23, 4: 241–256.

Lazarsfeld, P. F. (1940) *Radio and the Printed Page*, New York: Duell, Sloan & Pearce.

— (1941) "Remarks on administrative and critical communication research," *Studies in Philosophy and Social Science* 9, 1: 2–16.

Leiser, E. (1986) "The Way It Is: Networks' News Coverage Fizzles," *San Jose Mercury News*. 17 August: 3C.

— (1988) "Little network making it big," *New York Times Sunday Magazine* 20 March: 30–38.

References

MacBride, S. (1980) *Many Voices One World*, New York: Unipub.

McManus, J. (1986) "Compromised news: selection values in a television newsroom," report, Institute for Communication Research, Stanford University, CA 94305,USA.

McQuail, D. (1977) *Analysis of Newspaper Content*, Royal Commission on the Press, Report Cmnd 6810–4, Her Majesty's Stationery Office, London.

Meyrowitz, J. (1985) *No Sense of Place*, Oxford: Oxford University Press.

Milne, A. (1988) *Memories of a British Broadcaster*, London: Hodder & Stoughton.

Mowlana, H. (1986) *Global Information and World Communication*, New York, Longman.

Ohlsson, A. (1988) "Politiska nyheter till nytta och noje," ("Political news items for both use and fun"), Department of Political Science, Gothenburg University.

Postman, N. (1985) *Amusing Ourselves to Death*, New York: Viking.

Powers, R. (1977) *The Newscasters*, New York: St Martin's Press.

Real, M. (1986) "Demythologising media: Recent writings in critical and institutional theory," *Critical Studies in Mass Communication* 3, 4: 459–481.

Remdahl, B. and Mosander, J. (1987) "Svenska Freds och Bofors" ("The Swedish Peace Association and the Bofors Company") *Antennan*, Sveriges Radio's in-house weekly staff magazine, Stockholm, 6 November 1987.

Riffe, D. (1984) "International news borrowing: a trend analysis," *Journalism Quarterly* 61, 1: 142–148.

— and Shaw, E. (1986) "Conflict and Consonance: Coverage of the Third World in two US papers," *Journalism Quarterly* 63, 4: 617–626.

— et al. (1986) "Gatekeeping and the network news mix," *Journalism Quarterly* 63, 2: 315–321.

Ruth, M. (1986) "Covering foreign news," *Presstime*, April: 28–35.

Scheer, S. J. and Eiler, S. W. (1972) "A comparison of Canadian and American network television news," *Journal of Broadcasting* 16, 2: 159–164.

Schlesinger, P. (1987) *Putting Reality Together*, London: Methuen.

Semmel, A. K. (1976) "Foreign news in four US elite dailies: some comparisons," *Journalism Quarterly* 53, 4: 732–736.

Selznick, P. (1957) *Leadership in Administration: A Sociological Interpretation*, Evanston, IL: Row, Peterson.

Siebert, F. S., Peterson, T. and Schramm, W. (1956) *Four Theories of the Press*, Urbana, IL: University of Illinois Press.

Smith, A. (1974) *British Broadcasting*, Newton Abbot: David & Charles.

Sparkes, V. M. and Winter, J. P. (1980) "Public Interest in Foreign News", *Gazette* 26: 149–179.

Stein, M.L. (1986) "The MTV generation," *Editor and Publisher* 119, 19: 16.

Stevens, J. and Porter, W. (1973) *The Rest of the Elephant*, Englewood Cliffs, NJ: Prentice-Hall.

"Sunday Times editor to take charge of Sky TV," (1988) London, the *Independent*, 18 November.

Tate, C. (1989) "On Chris Whittle's school-news scheme," *Columbia Journalism Review* 28, 1: 52.

"Tracking news media," (1986) USIA Report, Washington.

Tottmar, M. (1989) "Television, Cable and Satellite," *Dagens Nyheter*, 14 April, p. 2.

Tuchman, G. (1974) *The TV Establishment: Programming for Power and Profit*, Englewood Cliffs, NJ: Prentice-Hall.

Tunstall, J. (1971) *Journalists at Work*, London: Constable.

— (1977) *The Media are American*, London: Constable.

— (1983) *The Media in Britain*, London: Constable.

— (1985) *Communications Deregulation*, Oxford: Blackwell

— (1986) "American Commmunications Deregulation; How to copy and misunderstand it." *Nordicom Information* No 3: 31–34. Gothenburg University, Sweden.

Turow, J. (1983) "Local Television: Producing Soft News," *Journal of Communication* 33, 2: 111–123.

UNESCO (1986) "Television in the Caribbean: St Lucia," Regional Office Report, Kingston, Jamaica.

Urwick, F. (1953) *Profitability Using the General Staff Position in Management*, New York: AMA General Management Series 165.

Wade, G. (1989) "The Region Legion," *TV Product*, April: 41–45.

Wallis, R. and Malm, K. (1984) *Big Sounds from Small Peoples*, London: Constable.

Wallis, R. and Malm, K. (1988) "A systems approach to the relationship between the phonogram/videogram industry and music television," *Popular Music* 7, 3: 267–284.

Weaver, J., Porter, C. and Evans, M. (1984) "Patterns in foreign news coverage on US network television: A ten year analysis," *Journalism Quarterly* 61, 2: 356–363.

Weibull, L. *et al.* (1987) "News diffusion in Sweden: the role of the media," *European Journal of Communication* 2, 143–170.

Weiss, P. (1988) "Party time in Atlanta," *Columbia Journalism Review* 27, 3: 27–34.

Westerståhl, J. and Johansson, F. (1986) *News Ideologies as Moulders of Domestic News*, European Journal of Communication, London: Sage, 1: 133–49.

Westin, A., (1982) *Newswatch: How TV Decides the News*, New York: Simon & Schuster.

— (1987) "Days of penury, days of affluence," American Broadcasting Company internal memo, New York.

Wilhoit, G. C. and Weaver, D. (1983) "Foreign news coverage in two US wire services: An update," *Journal of Communication* 33, 2: 132–148.

Williams, F. (1969) *The Right to Know*, London: Longmans.

"The world of the news – the news of the world," (1980) UNESCO–IAMCR Report, Leicester, United Kingdom.

Wylie, M. (1939) *Radio Writing*, New York: Farrar & Reinhart.

Index

265

Index

Index

PBS (Public Broadcasting System) 36–7

Peacock Report 58

Perry Report 130

Persson, Per 75

pirate radio 75

Pittman, Robert 13

Planter, Ed 57, 251

Plato 2

Postman, Neil 7–8

Powers, Ron 29, 120

Protheroe, Alan 47–8

Radio Free Europe 135–7

Radio Leeds 101–2

Radio Liberty 135–7

Radio Moscow 121, 140–3, 153

"Rapport" 10, 77, 93, 169–207

Rather, Dan 18, 22, 24, 30

Reagan, Ronald 14, 25, 27–8, 37, 41–2, 53, 96–8, 151, 202, 208–9, 213

recording industry 245–50

Riffe, Daniel 161–2, 168, 192

Ruth, Marcia 10–11

Rydbeck, Olof 77

satellite television 108–15

Sawyer, Dianne 22

Scansat 94, 113–14

Schorr, Daniel 30

Schlesinger, Philip 62–3

Schramm, Wilbur 157

short wave radio 116–20, 122

"60 Minutes" 13, 21

Sky Channel 55, 69, 111–12

Sky News 113, 247

Sloman, Ann 70, 240

SNG (Satellite news gathering) 1, 57, 219, 223

Spaull, David 129, 133, 213

Spycatcher 133, 151, 178, 195, 206

Sung, Kim Il 153–4

"Svepet" 84

Sveriges Radio 73–4, 85–6, 94

Swedish Radio, 6, 13, 72–85, 91–4, 120–2, 169–207, 225

Swedish Television 6, 72–8, 85–94, 169–207; Channel 1 10, 77, 93; Channel 2 10, 31, 77, 93

Sytchev, Alexandre 138–40

TASS 138–40

Television News Index and Abstracts 156–7

Thatcher, Margaret 47, 53, 143, 208, 233

Third Tier Radio 94

Tisch, Laurance 21, 24–5

TTT (Trinidad and Tobago Television) 143–4

TT 74–5, 221

Tuchman, Gaye 31

Tunstall, Jeremy 10, 35, 44–5, 167

Turner, Ted 24, 105–7

Turow, Joseph 103

"20/20" 13

Udana, the 2

UNESCO 145–7, 160, 162–3, 179–81

USIA (United States Information Agency) 123, 135, 145–6, 213

USA Today 11

"USA Tonight" 104–5

van Sauter, Gordon, 25

VISNEWS 34–5, 55–8, 87–8, 95, 104, 143, 147, 149, 194

VOA (Voice of America) 117–18, 121–5, 134–7

VOK (Voice of Kenya) 147–8

Weiss, Philip 16

Wenham, Brian 61

Westin, Av 18, 23, 26, 99

Westmorland, William 31, 48

Wick, Charles Z. 137, 213–4

Williams, Francis 64

Worldnet 137

WTN 34, 55–8, 87–8, 143, 147, 149

Wylie, Max 17